P9-DVV-981

How to Carve Wood

How to Carve Wood

A book of projects and techniques

Richard Bütz

The Taunton Press

All cover and text photos by Richard and Ellen Bütz,
except where noted.

Taunton
BOOKS & VIDEOS
for fellow enthusiasts

© 1984 by The Taunton Press, Inc.
All rights reserved.

First printing: October 1984
Second printing: April 1985
Third printing: September 1986
Fourth printing: June 1987
Fifth printing: March 1988
Sixth printing: December 1988
Seventh printing: May 1990
Eight printing: August 1991
Ninth printing: December 1992
Tenth printing: August 1993
Eleventh printing: February 1995
Twelfth printing: October 1995
Thirteenth printing: August 1997

International Standard Book Number: 0-918804-20-5
Library of Congress Catalog Card Number: 83-050680
Printed in the United States of America

A FINE WOODWORKING Book
FINE WOODWORKING® is a trademark of The Taunton Press, Inc.,
registered in the U.S. Patent and Trademark Office.

The Taunton Press, 63 South Main Street, Box 5506,
Newtown, CT 06470-5506

To Ellen, for her help, understanding and support

I would like to thank all the woodcarvers who have been so generous in sharing their time and knowledge with me through the years. This willingness of the masters to share their secrets with young carvers will help to keep woodcarving from becoming a lost art.

I would also like to thank all the people who helped me obtain historical photographs for this book—in particular, Darrel D. Henning of Vesterheim, The Norwegian-American Museum, Mary Doherty of the Metropolitan Museum of Art, Tom Shelton of the Institute of Texan Cultures at San Antonio, Ed Gallenstein, president of the National Woodcarvers Association, and Craig and Alice Gilborn and the staff of the Adirondack Museum.

I'd also like to thank my neighbor Emery Savage for all his help and support.

Finally, a thank-you to Ellen, my wife, for her many hours of work as a photographer, and my daughter, Juliana, for her patience and understanding during all the times I've been busy for the past three years.

Richard Bütz
Blue Mountain Lake, New York
July 1984

Contents

Introduction   **1**

Tools and Work Space   1   **2**

Sharpening   2   **24**

Woods and Finishes   3   **38**

Design   4   **54**

Whittling   5   **70**

Chip Carving   6   **90**

Relief Carving   7   **114**

Wildlife Carving   8   **146**

Lettering   9   **184**

Architectural Carving   10   **196**

Bibliography   **213**

Index   **214**

Introduction

Sometimes it seems we have encumbered and complicated our lives so much through necessity and technology that we have lost one of the greatest pleasures of all—simply sitting and enjoying the satisfaction of making something of lasting beauty with our hands. Woodcarving allows us to do this. Of all the artistic mediums used today, I feel that wood is the most expressive and sensitive, and yet it is the least understood and perhaps the most neglected. Woodcarving is a solitary pursuit, but it is an experience that goes beyond just shaping a piece of wood. You will discover that it can become a much deeper, almost spiritual exercise. This is because wood is a living material. Each piece has its own beauty and individuality, and you must develop a feeling for working in cooperation with it. A person working in clay or metal can force it into any shape desired. Not so with wood. The carver must work along with the character of each piece.

You do not have to be an experienced artist or craftsman to enjoy woodcarving. All that is required is natural curiosity, a desire to learn and a little time. Unlike other art forms, woodcarving doesn't require a lot of tools and equipment. All you need to get started is a small pocketknife and a piece of wood. For centuries, people around the world have used these same materials to create folk art of subtle and complex beauty. On the other hand, you can acquire dozens of carving gouges and make large, sophisticated works of art. There is no limit to the potential of wood.

I wrote this book for anyone who wishes to understand and master woodcarving. You will find information on tools, wood and design, along with projects that teach the skills needed by every woodcarver. These skills are the building blocks that enable you to develop your carving ability. The secret to woodcarving is to develop your own personal style by experimenting with the tools and techniques until you feel comfortable with them. When this happens, you will have greater control and freedom in shaping wood. If you're a beginner, start with the projects in Whittling and Chip Carving. As you progress through the book, you'll see that the projects become more difficult, but if you have mastered the fundamental skills, you shouldn't have any trouble with them.

Each skill is introduced at the beginning of the chapter, then taught by working step by step through exercises and projects. The photographs show the work as it would appear if you were holding the tools, or looking over a woodcarver's shoulder. A scaled pattern for each project is provided at the end of the chapter, along with a gallery of carvings you could make using the same techniques. Don't feel that you must copy every project exactly. Feel free to make modifications in the patterns, or better yet, create your own designs. One of the real joys of working with your hands is seeing your own ideas take on a physical form.

So, enjoy reading through these chapters and studying the methods. There is no need to follow the book page by page unless you want to. If you see a project you want to try, go right ahead. If you get stumped on a technique, use the index to find the section where that method is introduced, and work your way through it. And don't be afraid to talk with other woodcarvers who live in your area. Most of them will be willing to help you if they can.

Above all, use this book as a tool to help bring you closer to the enjoyment and satisfaction of woodcarving.

Tools and Work Space   1

From the first time our Paleolithic ancestors picked up a sharp-edged stone, we began developing an instinct for using tools. The ability to hold tools and use them with skill is our source of power in shaping our environment, and is what distinguishes people from animals. Humans have the ability to be creative; we can visualize an idea, shape the necessary materials to bring it into physical existence, and then step back and take pleasure in what we have created. Who knows? Maybe my cats would like to take up woodcarving. But they can't—they simply don't have the physical means to hold tools. Jacob Bronowski, author of *Ascent of Man*, sums it up, "The mark of man is the refinement of the hand in action...." Perhaps it would be more accurate to say that the mark of man is the refinement of the tools in action.

Tools are the heart of woodcarving, and you will soon discover a strong bond between them and your hands. As this bond develops, so does respect for the tools. You can feel it whenever you walk into the workshop of an old woodcarver. You can sense the kinship the craftsman has with the tools. Surrounded by the sweet, clean fragrance of wood shavings, you find rows of planes and gouges with handles that have been polished by years of constant use. There's a mood of respect that is almost like the quiet reverence you feel in an old English countryside church.

Respect for the tools is what distinguishes a serious woodcarver from all others. If you look at the tools of a mediocre carver, you'll notice they are dull and nicked, a spot of powdery rust here and there. The handles might be splintered and frayed—a sure indication of abuse. A carver's attitude toward the tools comes across in the work, too, so it is likely this carver's woodcarvings will look coarse and incomplete. Most of the time, however, the

Keep your tools in good condition, your bench well organized and your work space well lighted—your carving will go more smoothly and the quality of your work will improve.

problem is only the result of a lack of experience. Usually, as soon as a carver understands the direct relationship between the tools and the quality of workmanship, the problem disappears.

But always remember, *you* create the woodcarving, not the tools. Don't allow yourself to become intimidated by the seemingly endless variety of tools, and then spend more time collecting them than using them. You don't need to buy all the woodcarving tools that you will ever need in your life at once. A few carefully chosen carving tools will be more useful than racks of highly specialized ones you don't yet need. It's better to start with a good knife and a couple of gouges, and then add tools when you discover the need for them. This way, you can build up a set of tools tailored to your own personal style of woodcarving.

When you purchase tools, make sure you get the best you can afford—it's hard to carve with a tool that won't stay sharp or bends when you use it. Good hand tools are expensive, and always have been (cheap tools often sell for one-third to one-half the cost of better tools), but high-quality tools are worth the investment. You can sometimes find good bargains, particularly in used tools, but your best bet is to deal only with reliable hardware stores or mail-order tool companies. Good tools maintained in perfect working condition will last a lifetime, and help produce carvings of superior quality.

Here is a brief introduction to the basic tools you'll need for the projects in this book. The specific tools and materials needed for each of the projects will be discussed again at the beginning of each chapter.

Knives—The first tool you'll need is a knife. Knives are useful for whittling, wildlife carving, chip carving and cleaning up details in relief carvings. They'll probably be your most frequently used pieces of equipment.

There are many different types of knives that are equally useful, but most people find one that they like and use it for everything. A pocketknife (also called a jackknife) or a fixed-blade whittler's knife is good for general-purpose work, provided the handle is large enough to fit your hand comfortably. I like to use a German-style chip-carving knife, which I modify slightly by shortening the blade and reshaping the handle, as discussed on p. 72. An X-acto is also a good general-purpose knife.

A knife blade should be made of good-quality, high-carbon steel, which will stay sharp longer than stainless steel. In general, the blade should be no longer than 1½ in. A long blade is more difficult to control because your leverage point on the handle is farther away from the work. Also, because only a very small portion of the blade is used to cut through the wood, the extra length is unnecessary and a potential safety hazard.

Custom knives, handmade by professional knife makers, are available in many different shapes intended for specific uses. For example, the one I had made for me (at left in the bottom photo) was designed for scooping out wood under the tail feathers of a bird carving—a difficult place to reach with a straight knife or gouge. This tool saves me a lot of trouble.

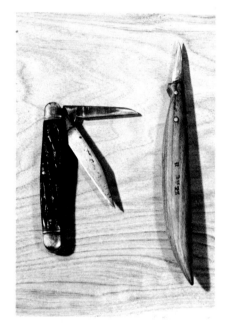

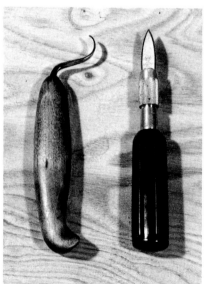

Top: a two-bladed pocketknife (left) and a modified German chip-carving knife (right). Bottom: a custom-made knife designed for scooping wood out from under the tail feathers on bird carvings (left) and an X-acto knife (right), available with interchangeable blades.

Gouges—Gouges are the real workhorses of woodcarving. They consist of a piece of metal sharpened at the tip and fitted to a wooden handle. The cutting edges of most carving gouges are curved along their width to allow the gouge to scoop out the wood without the corners of the tool digging into and splitting it. The best gouges are hand-forged, and they come in hundreds of different shapes. Gouges are categorized by size, which is the width of the cutting edge, and sweep, which is the amount of curvature of the edge. Size is measured in inches or millimeters, and sweep is indicated by an arbitrarily assigned number, as shown in the chart on p. 6. In addition, the blade of a gouge can be either straight or curved along its length. When identifying or ordering most gouges, you need to indicate the size and sweep, as well as whether the blade is straight or curved—for example, you would ask for a 5mm No. 9 straight gouge.

The tool I use most often is the fishtail gouge. The straight blade flares out at the cutting edge and then tapers back for about 1 in., so it can get into tight areas without damaging any of the shapes nearby. These gouges are also lighter and more comfortable to use than a gouge that is full width along its blade. They get their name from their fishtail shape, and have a nice streamlined look. Fishtail gouges are available with or without sweep, and I use them for a lot of general-purpose work, including roughing-out and detailing.

The flat, flared blade of a fishtail gouge makes it easy to get into small areas that would be difficult to reach with a regular gouge.

A few of the many different types of chisels and gouges used for carving are, from top to bottom: a 12mm firmer or woodcarver's chisel, a 12mm skew chisel, a 15mm No. 9 straight gouge, a 20mm No. 5 fishtail gouge, and a 50mm No. 7 straight gouge.

PARTS OF A GOUGE

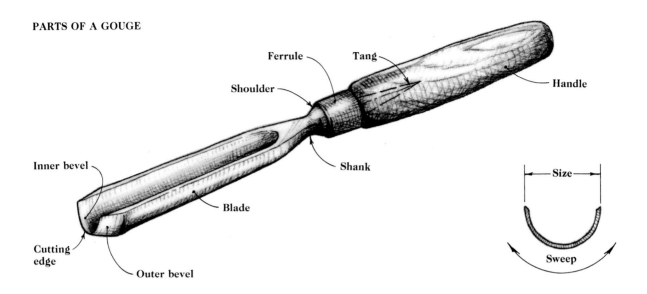

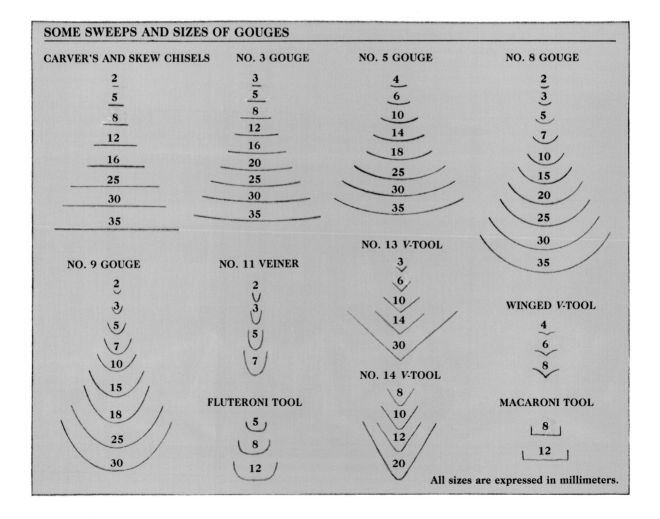

SOME SWEEPS AND SIZES OF GOUGES

CARVER'S AND SKEW CHISELS	NO. 3 GOUGE	NO. 5 GOUGE	NO. 8 GOUGE
2	3	4	2
5	5	6	3
8	8	10	5
12	12	14	7
16	16	18	10
25	20	25	15
30	25	30	20
35	30	35	25
	35		30
			35

NO. 9 GOUGE

2
3
5
7
10
15
18
25
30

NO. 11 VEINER

2
3
5
7

FLUTERONI TOOL

5
8
12

NO. 13 *V*-TOOL

3
6
10
14
30

NO. 14 *V*-TOOL

8
10
12
20

WINGED *V*-TOOL

4
6
8

MACARONI TOOL

8
12

All sizes are expressed in millimeters.

There are several gouges with straight blades and cutting edges having no sweep, known as carver's chisels. These tools resemble carpenter's chisels, except the cutting edge is beveled on both sides instead of just one. The two bevels make the tool easier to control when carving. The standard carver's chisel, also called a firmer, has a cutting edge that is square to the side of the blade. The skew chisel has a cutting edge ground at an angle of about 25° to 35° to the side of the blade. Some woodcarvers prefer this angled cutting edge for cleaning up recessed backgrounds or small details, but I find my whittling knife can do this work just as well.

Gouges with *U*-shaped blades (that is, having such a severe sweep that the blade resembles a *U*) are called veiners. They were originally used by medieval and Renaissance carvers to make the veins on leaves, which is how they got their name, and are now used by some craftsmen for outlining relief carvings. However, I prefer to use *V*-parting tools, or *V*-tools (tools with a sweep resembling a *V*), for outlining because they are easier to control. I occasionally use a veiner for detail work.

GOUGES WITH STRAIGHT BLADES

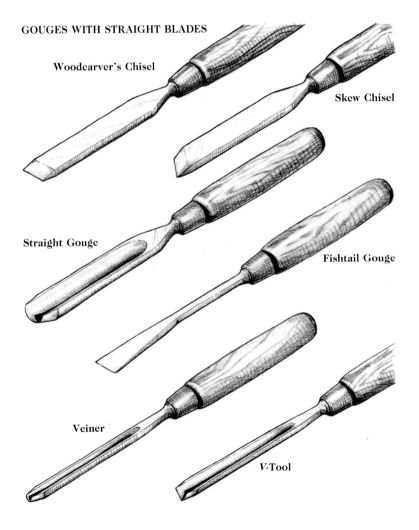

Woodcarver's Chisel

Skew Chisel

Straight Gouge

Fishtail Gouge

Veiner

V-Tool

SPOON-BENT GOUGE

BACK-BENT GOUGE

Gouges with blades that are curved along their length are used to remove wood in places where a straight gouge won't fit. For example, as shown in the drawing below, the curved gouge, or long-bent gouge, has an even curve along the blade of the tool and is useful for scooping out bowls or the concave surfaces of a sculpture. The blade of the front-bent grounder, also shown below, has more of an *S*-shape than the curved-gouge blade. This tool is useful for carving out backgrounds because the curve allows your hand to clear the wood while keeping the cutting edge at a low angle to the background. A spoon-bent gouge, shown at left and in the drawing below, has a straight blade with a deep curve just behind the cutting edge. This makes it useful for getting into deeply recessed sections of relief carvings and sculptures, because you can position this tool almost vertical to the wood, and avoid damaging surrounding areas. A back-bent gouge, shown in the drawing at left, looks much like the spoon-bent, except the curve is reversed. This gouge is useful for scooping out the underside of a carving, a place difficult to reach with any other shape of tool, and although it's not used very often, it's handy to have when you need it.

SPOON-BENT GOUGE

FRONT-BENT GROUNDER

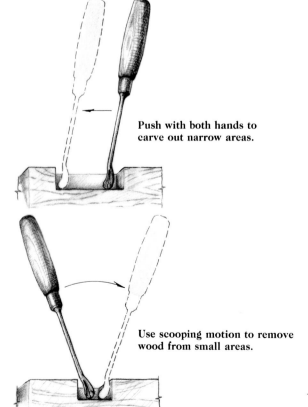

Used to level and smooth background areas

Push with both hands to carve out narrow areas.

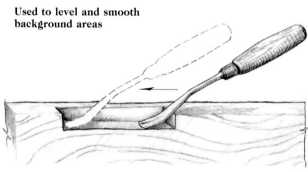

CURVED OR LONG-BENT GOUGE

Use scooping motion to remove wood from small areas.

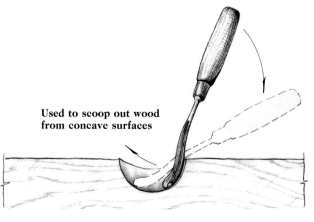

Used to scoop out wood from concave surfaces

There are also many specialized tools originally designed for very specific uses that eventually became standard among woodcarving tools. The macaroni tool (straight or curved) is used to smooth background areas on relief carvings and to cut moldings. The dogleg chisel is used to level backgrounds on relief carvings where clearance is restricted. The fluteroni tool (straight or curved) is used to carve fluting or molding on curved shapes. The winged *V*-tool is used to carve various types of beaded moldings and fan shapes. Most woodcarvers find that even though they may own several dozen different gouges, most of the time they use only half a dozen or so.

For roughing-out large blocks of wood for a three-dimensional carving, I generally use 25mm to 50mm, No. 7 to No. 9 straight gouges. For shaping and smoothing two-dimensional and small three-dimensional work, I use 10mm to 20mm, No. 5 to No. 7 straight gouges. For final detail work, I generally use 4mm to 8mm, No. 2 to No. 5 straight gouges. For most of my two-dimensional work, I use a 6mm *V*-tool for outlining and detailing, a 20mm No. 5 fishtail gouge for roughing-out and smoothing backgrounds, and a 6mm No. 3 straight gouge for finishing details. (The chart on p. 23 gives a listing of the recommended sets of tools required for different types of carving.) The most important thing to remember is to use the correct-sized tool for the type of work you are doing. Don't use a small, 3mm gouge to rough-out a large sculpture; it wasn't designed for heavy-duty work and can easily be broken or damaged. Likewise, a large, 35mm gouge is totally unsuitable for carving delicate details.

When you're selecting gouges, look for the full-sized professional tools, which are about 9 in. to 11 in. long from the cutting edge to the end of the handle. These sizes are much easier to work with, and therefore the tools are more versatile than the miniature "beginner" or "student-sized" tools, which are only about 6 in. to 8 in. long.

Gouge handles—Some gouges are sold without handles, but you can buy handles from any tool supplier (or you can make your own from pieces of hardwood). There are several different types to choose from, made in a variety of different woods, such as boxwood, maple, beech and rosewood—choice of wood is really a matter of personal preference. Traditionally, English handles are round, whereas Swiss and German handles are octagonal. I prefer octagonal handles because they are less likely to slip in my hand and won't roll off the workbench. Most gouge handles have metal ferrules at the tang end to prevent the wood from splitting. Heavy-duty gouges, which are driven with mallets, often have ferrules at the striking end of the handle, too. Small gouges are pushed by hand or only lightly tapped with a mallet, so splitting is not usually a problem, as long as the wood is properly sealed (p. 10) and the tools are correctly used and stored.

Handle lengths vary, so choose whatever is comfortable for your hand. They are available in small, medium and large diameters—the ones I use are about ⅞ in. to 1½ in. in diameter. Always choose a handle with a diameter proportional to the size of the

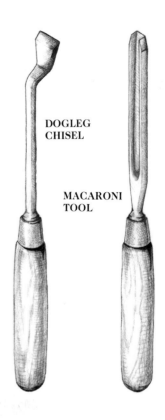

DOGLEG CHISEL

MACARONI TOOL

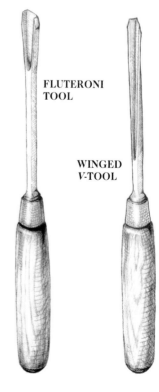

FLUTERONI TOOL

WINGED V-TOOL

tool. A small, delicate blade requires a small handle of 1 in. or less in diameter for better control; a large handle would allow you to put too much pressure on the tool and could cause the blade to break. A wide blade needs a large handle, about 1¼ in. to 1½ in. in diameter; a small handle would be difficult to grip firmly enough to control the blade. You might need to replace the handle on a new gouge to fit the scale of the blade. I once purchased a 30mm No. 9 gouge with a handle ¾ in. in diameter, but because the handle was so small, it was uncomfortable to work with. Once I put on a larger handle (1³⁄₁₆ in.), the gouge was much easier to use and it is now one of my favorites.

Fitting a new handle is simple. Drill a small hole about ⅛ in. in diameter down the center of the handle to a depth of 1½ in. or so—make this hole as straight as you can. Next, wrap several layers of cloth around the blade as protection, and secure it in a vise with the tang pointing up. Position the pilot hole in the handle on the tang and press down, turning the handle as though you were screwing it on. Check from a few different angles to make sure the handle and blade are aligned. If they aren't, pull the handle a little to one side and turn it to ream the hole straight. When the hole is large enough to take all but ¼ in. of the tang, remove the handle, clean out any chips and sawdust, replace it on the tang, and tap it the rest of the way home with a wooden mallet. This will give a tight fit without splitting the handle.

Some handles you buy already have ferrules on them, but if you want to put a ferrule on a homemade handle, use a piece of brass or metal tubing about ½ in. to ¾ in. long. Use a file or sharp knife to shape the end of the handle. Then tap the ferrule onto the handle with a hammer before putting the blade on. I like the way ferrules look, but they are only necessary on tools that will have to endure a lot of force from heavy mallets.

You will discover that a good-quality gouge with a comfortable handle actually produces a better woodcarving. I'm not sure if this is purely a psychological reaction, or if it is because you have better control of a tool that feels comfortable. But having a good tool and the right handle does make a difference and gives your work an extra edge of quality.

One of the first things I do when I get a new gouge is check the blade and handle for any rough spots. Often there are burrs of metal left over from the forging process, which can give you a nasty scratch and should be filed smooth. It's also not unusual for a new handle to have bits of sawdust and splinters embedded in the varnish. Handles should be sanded smooth with very fine sandpaper. (I use 220-grit garnet paper.) Heavily varnished wood also creates a lot of friction, and many old-timers would take the finish right off the handle to prevent blisters and calluses on their hands. I scrape the finish off with a pocketknife and then lightly sand the handle. Then I soak the exposed wood in boiled linseed oil and wipe it clean. This not only seals the wood, but leaves a porous finish that is comfortable to work with for hours on end. The oil also hardens the end of the handle as heat is generated by the striking mallet. This helps prevent fraying and splitting of the end grain.

Storage—It's important to have your tools organized to keep them from knocking against each other—a sure way to dull or nick them. I store mine in a cloth roll with individually sewn pockets. You can buy one of these from a tool supplier or make it yourself. My wife, Ellen, made mine from a piece of brown velveteen, and it holds 20 gouges. Its finished length is about 22 in., and its finished width about 12 in. Each pocket is 4 in. deep and 2½ in. wide. Store the gouges with their blades exposed so that you can easily identify them. Whenever you are working away from your bench, you can just spread out the cloth roll and have each gouge easily accessible, but well protected.

For fastening, the cloth roll in the photo below and in the drawing at right, has fabric ties about 25 in. long. Position them about 2 in. from the folded sides of the roll. Sew them 1 in. in from the end of the roll, leaving 12 in. of tie free on either side of the stitching. Once the tools and cloth are rolled up, wrap the two ties a few times around the roll and knot them with square knots. These ties are much more useful than buckles or snaps, because the roll doesn't need to be full of tools to be secure.

In my workshop, I also use notched wall racks, designed to fit the tool at the shank between the blade and the handle. When I'm carving a commission away from home, I carry my tools in an antique toolbox. It has shallow drawers fitted with racks that will hold about 40 gouges securely, and a large drawer for mallets, sharpening stones and oil.

Always keep your gouges clean. Every few months, the blades and handles should be wiped down with a clean rag moistened with a light machine oil like 3-in-1. This will protect the tools against rust or moisture build-up.

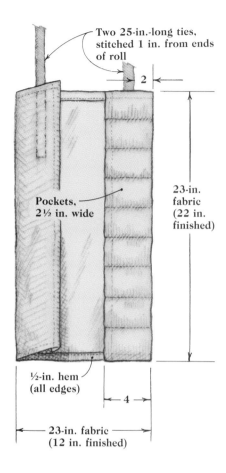

Two 25-in.-long ties, stitched 1 in. from ends of roll

Pockets, 2½ in. wide

23-in. fabric (22 in. finished)

½-in. hem (all edges)

23-in. fabric (12 in. finished)

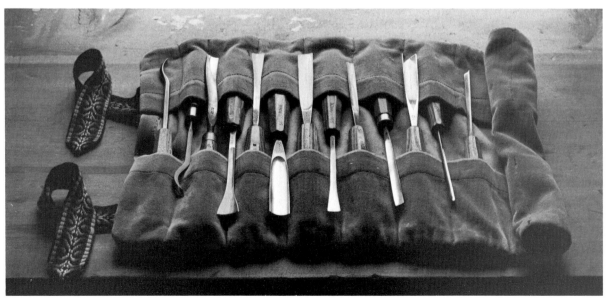

Protect your gouges by storing them in a cloth roll with individually sewn pockets. The pockets should be deep enough to hold the handles securely—about 4 in.

Sharpening stones—The steel edge of a tool is sharpened by rubbing it against abrasive stones that wear off metal and form a sharp beveled edge. Sharpening stones, also called whetstones, are made from either man-made or natural materials, and come in a variety of textures, ranging from coarse to very fine and sometimes graded by grit number. You will need a medium-coarse stone (200 grit) and a fine stone (400 grit) to prepare your tools for carving the projects in this book. These two stones can be purchased as a single sharpening stone, called a combination benchstone, with the coarse texture on one side and the fine texture on the other. A combination stone about 2 in. wide and 8 in. long is a good size for sharpening the tools you'll be using. You will also need a small can of light machine oil such as 3-in-1 to lubricate the stone while sharpening. For the final polishing of a cutting edge, woodcarvers use a leather strop. A strop is a piece of leather 1 in. to 2 in. wide and about 12 in. long. You can purchase a strop or make one yourself, as discussed on p. 27. (See Chapter 2 for more information on sharpening materials.)

Mallets—Most carving is done by pushing the gouge with your hand, but sometimes when carving a very hard wood or using a gouge with a wide cutting edge, the tool needs to be driven by tapping the end of the handle with a wooden mallet. (Never use a steel hammer on your gouges; the metal doesn't give and will rapidly damage wooden tool handles.)

Mallets are square or cylindrical pieces of wood with handles. They come in a variety of shapes and sizes, and in two basic styles. The English-style mallet is made in two parts, with an ash handle secured to the head with a wooden wedge. I think this style is a carry-over from the days of stone masonry, when mallets were used against solid-iron chisels and their heads needed to be replaced frequently because of wear. The type of mallet I use, shown in the photo on the facing page, is turned from a solid piece of wood, so I don't need to worry about the head's loosening.

Square-headed mallets are traditionally used by cabinetmakers and carpenters, and not recommended for carving. The square face is designed to strike chisels held vertically. The face is perpendicular to the tool, and transfers force straight down like a hammer. Carving gouges, on the other hand, are held at lower angles to the work, and it is difficult to position a flat surface squarely on the tool. The rounded face of a woodcarving mallet can be held at any angle and still make solid contact.

Mallet weight is determined by how much wood you need to remove and the size of the tool. The larger the cutting edge, the more force you need to drive it through the wood—you don't need more of an arm swing, you need a heavier mallet. Make sure you never use a large mallet with a small, delicate blade. (I speak from experience. I have only broken one tool, and this is how I did it.) I have three mallets I use most often: an 18-oz. mallet I use with small gouges; a 28-oz. mallet for 12mm to 30mm gouges; and a 36-oz. mallet I use with larger gouges. A 16-oz. to 24-oz. mallet is good to start with, although if you plan to do a lot of heavy-duty sculpture using large gouges, you may want a larger mallet, too.

Mallets are available in a variety of woods, including hickory, maple and osage orange. One of the best woods for mallets is lignum vitae, a heavy, dense tropical wood with close, interlocking grain fibers that prevent it from splitting under stress. Its beautiful yellowish color seasons to a rich amber. A newly purchased lignum vitae mallet arrives coated with a thick paraffin wax, which protects it during shipping. Remove this by gently scraping with a blunt metal edge such as a table knife or the edge of a coin. Then rub the mallet down with fine, 000 steel wool. This cleans off the sticky wax, but the wood still has to be sealed to keep its moisture in; if lignum vitae dries out too quickly, it may crack and check. So apply a liberal amount of boiled linseed oil and let it soak in overnight, then wipe it dry with a clean rag.

The mallet is now ready to use, although it's a good idea to oil it once a week for the first month or so. If you notice any cracks appearing in the end grain, try storing the mallet in a plastic bag with a few drops of water when not in use. It may take several months for the lignum vitae to stabilize to your particular climate.

Carving mallets are used to drive gouges through the wood when you're working in very hard wood, when you need to remove large amounts of wood or when you're using a very large tool. These mallets, of three different weights, are turned from a solid piece of lignum vitae, which is a dense, tropical wood.

There are several different types of saws that are useful to woodcarvers. From left to right: a carpenter's crosscut saw, a Japanese ryoba *saw, a coping saw and a keyhole saw.*

A bandsaw is used to cut a piece of wood to size and to its rough shape.

Saws—I use handsaws to cut wood for relief panels or to get a small enough piece to work on the bandsaw. Woodcarvers use several types of saws. A carpenter's crosscut saw, shown at far left in the photo, is good for trimming down boards because it has a wide, stiff blade and cuts in a straight line if it's sharp. These saws are fairly inexpensive and good used ones are easy to find.

Japanese *ryoba* saws are used the same way as a carpenter's saw except they cut on the pull stroke instead of the push stroke. The one I use has a blade about 9½ in. long. These saws have two edges—one for ripping, one for crosscutting. They're a delight to use, though I find they are somewhat delicate because of their thin, brittle blades. I use them for light work around the shop.

A coping saw is made from a replaceable, high-carbon-steel blade fitted to a metal frame with a wooden handle, usually beech. Because the blade is so thin, it can cut curves in wood up to 3 in. thick. This is a handy saw, but takes a bit of patience to use—you need to work slowly because it's easy to jam, bend or break the blade if you're sawing too fast or using too much pressure.

A keyhole saw has a strong, thin blade about 6 in. to 14 in. long that tapers to a point. It's used for cutting out circles or curved shapes inside a piece of wood. To use a keyhole saw, first drill at least a ½-in. hole within the area to be removed (any smaller, and it will take too long to get the cut started—you can only work a few teeth at a time). Then insert the blade and cut out the waste. You can also use a compass saw, which is similar to the keyhole saw, and available in blade lengths of 10 in. to 18 in. The Japanese version of the keyhole saw is known as a *mawashibiki*. I sometimes use the Japanese saw, but it has coarse teeth that can tear the wood and cause splinters to run into small designs.

A bandsaw is a large machine with a long, vertical sawblade. The blade is welded into a loop and runs over two large wheels. A bandsaw does the work of a continuously cutting coping saw, only much quicker. Bandsaws are usually powered by an electric motor, which enables the saw to cut wood that is several inches thick. Small bandsaws suitable for a home workshop have limited clearance between the blade and the housing, so you can only cut pieces about 10 in. to 14 in. wide. Generally, I don't like to use power tools, not because of any aesthetic prejudice, but because I find the noise and dust a nuisance. The bandsaw, however, is probably the best invention to come along for woodcarvers since steel. It can cut a piece of wood down to a workable size more quickly, efficiently and safely than any other tool. I consider it a wise investment for any serious carver.

Planes, spokeshaves and drawknives—Woodcarvers use a number of planes at various stages in their work. I use them to clean up boards or logs, or to smooth and bevel edges of a carving prior to finishing. Planes come in several different shapes and sizes. I find antique wooden planes more comfortable to use than metal planes. They are lighter in weight, their edges are rounded and smooth—easy to hold onto while working—and they feel more natural in my hand, especially older planes that have been broken in.

Molding planes, at far left in the photo at right, have irregularly shaped soles and cutting edges that produce long hollows and curves instead of flat surfaces. I use them only occasionally for architectural work, such as planing molding and linenfold designs. (For molding, I also use a beading plane, which has a *U*-shaped blade and a groove in the center of the sole. On linenfold panels, I also use the rabbet plane, plow plane and rounding plane to cut away background and shape contours.)

The smallest of the planes in both photos are called block planes, usually 6 in. to 8 in. long. I use this lightweight plane to touch up small areas and to chamfer the front and back edges of relief panels. I recommend having one handy if you are doing a lot of chip carving or relief carving, and need to smooth down board ends—block planes are easy to work on end grain, and the low angle of the blade makes them less likely to tear out the wood. Don't use these planes on large surfaces where you need a uniform flatness. Because the plane sole is short, it follows irregularities in the wood instead of leveling them.

The metal smoothing plane shown at center in the photo below, about 9 in. long, is good for general work. I use mine to smooth the flat edges of a finished carving. For smoothing a large, rough-cut block or preparing boards for lamination, I use a larger, jack plane, shown at far right, which is about 13 in. long.

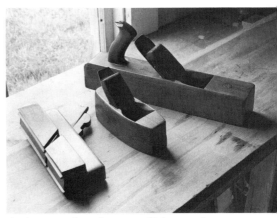

Antique wooden planes are lighter and more comfortable to use than their metal counterparts for smoothing, flattening, and shaping wood. From left to right: a molding plane, block plane and jack plane.

The metal block plane (left) is used to touch up or chamfer small areas and plane across end grain. The smoothing plane (center) and the jack plane (right) are both used for smoothing large areas.

Spokeshaves and drawknives are also useful tools. Originally, spokeshaves were designed to shape spokes for wagon wheels, hence the name. They have a small blade secured into a stock with handles; you grip the handles with both hands and either pull or push the tool (I find pulling easier). When spokeshaving, always secure the wood in a vise or with clamps.

I use a spokeshave for smoothing areas that are difficult to reach with a plane. A spokeshave will cut in a smaller radius than a plane, and is useful on inside and outside curves because of its narrow sole. I also use one for cleaning edges and rounding corners. The thickness of the shaving is controlled by the amount the cutting edge protrudes from the sole.

Spokeshaves are available in a variety of sizes, but the one I use most often is 11 in. long, made of wood and about 150 years old. The 2½-in.-long blade is positioned almost flat to the wood so that it cuts like a knife; the blade of a metal shave is angled higher and cuts more like a plane. The advantage of a lower-angled blade is that it can cut more easily across end grain or irregular grain.

The drawknife, an ancient tool, has two handles set at right angles on each end of a long blade. Although they are available with a curved blade, my two drawknives, shown at top in the photo below, have straight blades 12 in. and 9 in. long. Like a spokeshave, a drawknife can be pulled or pushed. I use it to remove bark from logs. Some people use drawknives for roughing-out large blocks of wood for decoys, but I don't like using them this way because there is so much exposed cutting edge. I find it easier to remove bulk wood with a gouge.

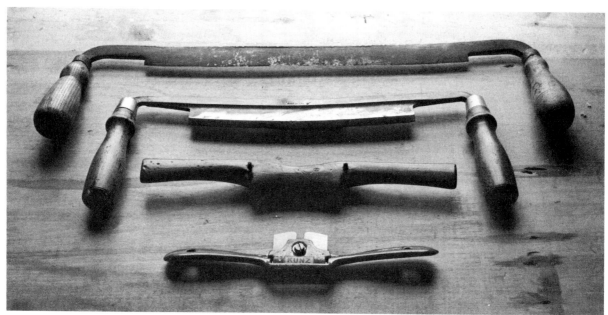

The two drawknives, at top, have blade lengths of 12 in. and 9 in. respectively, and are useful for removing bark from logs. The two spokeshaves have blade lengths of 2½ in. and 1¾ in. respectively, and are useful tools for smoothing areas difficult to reach with a plane.

Files, rasps and rifflers—These tools are also used to remove wood. A file is a piece of high-carbon steel with teeth cut in ridges across its surfaces. Rasps are similar except each tooth is cut individually into the steel, making a coarser and faster cutting surface. I use a 4-In-Hand rasp, which has flat and curved surfaces with fine and coarse teeth, but these tools aren't really necessary for beginners.

Rifflers are specialized tools that combine the cutting surfaces of the file and rasp. They have thin, steel handles with both ends forged flat and set with cutting teeth. They are made in about 40 shapes and styles—some with tapered and curved cutting surfaces for smoothing corners or small rounded areas. Some fine-toothed rifflers can be used instead of sandpaper in hard-to-reach places, and are good for smoothing end grain. These tools are used mostly on sculpture and carved furniture and can be useful, although they're not essential. I don't use them very often because I prefer to let the tool marks of the gouges stand out.

Sandpaper—I use sandpaper for finishing a carving, and sometimes to reach areas that are difficult to reach with tools. The best sandpapers use garnet, a finely ground, reddish-orange crystal and a semi-precious stone, mined in the Adirondack Mountains of New York State. Garnet, unlike some abrasives, has the advantage of not dulling with use. Instead, as the material is worn away, the tiny crystals fracture, and expose new sharp cutting edges. I also use silicon-carbide sandpaper; in the finer grits (between 220 and 400 grit), I find it lasts longer than garnet. Either of these are fine to use, but never use cheap, bargain papers. They are easy to identify because the sand granules are highly visible, and the grit comes off as you work. Stick with the better-quality papers. They're worth the little bit of extra money.

Sandpaper is graded by the coarseness of its abrasive: No. 80 is coarse, No. 400 is very fine, and there is a range of grades in between. I stock most grades, although I find that I use No. 150, No. 220 and No. 320 the most. These grits are appropriate for most of the work you need to do. I don't really use No. 80 on carvings unless I want to obliterate the tool marks for some reason. If you want a very smooth surface, don't progress from a very coarse paper to a very fine paper without intermediate steps. You'll get the best results by starting with 150 grit for the rough work, going next to 220 and ending with 320.

Never use sandpaper on wood before carving. Tiny abrasive particles will get stuck in the wood fibers and quickly dull the cutting edges of your tools. Use sandpaper only for finishing, and even then, rub with the grain to prevent cross-grain scars, which are difficult to remove. Used properly, sandpaper can improve the appearance of a carving by cleaning out small splinters in hard-to-reach places. However, too much sanding can give crisp details a blurred look, which makes the carving look sloppy.

Steel wool, which works like fine sandpaper, is another useful abrasive. It is used for the final smoothing after a carving has been sealed with finish. Its grades range from 0 to 0000. (The more zeros, the finer the steel wool.) For most purposes, I use 000.

Stamps—Stamps, or punches, are used to texture the background of a carving. The stamp, a specially shaped piece of metal, is tapped with a metal hammer to make indentations in the wood. (Stamps will easily damage a wooden mallet.)

Stamping the backgrounds of carvings was a common practice of medieval woodcarvers and used extensively by Victorian furniture makers. I only use background stamps occasionally, but they create a nice effect, especially in relief carvings, when arranged in a pleasing and consistent pattern. I often use them to decorate the backgrounds of signs that have carved lettering. The stippled surface produced by the stamps will take more stain, and darken the background without being obvious or looking contrived. Stamping is useful on oak, ash and other stringy hardwoods as well as on softwoods, because it smooths down the fibrous splinters in small, hard-to-reach places.

The stamps shown in the photo at top left are the four standard shapes for decoration: two sizes of single-point diamonds (left and second from left), a rhomboid diamond (second from right), and a square diamond (right). Use the single-point diamonds close together to get a stippled effect.

Stamps can be purchased from woodcarving supply houses. You can also make your own by modifying leatherworking stamps or from large nail heads. Secure the stamp or nail in a vise, and use a small file to make the triangular, square or diamond shapes you want. You can also file the point of a large nail to make a single diamond or a circular stamp.

Drawing materials—You'll need to have some basic drawing supplies handy for making patterns and drawing designs. You'll need a ruler, sharp pencils, a gum eraser for removing lines from paper and wood, a sketchbook or two, carbon paper and tracing paper. I also recommend a mechanical drawing set with a good compass that can be fitted with a pencil lead. Dividers and calipers are useful for transferring measurements, and a *T*-square and a couple of plastic triangles will also come in handy.

Work Space

Getting started in woodcarving doesn't require a lot of space or equipment. All you need is a knife, a piece of wood and a place to sit. From this starting point, you can spend many pleasant hours whittling in your living room or outdoors. (Wood shavings sweep up easily without making dust.) This arrangement, however, limits you to working on small objects that you can hold in your hand. If you would like to carve larger and more complex pieces, you will need a special place to work where you can keep a sturdy workbench. The ideal work space should have natural lighting and a place to store hand tools when not in use. Power tools should have enough clearance around them to work in safety. The drawings on the facing page show a full shop setup (at left) and a possible setup for a small room or apartment (at right).

Having a quiet, well-lighted and comfortable place to work helps to create an atmosphere that encourages the highest-quality workmanship.

Stamps, or punches, are used to texture the background areas of relief carvings. At top are shown, from left to right: a large single-point diamond, a small single-point diamond, a rhomboid diamond, and a square diamond. The effects created by each of the stamps is shown in the photo at bottom.

LAYOUT FOR LARGE WORK SPACE

LAYOUT FOR SMALL WORK SPACE

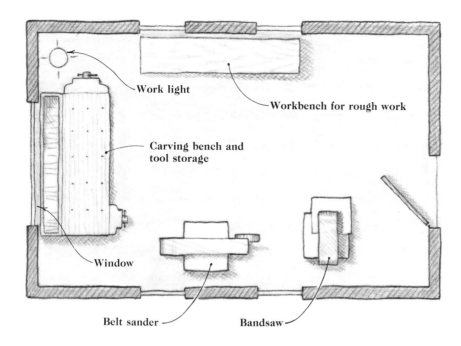

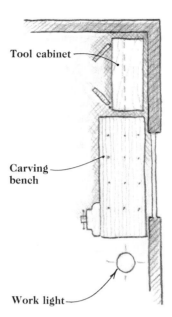

This locking tool cabinet hinges open for easy access to gouges and chisels. (Photo courtesy of Edmund McKamey.)

Lighting—Good light is essential for woodcarving. You really need to be able to see what you are doing, yet you need a light source that won't create harsh shadows. The best working light is found near a north window. This gives an even, indirect light source, which shows details well. If you are carving in relief, set up your work so you are facing the window, because this will illuminate the shapes most clearly.

If it's impossible to use natural light, use an electric 75-watt floodlight. It's best to have the light source at a 45° angle to your workbench, about 4 ft. to 8 ft. away. You may need additional lights as well, but try to have one primary light source. The lighting should let you see the tool's cutting edge and cast slight shadows so you can judge the depth and textures of your work. Don't use fluorescent lights as your main source of illumination—the light is too soft and doesn't show details clearly.

Workbenches—A sturdy work surface is essential for large or complicated woodcarvings. You can use a heavy kitchen table or garage bench or buy a carving bench. Your workbench should be heavy enough not to slide around while you're carving, or should be screwed to the floor. It should also have a way to clamp work to it to allow you to carve easily, with both hands on the tool. You can use a built-in vise or one bolted to the benchtop. A good-sized bench should be about 35 in. high, 14 in. to 24 in. wide, and 4 ft. to 6 ft. long. Modify these dimensions for your own comfort and preference. Sometimes you can find a workbench with locking tool drawers, a good idea if there are children around.

Keep your workbench neat and uncluttered. This will make your work go smoothly and efficiently. I arrange my gouges along the back of my bench in order of frequency of use with the edges towards me for quick identification. From left to right, I lay out the V-tools and fishtail gouges. Straight gouges are lined up according to size, from small to large, and the curved tools are at the end. Gouges I am using are placed near the work, with the blades pointing away for safety.

A craftsman needs the discipline of organized tools and work methods. Use whatever system feels comfortable to you, but always keep your tools ordered by size so you know where to look for them as you work. If tools are scattered all over the bench and rolling onto the floor, a lot of time can be wasted looking for a particular gouge. Organization makes your work simpler.

For efficiency in working, arrange your gouges on the bench in order of frequency of use, with the blade edges facing you for quick identification. Gouges that you are using are placed next to the work, with the blades facing away for safety.

WORKBENCH

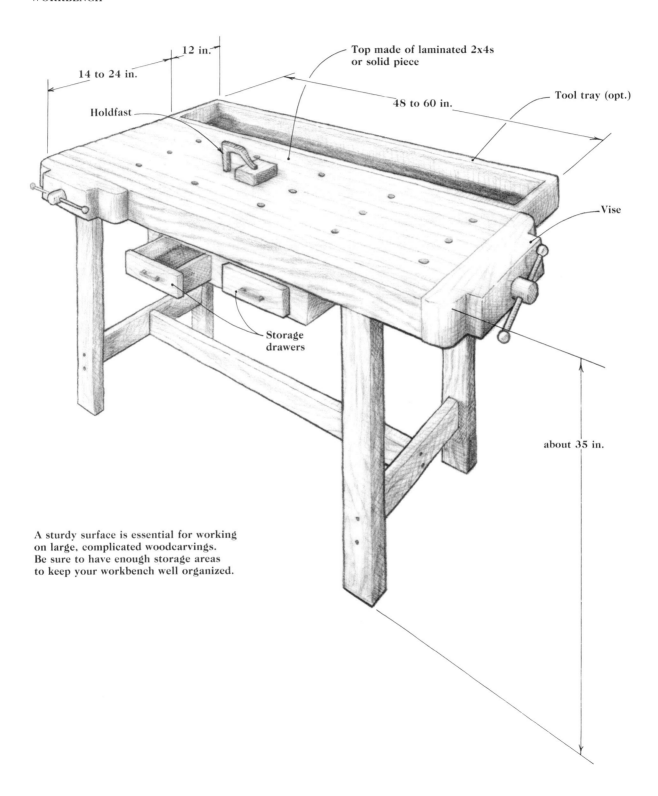

12 in.

14 to 24 in.

Top made of laminated 2x4s
or solid piece

Holdfast

48 to 60 in.

Tool tray (opt.)

Vise

Storage
drawers

about 35 in.

A sturdy surface is essential for working
on large, complicated woodcarvings.
Be sure to have enough storage areas
to keep your workbench well organized.

Vises and clamps—Whenever you are carving a large block of wood, you need to secure it to your workbench. One way to do this is to fasten the block in a vise, which has two wood or metal jaws to grip the wood. Wooden vises are built into traditional woodcarving benches. You can also use a portable, metal vise that bolts onto your work surface. Although metal vises aren't usually recommended for carving, I use a large one I found, and I've never had any trouble with it. The complaint is that it is easy for the tool to slip onto the metal and nick the cutting edge. Another problem is that the jaws of the vise will damage any wood surface they grip. When I use my metal vise for working on three-dimensional sculptures or decoys, I screw a block of hardwood to the base of the carving and fasten the jaws of the vise on the block, as shown in the photo below. This setup not only holds the carving securely, it elevates the piece so the tools will clear the vise if they happen to slip.

In addition to a vise, you will need a couple of C-clamps for holding the wood to the bench. When using clamps, always place a small piece of thin scrap wood between the metal and the work to prevent it from being damaged by the clamp jaws. I also use a simple bench hook made from scrap to secure small blocks. (I describe how to make a bench hook on p. 93.)

Either a bench holdfast (left) or a C-clamp (right) can be used to secure a piece of wood to the workbench when you are carving.

You can buy a carver's screw, or you can make one by sawing a slot in the end of a ¼-in. lag screw.

To secure a carving to the bench in a vise, screw a block of hardwood to the base of the carving and fasten the vise jaws on the block.

Another useful device is a bench holdfast, a traditional tool made of a single piece of forged iron. It's shaped like an inverted *L,* and fits into an oversized hole drilled in the benchtop. Once it is tapped into place with a hammer, it firmly holds down a flat piece of wood by means of friction. To release the holdfast, strike the back of it lightly. I use a pair of holdfasts for planing boards or carving panels. One of my workbenches, an old family design, has a series of ¾-in.-diameter holes drilled through the top. Holdfasts fit into any of these holes, which allows me to secure boards and panels of any dimension or shape to my bench.

Wood can also be secured with a carver's screw, a piece of steel with wood-screw threads at the pointed end and machine threads at the other. You can purchase a carver's screw, or make your own from a ¼-in. lag screw. Cut a slot in the blunt end with a hacksaw so it can be screwed into the carving block about ¾ in. with a screwdriver. Insert the screw through one of the bench holes, then use a large washer and wing nut to lock it down from underneath. This arrangement allows you to turn the carving so you can work on it from different directions. The only drawback is that the wood can pivot when you're carving, especially if you're using a heavy gouge and mallet. In this case, I secure the work with a holdfast or *C*-clamp for additional support.

HOLDFAST

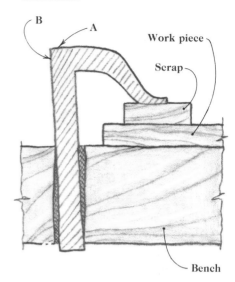

Tap at point A to set the holdfast in place; tap at point B to release it.

RECOMMENDED TOOLS FOR:

WHITTLING
Straight-bladed knife
X-acto knife
3mm and 6mm *V*-tools

RELIEF CARVING
Beginning
6mm #3 gouge
12mm #5 fishtail gouge
6mm and 12mm #7 gouges
6mm *V*-tool
Advanced
8mm and 15mm #3 gouges
18mm #5 spoon-bent gouge
20mm #5 fishtail gouge
10mm #7 spoon-bent gouge
14mm, 18mm, 25mm
   #7 gouges
10mm #8 gouge
3mm and 14mm *V*-tools
2mm and 7mm veiners
12mm carver's chisel

CHIP CARVING
Straight-bladed knife
Skew knife
Offset knife

WILDLIFE CARVING
Beginning
Straight-bladed knife
5mm #3 and #8 gouges
3mm *V*-tool
Advanced
15mm #3 gouge
12mm #5 fishtail
18mm and 25mm #7 gouges
3mm, 4mm, 6mm #8 gouges
6mm *V*-tool
12mm macaroni tool
12mm carver's chisel

LETTERING
Straight-bladed knife
14mm #5 gouge
10mm and 12mm
   #5 fishtail gouges
6mm, 14mm, 18mm #7 gouges
4mm #8 gouge
3mm *V*-tool
15mm #13 *V*-tool
6mm and 12mm
   carver's chisels
30mm chisel

ARCHITECTURAL CARVING
5mm #3 gouge
12mm and 20mm #5 gouges
10mm #5 fishtail gouge
8mm #5 back-bent gouge
6mm, 14mm, 18mm #7 gouges
6mm #9 gouge
6mm *V*-tool
12mm carver's chisel

Sharpening

I f there were one skill that could be called the greatest secret to fine woodcarving, it would be sharpening your tools correctly. A sharp cutting edge will cut cleanly through wood fibers and leave a polished facet that reveals the beauty of the wood. If your tools are not sharp, a block of wood will seem obstinate and unyielding—dull tools make woodcarving a frustrating experience rather than a pleasure.

Even a casual observer can tell the difference between a carving made with sharp tools and a carving made with dull ones. A woodcarving made with sharp tools shines with crispness and vitality. Dull tools crush the wood fibers and leave a rough, splintered appearance, so the work looks sloppy and amateurish, no matter how skillfully the design is carved.

Mastering the skill of sharpening is extremely important to any serious woodcarver. It is not difficult to learn. There are no mysteries—all it requires is starting with the right basic technique, and the rest comes with practice.

Materials

The cutting edge of a tool is sharpened by rubbing it against lubricated abrasive stones. Sharpening stones are available in a number of shapes and sizes, different types of materials and degrees of abrasiveness (sometimes graded by number). Stones intended to be lubricated with oil are called oilstones; those with water, waterstones. I prefer to use oilstones because they are generally harder, and don't wear down as quickly. Waterstones require a different sharpening technique than the one I will explain here. (Japanese craftsmen have made sharpening with waterstones an art in itself.)

Sharpening is not a difficult skill— learn the basic techniques, and the rest comes with practice.

Benchstones, about 2 in. wide and 6 in. to 10 in. long, are used for sharpening knives and the outer bevels of gouges. From left to right: a soft Arkansas stone, a man-made Japanese water-stone, and a 200/400-grit combination India stone.

Oilstones are made of either man-made materials, such as silicon carbide or aluminum oxide, or natural materials, such as novaculite. Silicon carbide, one of the hardest industrial abrasives, cuts metal quickly, but leaves a coarse, rough edge. The abrasive particles loosen with use, so stones made from silicon carbide tend to wear away quickly, and may need to be replaced every few years. (Carborundum and Crystolon are trade names for silicon-carbide stones.) India stones, made from aluminum oxide, have a finer texture and last longer than silicon-carbide stones.

Sharpening stones are available in a variety of grits. Grit is the degree of abrasive quality of a stone, and ranges from coarse (about 100 to 200 if graded by number), medium (about 200 to 400), fine (about 400 to 800) to very fine (about 800 to 2000). Sometimes, two stones of different grits are fused together to make a combination stone. I use a 200/400-grit combination India benchstone, about 2 in. wide and 7 in. long.

The most common natural sharpening stones are made from novaculite, a type of quartz found near the hot springs area in

OILSTONES

NAME	COLOR	TEXTURE AND MATERIAL	USE
Carborundum or Crystolon	Dark grey	Coarse (100-200 grit). A soft stone, man-made from silicon carbide.	Coarse-sharpening. Used for preliminary shaping of a bevel or repairing a nicked edge.
Washita	Cream with dark stripes	Medium (350 grit). A soft, natural stone.	Whetting. Used for smoothing the bevel and producing a burr edge.
India	Reddish brown	Medium (400 grit). A hard stone, man-made from aluminum oxide.	Whetting. Used for smoothing the bevel and producing a burr edge.
Soft Arkansas	White or grey speckled	Fine (800 grit). A soft, natural stone.	Honing. Used for removing the burr edge.
Hard Arkansas	White	Very fine (1000 grit). A hard, natural stone.	Honing and Polishing. Used for the final honing and polishing of the edge.
Black Arkansas	Black	Extremely fine (2000 grit). A very hard, natural stone.	Polishing. Used for the final polishing of a sharpened edge.

Arkansas. These stones are known as Arkansas stones, and for centuries have been considered the finest and most sought-after sharpening stones in the world. Unfortunately, because novaculite is rare and difficult to work, natural sharpening stones can be quite expensive. The abrasive quality of these stones is graded by hardness and color—the soft white and hard white Arkansas stones are not as finely textured as the hard black Arkansas.

Basically, the process of sharpening the cutting edge of a tool can be broken down into four steps: coarse-sharpening, whetting, honing and polishing. Coarse-sharpening removes the bulk of the metal, produces the tool's rough shape and bevel and removes any nicks in the edge. (If an edge is severely damaged, you may need to repair it on a grinding wheel.) For coarse-sharpening, you need a stone of about 100 grit to 200 grit, so I use the coarse side of the combination India stone. You can also use a Carborundum or Crystolon stone.

Whetting smooths the bevel and produces the burr or wire edge that is essential to getting a tool sharp. For this step, you need a stone of medium grit (200 to 400), and I use the 400-grit side of the combination India stone. Honing removes the burr and produces the final, razor-sharp edge. For this, you need a fine stone; I use either a soft or hard white Arkansas. I have found that Arkansas stones are useful in the shape of small stones called slipstones, or slips, ranging in size from 2 in. to 4 in. long. Slipstones come in a variety of shapes, as shown in the photo and drawing at right, but the slips with rounded edges are especially useful for honing the inner and outer bevels of a gouge.

Polishing, the last step, buffs away the minute scratches left from the earlier stages of sharpening, and leaves the tool with a mirror-bright surface that glides easily through the wood. For polishing, I use a very fine stone, like the black Arkansas, or a leather strop, which is a strip of leather fastened to a length of wood. You can easily make a strop by taking a piece of belt leather approximately 2 in. wide and 12 in. long and securing it to each end of a piece of wood with glue or tacks. (For polishing gouges, I also sometimes use a cloth buffing wheel, as described on pp. 32-33.)

For sharpening on oilstones, you'll need a can of light machine oil, such as 3-in-1. (Some carvers use kerosene, but light machine oil is a better lubricant, doesn't smell as bad and isn't as flammable.) Keep your stones well oiled with a few drops of 3-in-1 when sharpening. The oil not only lubricates the blade, it floats away the metal filings and prevents them from clogging the pores of the stone, which would eventually ruin it. Wipe off excess oil and metal filings after each use with a rag or paper towel. I use paper towels because they are less of a fire hazard, and I discard them when I'm through. If you use cloth rags, be sure to store them after use in an airtight metal container to prevent spontaneous combustion.

Protect your stones from dust and chipping by storing them in a wooden box. Be sure to keep them well lubricated when sharpening, and clean away excess oil after every use. With proper care, your sharpening stones will last a long time.

SLIPSTONES

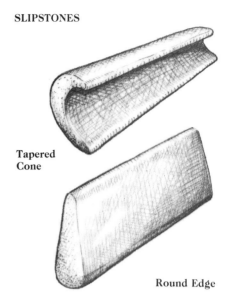

Tapered Cone

Round Edge

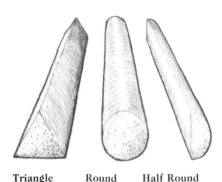

Triangle   **Round**   **Half Round**

Slipstones are used to sharpen inner bevels, and are available in different shapes. From left to right: a black Arkansas with a knife edge, a hard white Arkansas and a soft Arkansas slip, both having one round edge and one knife edge (for inner bevels of V-tools), and a round-edge India slip.

Keep the cutting edge flat
and the back of the blade
20° to 30° to the stone.
Move the knife in a
circular motion.

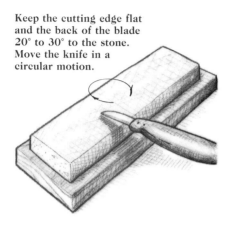

Sectional Front View

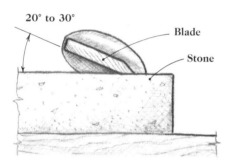

20° to 30°

Blade

Stone

*Keep the entire cutting edge flat against
the stone and the back of the blade angled up 20° to 30° as you sharpen in a
circular motion.*

Sharpening a Knife

The best tool for learning how to sharpen is a knife. If the knife is new, or the edge isn't too badly nicked or neglected, begin sharpening with a medium stone and finish with a fine stone or the strop. If the edge is badly dulled, nicked or rusted, use a coarse stone before the medium stone. The techniques are the same for both coarse-sharpening and whetting.

Place two or three drops of oil on the stone to make a small pool, and rub the entire cutting edge against it in a circular motion, as shown in the drawing at left. Position the knife in your hand as if you were spreading jam with a table knife. The entire cutting edge should be flat on the stone, but the back of the blade should angle up about 20° to 30°. The angles are difficult to measure, so estimate. (At first, just concentrate on getting the edge sharp; the rest will develop with practice and experience.) When rubbing the knife on the stone, you don't have to press down with a lot of force; just use the same amount of pressure you would use when writing with a pencil. When the stone's surface looks dry, add a few more drops of oil; otherwise, the stone will clog with the metal filings being removed from the blade.

Sharpen both sides of the blade equally and at the same angle. As the stone wears away the blade, you'll notice that a thin layer of metal begins to form at the cutting edge, curling up on the side opposite the one that you're sharpening. This is the burr or wire edge. A burr indicates that the steel has been brought to as sharp

*Sharpening will produce a burr on the cutting edge (left). Once the burr
has been removed, the edge will be razor-sharp (right).*

an edge as the grit of your sharpening stone will produce. The burr is virtually microscopic, so check for it by lightly dragging your fingertip across the width of the blade, toward and over the cutting edge. (Don't stroke along the edge or you can be easily cut.) The burr will feel rough, as though it were catching on the ridges of your fingerprint. Continue sharpening until you can feel the burr along the entire length of the blade.

If you were to use this knife now, the burr would fold over and break off, leaving a dull cutting edge. Therefore, you must hone off the burr with a stone of finer grit. For honing, I use a white Arkansas stone, either soft or hard. The hand position, the circular motion and the need to add oil is the same as when whetting.

If you don't have an Arkansas stone, you can progress directly from the medium stone to the strop—it will just take a little more time to get the sharp, polished edge you need.

To use the strop, hold the blade at the same low angle you used on the sharpening stone and slowly stroke the blade up and down the length of the strop. Always stroke away from the cutting edge, otherwise the knife will cut into the leather and ruin it. I usually work the blade ten strokes on one side, turn the blade over and repeat on the other side, and then work the first side again. (This ensures each side is worked evenly.) I stroke the blade away from me with the edge facing me; when I change direction, I flip the blade over and stroke it toward me with the edge facing away. The important thing is to remove the burr and polish the bevels that form the cutting edge. This may be accomplished sooner, but I usually strop each side of the blade a total of about 50 times, then test the edge for any remnant of the burr. If there is none, the blade is razor-sharp and ready to use.

Although the strop can be used without any lubricant, I sometimes rub a little polishing compound into the leather to speed up the process. I use Tripoli compound, which is a waxlike substance that comes in stick form. It is normally used for dressing buffing wheels when making jewelry. You can also use an automotive buffing compound, silver polish or even cheap toothpaste, all of which have enough grit to make the strop cut better and speed up polishing.

When polishing a knife on the strop, stroke away from the cutting edge.

Testing for sharpness—After stropping, test the blade for sharpness. There are two good methods for testing. One is to try carving across the end grain of a soft piece of wood, like pine or basswood. (The end grain is the surface where the annual rings are visible.) If your knife is sharp, it will remove a nice, clean chip and leave a polished surface. However, if the edge is dull, the wood will crunch and tear.

The second test for sharpness requires more sensitivity. Drag the cutting edge lightly down the surface of your thumbnail, holding the blade almost vertical. If the edge slides over the nail surface, it's still too dull, and needs more work. If you can feel the edge grip the nail slightly, the blade is sharp. The more vertical the angle at which the edge grips the nail, the sharper the edge.

Don't become discouraged if it takes a while to get a sharp edge. I can still remember the first time that I ever tried to sharpen a

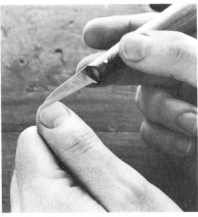

Test for sharpness by dragging the cutting edge lightly down your thumbnail.

knife. I thought it would be quite easy because the knife is such a basic tool. As it turned out, it took nearly three hours to bring it to a razor-sharp edge. Now, many years later, the same work requires only a few minutes. It's a good idea to keep the strop nearby and stroke the blade 20 to 30 times after each half hour of woodcarving. This will help maintain the sharp edge of your knife while you're carving.

Sharpening Gouges

Woodcarving gouges are sharpened in much the same way as a knife. The only difference is that you are working with a curved cutting edge rather than a flat one. You begin with a coarse stone to shape the bevel or if the edge is dull or nicked, proceed to a medium stone until the burr forms, then hone on a fine Arkansas slipstone and polish on the strop or cloth wheel.

To coarse-sharpen, fasten a coarse stone to the bench so that it doesn't slide around as you work. (If the stone is in a wooden box, as most are, clamp the edges of the box to the workbench with two *C*-clamps.) Place a few drops of oil on the stone and hold the handle of the gouge in your right hand (if you are right-handed), placing the fingers of your left hand on the shaft, as shown in the photos at left. With a light, but firm downward pressure, rub the edge along the length of the stone. By twisting your right hand, you will create a rolling motion that causes the entire curved edge to contact the stone. However, be careful not to roll the blade too far on either side when sharpening, because this will round off the outside corners of the blade and reduce the width and effectiveness of the cutting edge.

Most tools come with a bevel already ground. To determine the bevel angle, place the bevel flat on the stone. The angle the blade makes to the stone is the bevel angle. (This is the angle at which the tool enters the wood as it starts to cut.) The correct bevel angle varies with personal preference, but also depends on the type of wood you will be carving. For example, straight gouges used mostly with softwoods or for carving fine details should have a bevel angle of 15° to 20°. This makes for a thin cutting edge, which is okay because it doesn't take a lot of pressure to move a gouge through softwood. Straight gouges used with hardwood or for heavy-duty roughing-out should be beveled at an angle closer to 25° or 30° to more easily sever the coarse fibers. This angle makes for a slightly thicker cutting edge, which is less likely to chip or break. Some woodcarvers make the mistake of making the bevel on a gouge a perfectly flat surface. Instead, the bevel should be rounded slightly at the back so that it blends smoothly into the bottom surface of the blade and doesn't have any sharp angles that can drag on the wood. This also makes it easier for the gouge to come out of the wood when you want to stop a cut.

After the bevel has been shaped to the correct angle, proceed to the medium stone and sharpen with the same rolling motion until a burr forms on the inside of the cutting edge. Remove the burr with a soft or hard white Arkansas slipstone. I begin by rubbing the stone against the inner bevel. Place a few drops of oil on the bevel, and hold the blade in your left hand so that it points slightly

When sharpening a gouge, hold the handle in one hand and place the fingers of your other hand on top of the blade. Roll the tool as you move it along the stone so that the entire cutting edge will be sharpened.

upward, as shown in the photo at top right. In your right hand, take a slipstone with a rounded edge that fits inside the tool's curve—it doesn't need to fit tightly. Brace your left elbow against your body to hold the gouge steady, and briskly rub the stone back and forth across the bevel at a 10° to 20° angle to the inside surface. Rolling the gouge in your fingers as you rub will let you bring the entire surface of the bevel against the stone. Use the flat surface of the slipstone to hone the outer bevel using the same motion. The Arkansas stone will smooth out the scratches left by the previous stone and wear away any remnants of the burr.

For the final polishing of both inner and outer bevels, you can use a black Arkansas slipstone in the same way, although this can be a slow process because the grit is so fine. You can also polish the inner bevel with a folded piece of leather, held in the same way as the slipstone, and polish the outer bevel on the strop. Hold the strop steady on the bench with one hand, and hold the gouge in the other hand about halfway down its total length, at an angle of 15° to 30°. Curl your fingers around the handle, and extend your index finger straight along the blade, applying pressure near the cutting edge. Stroke the gouge toward you along the leather, rolling the blade slightly to polish the entire edge. Repeat this motion with a brisk, stroking action until the tool is razor-sharp. Test for sharpness the same way as for a knife.

To hone the inner bevel of a gouge, use a soft or hard Arkansas slipstone with a rounded edge. Briskly rub the stone back and forth with one hand as you roll the gouge slightly with the other.

SHARPENING A GOUGE

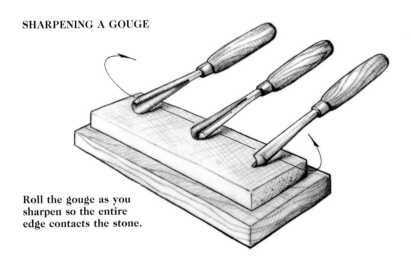

Roll the gouge as you sharpen so the entire edge contacts the stone.

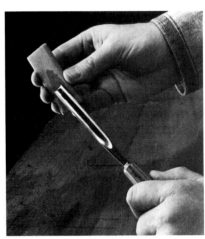

Hone the outer bevel of a straight gouge using the flat surface of the slipstone.

BEVEL ANGLES FOR STRAIGHT GOUGES

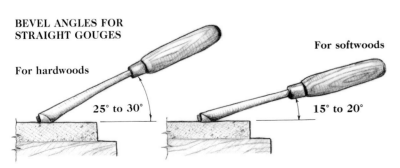

For softwoods

For hardwoods

25° to 30°

15° to 20°

To polish the outer bevel of a straight gouge, hold the tool at a 15° to 20° angle to the strop and roll the blade slightly as you stroke it toward you.

Buffing wheel—A faster way to achieve the same results is to polish the bevel on a cloth buffing wheel that has been rubbed with a little polishing compound. I use a flannel wheel fitted to an old electric motor. It does an excellent job of polishing the edge to a perfect sharpness, and it is also the best method for removing tiny scratches left by the sharpening stones.

You can make your own buffing-wheel setup by removing the emery wheel from an electric grinder and fastening a 6-in.-diameter cloth wheel to the shaft. Cloth wheels are about 1 in. thick and made of layers of felt or cotton discs sewn together. You can purchase these wheels at hardware stores or craft and jewelry-supply houses.

The wheel will be rotating at a speed of approximately 2000 revolutions per minute, so you need to follow several safety precautions. Always wear goggles when working with any power tools. Keep sleeves rolled up and out of the way, and don't wear any loose clothing that could get tangled in the wheel. The direction the wheel is turning is important for safety, too. It should be moving so that the surface you are facing is turning downward. The wheel can grab whatever you're holding against it and throw it out of your hands; with the wheel turning downward, objects are thrown toward the floor instead of up in the air and toward you. To prevent work from being thrown by the wheel at all, always hold it firmly with both hands. Use a light pressure against the wheel and always keep the work below the wheel's center, as shown in the photos below.

To polish on a cloth buffing wheel, press the bevel against the wheel, always keeping the tool's edge below the wheel's center.

To polish gouges on the buffing wheel, lightly press a stick of Tripoli, jeweler's rouge or another fine polishing compound against the revolving wheel for a few seconds. Next, hold the gouge handle firmly in one hand, with the bevel you want to polish facing up. With the other hand, hold the blade about 2 in. back from the cutting edge. Position the gouge so it makes an angle to the floor of about 45° (for outer bevels) or 65° (for inner bevels). Stand in front of the wheel and carefully bring the bevel up to the revolving wheel. Lightly roll the bevel back and forth across the width of the wheel so that the entire surface is polished. It should have a mirror shine in one or two minutes. (When carving, I often use the buffing wheel to touch up a cutting edge. I hone the inner bevel with a slipstone, then polish the inner and outer bevels quickly on the wheel.) Polishing on a buffing wheel is a technique used by professional carvers; if you want to try it, take your time, and observe all safety precautions.

The drawing at right shows what a properly sharpened gouge should look like, and the chart below shows examples of improperly sharpened gouges. As you are learning, you might find it useful to refer to this list of common problems encountered in sharpening, and their causes and solutions.

CORRECTLY SHARPENED GOUGE

Cutting edge is even and perpendicular to shaft.

Bevel is the correct angle.

Corners of cutting edge are sharp.

Bevel is slightly rounded at bottom to blend into surface of blade.

COMMON PROBLEMS IN SHARPENING GOUGES

PROBLEM	CAUSE	SOLUTION
Cutting edge is uneven.	Bevel has been sharpened in some areas more than others.	Square up the edge by holding the gouge vertically against a medium stone and rubbing the edge back and forth until the corners are at right angles to the blade. Resharpen, making sure to work the entire bevel evenly.
Edge is not perpendicular to the blade.	Sides have been sharpened too much, or the sharpening was begun without squaring the cutting edge first.	Square up the edge, as described above. Then resharpen, being careful not to roll the tool too far on either side.
Corners of the cutting edge are rounded.	The gouge was rolled too far on its sides during sharpening.	Square up the edge, then resharpen, being careful not to roll the tool too far on either side.
Bevel angle is too short.	Gouge was held at too high an angle during sharpening.	Resharpen on a coarse stone, holding the gouge at the correct angle (see pp. 30-31).

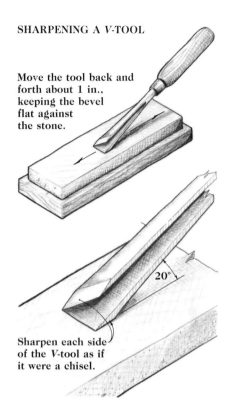

Move the tool back and forth about 1 in., keeping the bevel flat against the stone.

20°

Sharpen each side of the *V*-tool as if it were a chisel.

Sharpening a Chisel and a *V*-Tool

To sharpen a woodcarver's chisel, hold the tool as you would when sharpening a gouge (p. 30). (You can also hold the tool blade in one hand with the index finger extended for support, as shown in the photo below.) Sharpen the bevel on each side to an angle of about 20° by rubbing it back and forth along the stone. Don't roll the blade; keep the bevel flat against the stone. You only need to travel about 1 in. or so, which will help you keep the angle of the tool consistent. Sharpen the bevel on each side equally. Use the same motion on the medium and fine stones for whetting and honing, and polish on a strop or buffing wheel.

The *V*-tool is tricky to sharpen. It's easy to take off too much metal from one side, especially during the final stages of sharpening, resulting in an off-center cutting edge that will prevent the tool from cutting properly. You'll find a sharp *V*-tool especially useful, so it's well worth the extra trouble to sharpen it.

The two flat sides that meet to form the *V* of the *V*-tool call for a slightly different approach to sharpening. The best method is to treat each side of the *V* as if it were a single flat chisel. Sharpen

To sharpen a chisel or V-tool, you can hold the tool with one hand, as shown, or with two hands, as you would when sharpening a gouge.

the bevels on each side to an angle of 20° by moving the tool back and forth along the stone, as described for the carver's chisel and as shown in the drawing and photo on the facing page.

When a burr has formed on each side of the *V*, there will be a thick hook of excess metal at the center. Remove the hook by treating the base of the *V* as if it were a miniature gouge that needs sharpening. Roll the tool slightly as you move it back and forth across a medium stone, as shown in the drawing below, to create a center outer bevel. (This bevel should be about 10° for softwood, and 20° for hardwood.) Continue sharpening the center bevel until the hook wears away and leaves a sharp edge. Continue to roll the gouge as you sharpen so that the bevel blends into the sides of the *V*. Be careful not to oversharpen or you'll create a gap at the center of the tool—if this happens, square up the cutting edge and start again.

Hone the inner bevels of the tool with an Arkansas slipstone that fits inside the *V*. Remove the burr and put an angle of about 5° on the inner bevels. Then use the edge of the strop or buffing wheel to polish the inner and outer bevels to a mirror shine.

To remove the hook of excess metal and create the center outer bevel, roll the tool slightly as you move the base of the V across a medium stone.

REMOVING THE HOOK

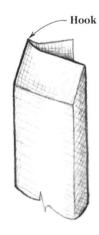

— Hook

After each side of the *V*-tool has been sharpened, a hook of metal forms at the center.

To remove the hook, roll the tool slightly as you move it across the medium stone.

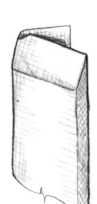

If you oversharpen the center outer bevel of the tool, square up the edge and try again.

10° to 20° center outer bevel —

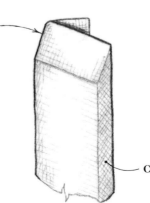

— Correctly sharpened *V*-tool

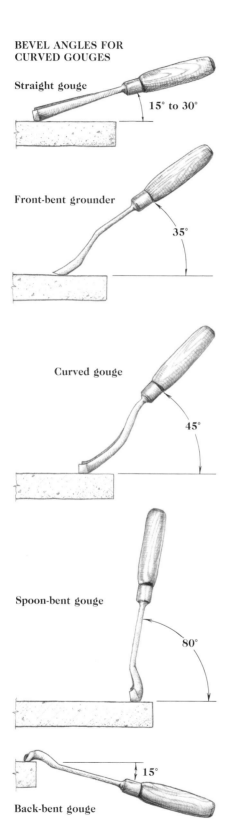

BEVEL ANGLES FOR CURVED GOUGES

Straight gouge

15° to 30°

Front-bent grounder

35°

Curved gouge

45°

Spoon-bent gouge

80°

15°

Back-bent gouge

Sharpening Gouges with Curved Blades

Gouges with front-bent, curved (long-bent), spoon-bent and back-bent blades are sharpened in the same way as straight gouges. The main difference is the angle at which each tool is held to the sharpening stone to compensate for its curvature, as shown in the drawings at left and the photos on the facing page. A straight gouge is sharpened to an angle of about 15° to 30°. For a front-bent grounder, the angle will be approximately 35°; for a curved gouge, about 45°; for a spoon-bent gouge, the angle will be closer to 80°. When the bevel of the back-bent gouge is flat against the stone, the tool will be at a 15° angle below the stone's surface. Of course, these angle measurements are approximate because the amount of bend in a blade varies among toolmakers. The bevel angle also depends on your preference, and on the type of wood you are carving. You'll probably have to experiment a bit in order to arrive at the correct angle for your own gouges.

The inner bevels of all these gouges are honed with a slipstone. Hold the tool in one hand and the slipstone in the other, as you did when sharpening the straight gouges (pp. 30-31). Rub the slipstone against the bevel at a 10° to 20° angle to the inside surface. The only problem may occur when honing the inner bevel of a deeply bent spoon gouge. The clearance between the cutting edge and the bend of the blade may be ½ in. or less, so you'll only be able to move the slipstone back and forth over a very short distance. In order to get the right results, you have to spend a little more time working with the slipstone.

I use either the leather strop or the buffing wheel to polish the outer bevels of these gouges, and a black Arkansas slipstone to polish the inner bevels.

Care of Tools

Always protect your gouges from banging against each other or hitting things that can dull their edges. The best protection is storing them in a cloth roll with individual pockets sewn in. A cloth roll can be purchased from any tool catalog, or you can make one, as discussed on p. 11.

When carving, always keep your tools in a place where they won't be knocked off your bench. Dropped tools invariably land point first, where the most damage can be done. If you do happen to drop a gouge, do not try to catch it. Just get out of the way and let it fall to the floor. A lot of accidents have occurred when people have tried to rescue a sharp tool in midflight.

A badly nicked or broken edge can be reshaped on an electric grinding wheel. This should be done only if the gouge has been so severely damaged that it would require a lot of time sharpening on a stone to repair it. The problem is that high-speed grinders cause the steel to heat up very quickly, and too much heat can permanently soften the steel by drawing out its temper. When this happens, the blade will no longer hold a sharp edge, and the tool will be ruined unless you take it to a blacksmith for retempering. If you must use an electric grinder, always keep some cool water nearby and dip the blade frequently. Never let the edge get too hot to touch.

The angle at which a tool is held to the stone varies with the shape of the blade. A straight gouge is held at an angle of 15° to 30° (top left); a front-bent grounder is held at an angle of approximately 35° (bottom left); a long-bent, or curved, gouge at an angle of about 45° (top right); a spoon-bent gouge at an angle of about 80° (center right); and a back-bent gouge at about 15° below the stone's surface (bottom right).

Woods and Finishes

3

For thousands of years, man has regarded wood with religious awe. Our ancestors believed trees were magical, somehow storing the sun's energy and releasing it in the form of fire. Many ancient societies believed wood was the home of powerful spirits of nature and worshipped trees as supernatural entities. Even our European ancestors thought that faeries and elves inhabited the trees and woods. They believed it was possible to drive out mischievous spirits by "knocking on the wood," a superstition still practiced today, though the original meaning is often forgotten.

In New Zealand, the Maori tribesmen have over a dozen taboos to observe while woodcarving. It's forbidden to leave food near a carving in progress, and woodcarvers cannot blow away chips or shavings, lest their breath offend the spirit of the wood. These beliefs and practices may seem unusual to us, but they underline the fact that wood has always inspired a sense of mystery.

There's a good reason why man developed this reverence for wood. Wood is a living material with a character unlike anything else—each piece has its own beauty and unique characteristics. Within one log, there can be sections with completely different colors and textures. Most people who have trouble carving just haven't taken the time to understand wood. I don't think this is simply a matter of impatience. Rather, in an age where we're accustomed to demanding and achieving instant results, it's hard to remember that some types of knowledge require time to learn.

Woodcarving isn't just shaping a block of wood; it's an act of cooperation between you, your tools and the fibers of a tree. Approach wood with understanding and respect, and carving will not develop into a battle of wills between you and your materials.

A variety of woods and finishes can be used for woodcarving, depending on the type of project and your personal preference.

HARDWOODS

NAME	HARDNESS	TEXTURE	DESCRIPTION
Ash	Hard	Medium coarse	Light grey. Tough and springy. Resembles oak. Often used for tool handles.
Aspen	Soft	Fine	White. Carves well but checks easily.
Balsa	Very soft	Coarse	Light tan. Too soft to carve.
Basswood	Soft	Fine	Cream. Also called limewood or linden. Good for whittling and relief carving.
Beech	Hard	Medium	Pink-tan. Moderately difficult to carve, checks and warps easily. Used for making wooden planes, tools, bowls and eating utensils.
Birch	Hard	Fine	Light tan. Good for carving, but straight-grained pieces are difficult to find.
Butternut	Medium	Medium coarse	Light cream to reddish brown with pink streaks. Excellent for carving. Beautiful grain. Good for sculptures and relief carvings.
Cherry, Black	Hard	Fine	Creamy tan. Ages to a dark reddish brown. Difficult to carve, but takes finishes well. Best for sculpture.
Chestnut	Medium hard	Medium coarse	Light brownish grey. Carves easily, takes finishes well. Rare because tree is nearly extinct.
Cottonwood	Soft	Fine	Light grey. Carves easily and holds detail well.
Elm, American	Hard	Coarse	Medium brown with dark streaks. Difficult to carve.
Hickory	Hard	Coarse	Brown. Tough and springy. Difficult to carve. Used for tool handles.
Mahogany: African, Cuban and Honduras	Medium	Medium coarse	Dark reddish brown. Beautiful figure and color. Some species difficult to carve because of hard and soft grain pattern.
Maple, Silver	Medium	Fine	Creamy white to light brown. Soft, straight grain. Carves well.
Maple: Black, Red and Sugar	Hard	Fine	Creamy white to light brown. Difficult to carve because grain is often wavy.
Oak: Black, Red and White	Hard	Coarse	Light brown to dark reddish brown. Difficult to carve, does not hold fine detail, but takes finishes well.
Osage Orange	Hard	Medium	Yellow-orange. Tough, with irregular grain. Difficult to carve. Suitable for sculpture.
Poplar	Medium soft	Fine	Light yellow. Easy to carve. Resists checking.
Teak	Hard	Medium coarse	Yellow-brown. Carves easily, but minerals in the wood will dull tools and react with some finishes. Weather-resistant.
Walnut, Black	Hard	Medium coarse	Dark to purplish brown. Excellent for sculpture.

The structure of wood—In order to choose woods to carve, you should know a few facts about wood structure. Basically, trees can be divided into two groups: hardwoods and softwoods. Hardwood trees, called deciduous trees, have broad leaves that change color and drop off during autumn. The oaks, maples and birches belong to this group. Softwoods trees, called evergreens or conifers, are resinous, cone-bearing trees with needles or scalelike leaves they retain all year long. Generally speaking, the fibers of hardwoods are hard and dense, while softwoods have a soft, more porous texture. (However, the botanical categories don't always indicate the actual hardness or softness of a piece of wood. As can be seen in the charts below and on the facing page, there are exceptions in each group.)

A tree trunk is made up of thousands of hollow, tubelike, fibrous cells. Moisture and dissolved minerals are absorbed by the roots, and transferred to the leaves through these cells. These materials are then processed into food with the aid of sunlight, and distributed back down through the cells to the roots. These microscopic bundles that run along the length of the trunk form the grain of the wood. The direction of the grain determines the strength of a piece of wood, and the direction in which a block of wood can be carved, which needs to be considered when laying out a design, as discussed on p. 60. Grain is also a factor in wood texture—the coarseness or fineness of the wood is determined by the average diameter of its cells.

In the center of the tree's trunk and branches is a soft core of spongy material called the pith. The pith is not very dense or stable, and has a tendency to chip out, so I usually cut it off

SOFTWOODS

NAME	HARDNESS	TEXTURE	DESCRIPTION
Cedar, Eastern Red	Medium	Fine	Red. Frequent knots, fragrant aroma. Oils in wood adversely affect many finishes. Used for lining cedar chests and closets.
Cedar: Northern White, Western Red	Soft	Medium coarse	Straight-grained and knot-free. Used in boatbuilding.
Fir: Balsam, Oregon White	Soft	Fine	Creamy white. Resembles white pine but has more pungent fragrance. Splits easily. A thoroughly miserable wood to carve.
Fir, Douglas	Medium	Medium	Reddish yellow. Difficult to carve because of hard and soft grain pattern. Used in house construction.
Pine: Sugar, White	Soft	Fine	Light cream. Fragrant aroma. Excellent to carve, holds detail well. Hard yellow pine is less suitable for carving.
Redwood	Soft	Medium fine	Reddish brown. Alternating hard and soft grain makes carving difficult. Weather-resistant.

blanks before I begin carving. Around the pith are concentric annual growth rings. By counting these rings, you can tell the age of a piece of wood, and it's interesting to know that the piece you are carving may have required 60 years or more to form. Earlywood, or springwood, forms the first portion of the growth ring, and the latewood, or summerwood, completes the ring. These alternating sections of the rings, and their varying densities, are part of what gives a wood its characteristic texture and beautiful color patterns.

The growth rings nearest the center of the trunk form the heartwood, and the outer rings make up the sapwood. Sapwood contains the living cells that conduct water and minerals through the tree; heartwood contains cells that are no longer active in conducting sap, but serve as support tissue for the trunk and branches. Heartwood is usually denser and darker than sapwood, especially in the hardwoods, although in some species of wood, you can't tell where the sapwood starts and the heartwood ends.

Sometimes you will find knots in a piece of wood. These dark, round or oval spots will distort the grain pattern for several inches around the knot's circumference, making the wood difficult to work. Knots are the remains of branches that were cut or broken off and around which the tree has grown, or the remains of new branches emerging at the time the tree was cut. Knots are hard and can damage your tools, so avoid them. Knotty wood is best saved for the fireplace—it burns much better than it carves.

CROSS SECTION OF TREE TRUNK

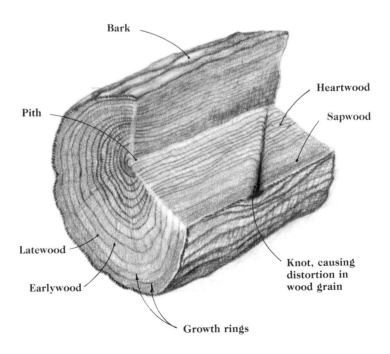

Carving wood–When carving wood, the trick is to carve away the excess in a smooth, controlled manner and avoid uncontrolled splitting of the wood fibers in front of the tool. This is done by carving with the grain, not against it.

The best way to figure out the way the grain is traveling is by trying to carve. If you are carving in the right direction, the wood will shear off in smooth curls. The tool will rise out of the wood, scoop out clean shavings and leave a smooth surface. If you reverse the direction, the tool will dig in, make jagged splinters and leave a rough surface.

The feeling of carving with the grain is a lot like petting a dog or a cat. When you move your hand in one direction, the fur feels smooth. But if you move your hand in the opposite direction, the fur feels rough and uncomfortable—and your pet doesn't like it much either. Carving with the grain is like that. One way feels right as the tool goes through the wood—the other way doesn't.

Look at the edge of a piece of wood and observe in which directions the grain patterns rise and fall. Then take a sharp knife and make a few sample cuts along the edge of the wood. Note that the cuts made in the direction of the rising grain make a clean, curling shaving; those made against the rising grain cause the knife edge to dig in and make splinters, as shown in the drawing below. With a little practice, you will be able to look at a piece of wood, and know which direction to carve it.

Learning to work with the grain is one of the most important skills in woodcarving and becomes easier with experience. The miniature duck decoy on pp. 74-77 is a good exercise to begin with to get a feel for working with the grain. The curved shapes and flat surfaces will give you a good sampling of some of the difficulties you may experience with changing grain directions.

CARVING WITH THE GRAIN

Grain ⟶

CARVING AGAINST THE GRAIN

Grain ⟶

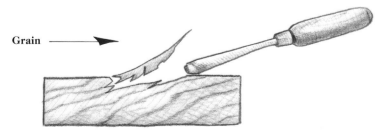

Choosing wood—One of the most frequently asked questions about woodcarving is "Which wood is best to carve?" Unfortunately there is no simple answer, because almost any wood can be carved—but some woods are better suited than others for certain projects, as shown in the chart on the facing page.

My favorite woods vary for different types of projects, but I always try to use pieces of wood with straight grain because it's easier to control the carving. As a general rule, use smooth, fine-textured woods such as pine or basswood for small projects or for carvings with fine details. These woods will hold detail better than coarse-textured woods, which are liable to split or crumble. Most fine-textured woods also have even color, which helps to emphasize the details of the carving.

The contrasting grain patterns of coarse-textured woods, such as oak, butternut and Honduras mahogany, although beautiful, can detract from fine details. However, these same woods, along with highly colored ones, such as cherry and walnut, are excellent for sculpture with bold, simple shapes and smooth outlines. The beautiful grain patterns and colors of the wood add to the drama of the finished piece.

Many woodcarvers prefer not to use pine or other softwoods because these woods can be easily damaged in the process of carving or when the carving is on display. However, because tools cut through the wood easily, softwoods are well suited for learning to carve. Working them provides excellent practice in developing coordination and hand control, because it's easy to carve away too much wood if you're not careful. A beginner will also get a lot of practice in sharpening, because softwoods require razor-sharp tools, otherwise the soft fibers will tear out and leave rough splinters on the surface.

Hardwoods are more difficult to carve because the wood is dense, and requires more effort to cut through. Yet in spite of the difficulties, carving hardwoods can be worth the effort, because of their beautiful colors and grain patterns.

With these guidelines in mind, you can choose many different woods for carving, depending on their availability and your own preference. Each part of the world has its own unique woods that are well suited to carving. For example, on the Pacific Coast of the United States, redwood and myrtlewood are frequently used. In the southwestern desert region, woodcarvers work with mesquite and ironwood—two beautiful but extremely hard woods. In the South, tupelo, sassafras and dogwood are common. So be on the lookout for new varieties, and always ask carvers you meet about the woods in their area. Don't be afraid to experiment with an unusual or unfamiliar wood.

Seasoning wood—Some woods, especially softwoods, are stringy and won't carve cleanly or take fine details when green. Any wood that you carve has to be relatively free of moisture, otherwise it may split or check as it dries—the fibers will shrink at varying rates and pull apart. Seasoning is the controlled process of removing moisture from wood, and can be done either by air-drying or kiln-drying.

SELECTING WOODS AND FINISHES

TYPE OF CARVING	SUGGESTED WOODS	SUGGESTED FINISHES
WHITTLING: (Carvings under 6 in.) Projects with detailed surfaces	Aspen, Basswood, Black Cherry, Cottonwood, Poplar, White Pine	Tint, Oil, Paste Wax
Projects with smooth surfaces or simple details	All woods above, plus Birch, Butternut, Chestnut, Maple, Oak, Walnut	All finishes above, plus French Polish
SCULPTURE: (Carvings over 6 in.) Projects with detailed surfaces	Basswood, Black Cherry, Honduras Mahogany, Pine, Walnut	Stain, Oil, Varnish, French Polish, Tint or Enamel Paint (on light woods only), Paste Wax
Projects with smooth surfaces or simple details	All woods above, plus Ash, Beech, Birch, Cedar, Chestnut, Douglas Fir, Elm, Mahoganies, Maple, Oak, Osage Orange, Redwood, Teak	All finishes above
CHIP CARVING	Aspen, Basswood, Butternut, Poplar, White Pine	Oil (with or without glazing), Paste Wax
RELIEF CARVING and LETTERING	Aspen, Basswood, Beech, Birch, Butternut, Cherry, Chestnut, Cottonwood, Elm, Mahogany, Maple, Oak, Pine, Poplar, Walnut	Stain, Oil (with or without glazing), French Polish, Varnish, Enamel Paint, Paste Wax
WILDLIFE CARVING	Basswood, White Pine	Stain, Oil Paint
ARCHITECTURAL CARVING	Cedar, Cherry, Pine, Redwood, Walnut	Interior: Stain, Oil, French Polish, Varnish Exterior: Marine or Spar Varnish, Stain

Most of the wood available in lumberyards has been kiln-dried—the wood is placed in an enclosed area and heated air is blown over and around it. With this method, commercial lumber can be dried in a few weeks—a process that might otherwise require several years. Kiln-drying offers many advantages to cabinetmakers and carpenters; however, the quick, hot air-drying can cause problems for the woodcarver. The heat (100°F-120°F) will often cook the resin of pine and other softwoods into the fibers, causing the wood to become hard and brittle, and much more difficult to work. On pieces of wood 2 in. thick or more, the internal stresses caused by fast drying may result in splits deep inside the wood, which are invisible until you carve into them. Therefore, especially when using softwoods, try to use only those that have been air-dried. Some local lumberyards carry air-dried wood, or you can purchase it from specialty wood dealers.

Rather than buying wood, you can often find good pieces that have been discarded by cabinetmakers. These leftover pieces are too small for furniture, but may be just right for carving. You can also get wood from felled trees. If you ask around, many people will give you wood that would otherwise be hauled away. Several years ago, I picked up over a dozen trunk sections of good black walnut this way. But if you decide to get your wood green, you'll have to dry it yourself.

To do this, place the wood in a sheltered area or cover it with plastic. (The bark should be removed from logs or log sections to prevent wood-boring beetles from attacking the wood—they are especially fond of softwoods.) If the wood has been cut into boards, place stickers made from 1-in.-square scraps of dry lumber between them to allow air to circulate, which will prevent warping and fungus growth. Pile blocks of green wood loosely so that the flat surfaces are not on top of one another; air should be allowed to circulate freely around the largest surfaces. (I stack small carving blocks in the rafters of my shop to dry.) Use small logs or scraps of wood to level stacks of lumber and raise them at least 6 in. off the ground to avoid fungus and insects.

Moisture leaves wood most rapidly through the end grain. To avoid uneven drying, and reduce the chances of splitting and checking, I seal the end grain of logs or boards with varnish or paint. Sealing the ends will force most of the moisture loss to take place on the lateral surfaces. This is especially important with hardwood, which is more likely to split. Softwood is better able to move in response to drying stresses, rather than resisting and checking, and if a piece does split, the split won't travel as far and as quickly as in hardwood. But softwood should be end-sealed, too, especially boards and logs over 3 in. thick.

As a general rule, allow one year of air-drying time for each inch of thickness. Naturally, this will vary with the relative humidity in your area and the type of wood you are drying. Softwoods dry faster than hardwoods; they usually have a lower moisture content and they're less dense, so moisture evaporates more quickly. According to Bruce Hoadley, professor of wood technology at the University of Massachusetts, air-dried wood reaches a moisture content in equilibrium with the relative humidity of its environment (Hoadley 1980, p. 72). I figure that, here in the Adirondacks, wood stored indoors will stabilize at a 6% to 12% moisture content during the winter.

I use white pine for a lot of my woodcarvings. I buy it green from the mill and then store it in my woodshed for one to two years. Because most of my carvings are meant to be displayed indoors, I store my wood inside for at least six more months. Wood left outside to dry in the Adirondacks, where there is a high humidity level, won't dry completely. After six months in my workshop, the wood is usually ready for carving, although I always make a few test cuts to be sure.

Deciding when wood is dry enough to carve isn't easy. I don't have equipment for measuring moisture content, so I rely on experience and intuition. I usually just make a couple of test cuts—wet wood is sticky and fibrous. If the wood carves cleanly, then I use it. Another way to judge whether the wood is dry is by weight and feel (wet wood is heavy and cool) or by smelling the wood (sometimes you can smell the cool dampness—although this takes some practice).

Finishes

Even centuries after a piece of wood has been cut and dried, it will continue to expand and contract with changing temperatures and humidity. But once a piece of wood has been properly finished, it will be preserved for centuries; even though the wood will continue to move, it will do so only slightly. A good finish seals the wood, slows the rate of moisture exchange and keeps the wood from checking and warping.

In addition to protecting the wood, a carefully applied finish also enhances its beauty. A piece of mahogany that has been skillfully carved is certainly interesting and pleasing to look at. But when it has been sealed and treated with a penetrating resin oil, the wood becomes truly beautiful. The deep colors and rich fire of the grain that would never show in the raw wood are revealed.

Finishing is an art in itself, but the process begins long before any material is applied to the wood surface—it begins with the final carving strokes of the tools and ends only when the last coat of finish has been applied. The finish enhances the workmanship, the changing textures and details of the carving, the smooth tool marks. Many people who admire the beauty of a carving are really admiring the way it has been finished. Rubbing a hand over a properly finished surface is a pleasure.

Choosing the correct finish—There are several different types of finishes that are appropriate for just about any woodcarving, so selecting the right finish is largely a matter of personal preference. However, I recommend that you avoid high-gloss varnishes or plastic finishes. At best, too much shine can make it hard to see subtle details; at worst, it can make the woodcarving look as though it were made of plastic. A well-applied, tasteful finish will improve the looks of any woodcarving, but the wrong finish or a sloppy, carelessly applied one will spoil even the best workmanship. Follow the manufacturer's instructions when you are using any finish. The chart on the facing page gives a brief description of some of the different finishes I have used, as well as some of the advantages and disadvantages of each. There are also several good books on the subject listed in the bibliography.

Because of the need to protect wood from moisture loss and gain, the carving should be finished the same on all sides. For example, if you apply varnish and paste wax to one side of a relief panel, then you must treat the edges and back exactly the same way. If you were to seal only the front, moisture would still be able to penetrate and escape from the back, which would increase the chances of the panel's warping.

Stains—Stains are used to change the color of the wood before applying a final finish of varnish, lacquer or paste wax. A stain is a solution of pigments or dyes that soaks into the fibers of the wood. You can buy stain in any color, dissolved in a solution of mineral spirits and oils. Some stains are sold as powders that can be mixed with water, but these shouldn't be used on woodcarvings. Water-based stains raise the grain of the wood—which means they cause the fibers to swell—and will make a carving look fuzzy.

The color of the stain you use is a matter of personal preference. I like to use a medium-brown stain on light-colored pine or poplar. These colors bring out the carved details and give the wood a warm tone. With light-colored hardwoods such as oak, birch or maple, staining is optional—although a fruitwood stain can warm up the color of the wood and enhance the grain. Dark woods, like butternut, walnut, mesquite, mahogany, cherry and teak, look best left natural and sealed with a clear finish.

Apply stain with a brush or cloth and allow it to soak in for a few minutes before wiping it off with a dry cloth. Repeat this process several times if you want the wood darker. Be careful, though, because it is difficult, if not impossible, to lighten the color once you've made it too dark. It's important to test the stain on a scrap piece of the wood you'll be using before applying the stain to the carving. The same stain might be entirely different on different types of wood. Most oil-based stains can be thinned with paint thinner or mineral spirits if you want a weaker color. (I don't use turpentine because it can leave a gummy residue.)

After the stain has dried, you can cover it with any compatible finish—wax, oil, varnish or lacquer—or you can leave it just as it is. Check the manufacturer's instructions to see what they recommend using with the stain you have.

PROPERTIES AND USES OF FINISHES

FINISH	DESCRIPTION	HOW TO APPLY	CARVINGS	COMMENTS
STAINS	Brown, red and ochre pigments in solution of oils and mineral spirits. Matte finish.	Apply with paintbrush or clean cloth. After a few minutes, wipe off excess. 1-2 coats. The more coats, the darker the stain. 1-6 hours drying time. Solvent in mineral spirits or paint thinner.	All carvings in light-colored wood.	Use only on raw wood. Apply wax, oil, shellac, varnish or lacquer over it.
OILS	Boiled linseed oil, with driers. Penetrating resin oil, from phenolic or alkyd resins in mineral spirits and natural oils. Matte to semigloss finish.	Apply with paintbrush or clean rag. After 10-15 minutes, wipe off excess. 2 coats. Allow 12 hours drying time between coats. Solvent in mineral spirits.	All indoor carvings. Detailed chip or relief carvings.	Use on raw or stained wood. Easy to apply. Can apply wax or special varnishes over it.
FRENCH POLISH	Shellac, methanol and boiled linseed oil. Semigloss to high-gloss finish, depending on number of coats.	Apply with wad of cotton cloth. 1-3 coats. Allow wood to dry ½ hour between coats. Solvent in wood alcohol (methanol).	Indoor carvings with even surfaces and few details. Also dark woods with strong grain patterns.	Use on raw wood. Can apply paste wax over it.
VARNISH	Mixture of synthetic resins in solution of linseed and tung oils and mineral spirits. Semimatte to high-gloss finish.	Brush on with natural-bristle paintbrush. 2-3 coats. Thin first coat. Allow several hours drying time between applications. Allow 1-1½ days drying time after final coat. Solvent in turpentine or mineral spirits.	Outdoor carvings (marine or spar varnish).	Use on raw or stained wood. Difficult to apply. Long drying time. This is a final finish.
LACQUER	Mixture of resins with acetone, alcohol and other volatile solvents. Semigloss to high-gloss finish.	Brush or spray on 1-6 coats. First coat dries quickly. Additional applications may need hours or days to dry. Solvent in lacquer thinner or acetone.	Wildlife or other carvings that will be painted.	Use on raw or stained wood. Rapid drying time of first coat. Hazardous fumes. Can't be applied over other finishes.
ARTIST'S OIL COLORS	Concentrated pigments in linseed-oil base. Semigloss to high-gloss finish.	Apply with paintbrushes ¹⁄₁₆-½ in. wide. 1 coat. Drying time 3 days to several weeks. Solvent in turpentine.	Wildlife carvings or decoys. Folk or relief carvings in light-colored woods.	Use on raw or sealed wood. Do not use with varnish or lacquer. Can apply wax over it.
ENAMEL PAINT	Opaque solution of pigments in varnish-like base. Matte to high-gloss finish.	Apply with paintbrushes. 1-2 coats. 1-12 hours drying time, depending on manufacturer. Solvent in turpentine or mineral spirits.	Outdoor signs and lettering.	Use on raw, varnished or lacquered woods.
PASTE WAX	Combination of natural and synthetic waxes. Semigloss finish.	Wipe on a very thin coat with cloth. 1 coat. After 15 minutes, buff with clean cloth or horsehair shoebrush. (Let homemade wax stand 1 day before buffing.) Solvent in mineral spirits or turpentine. (Do not thin.)	All carvings except wildlife.	Apply over raw wood or any finish, except paint. This is a final finish.

Penetrating resin oils, such as Minwax, create a durable finish and bring out the grain of the wood.

Oils—I think the best finish to use on most woodcarvings is some form of an oil finish. Nothing brings out the rich color of the wood grain like boiled linseed oil, tung oil or a penetrating resin oil. Unlike finishes that remain on the surface of the wood, such as varnish, an oil finish actually penetrates the wood fibers and hardens, forming a deep, strong finish. Scratches aren't as noticeable as on a surface finish either, because the color of the finish penetrates well into the wood. A deep scratch that cuts into the raw wood can be colored to blend with the rest of the finish just by rubbing a drop or two of oil into the scratch. Don't use vegetable oils or raw linseed oil on woodcarvings, because they don't polymerize—or harden—when exposed to air, and will always feel slightly gummy. Boiled linseed oil contains drying agents and can be used.

Penetrating resin oils consist of a thin liquid containing alkyd or phenolic resins in a solution of natural oils and mineral spirits. Not only do they bring out the color and grain of unstained wood, but they can also be purchased premixed with stains for coloring or darkening wood. Several companies make penetrating resin oils. Among the more popular are Minwax, Watco and DuPont. Some manufacturers also make varnishes that can be applied over the oils for even greater durability and protection—I use these on wood that will be exposed outdoors.

Oil finishes are the easiest of all finishes to apply, so they are perfect for highly detailed carvings. Swab the oil on the wood with a brush and let it soak in for about an hour. After the wood has soaked up as much as it will take, wipe off the excess with clean cloths. Let the carving air-dry for several hours, then repeat the process. Be sure to wipe off all excess—any pools left behind will dry to a gummy finish. (Oil-soaked rags are a fire hazard, so spread them out to dry, then store them in metal cans.)

French polish—The technique of French polishing was often used by Renaissance European craftsmen on carved furniture. As traditionally practiced, it is an involved process. I use a simplified French-polishing technique on carvings with simple details or on sculptures with smooth surfaces—it's hard to apply smoothly on carvings with irregular surfaces. French polishing is a slow process and takes a little careful practice, but the results are well worth it. The finish brings out more color and depth of grain than the penetrating resin oils.

My French polish is a solution of equal amounts of wood alcohol (methanol), boiled linseed oil and shellac. The oil brings out the rich colors of the wood, while the shellac gives a smooth, lustrous sheen. The oil provides a more durable coating than shellac would provide if used alone.

Shellac, an amber resin secreted by tropical insects, can be purchased either in powder form called shellac flakes or dissolved in a solution of wood alcohol. If you purchase liquid shellac, check the date of manufacture. The solution has a shelf life of approximately six months, after which time it won't dry when applied, but will leave a sticky film. I prefer to mix my own shellac solution so I can be sure it's fresh. To do this, pour ½ in. of dry shellac flakes (white or orange) into a jar, then cover them with 1 in. of wood alcohol. When completely dissolved, the solution should have the consistency of maple syrup. If not, adjust the mixture by adding more of either ingredient.

To make French polish, mix the dissolved shellac with equal amounts of boiled linseed oil and wood alcohol and shake well. Pour a few drops onto a wad of clean, lint-free cotton cloth and wipe it on the wood in a gentle, circular motion. Keep the cloth in constant motion, or it may stick to the wood. One coat will seal the wood; a second coat brings up a little shine. If you want a higher shine, use another coat. (Traditional French polishes, which were more dilute, were applied in dozens of coats.) I usually apply two coats and then lightly go over the finish with 000 or 0000 steel wool. If I want more sheen, I put a little paste wax on the wood and buff it with a cloth or shoebrush.

I like this finish. It's easy to mix up, dries quickly and looks nice. I've even brushed it over folk carvings that have been stained with thinned oil paints. The finish brings out the wood grain through the painted colors and leaves an even, semimatte sheen.

Varnish–Varnish is one of the most popular clear finishes for furniture, but it's also one of the most difficult finishes to apply correctly, so I don't recommend it for carvings. It takes a long time to dry, at least overnight and sometimes a day or two, which makes it susceptible to collecting dust or lint. However, there are two situations in which this finish is appropriate to use. If the carving is part of a piece of furniture that is to be varnished, then the entire piece should be varnished, preferably with a high-quality urethane or polyurethane varnish. Or, if the carving is going to be installed outdoors, it should be protected with several coats of a high-quality marine or spar varnish. This type of very durable varnish is formulated to resist the effects of sunlight and rain (but under these conditions, even the best varnishes may peel and flake off within two to five years).

Apply varnish by spreading it on with a paintbrush. Be sure to use a good, natural-bristle brush so as not to leave brush strokes in the dried varnish. Most manufacturers recommend thinning the first coat with turpentine or mineral spirits to help the varnish penetrate the wood. (You can also use turpentine or mineral spirits to clean the paintbrushes.) Dab the varnish well into the recesses and details of the carving, making sure not to miss any areas. Next, wipe the brush nearly dry and carefully lift out any puddles of excess varnish that have collected. Use a gentle brushing motion to draw these out and to clean up drips or runs. I usually apply a thinned, sealing coat and one or two full-strength finishing coats, depending on the manufacturer's instructions.

Lacquer–Lacquer can be difficult to work with—it's hard to brush on (although it can also be sprayed), the first coat dries quickly, and the fumes are hazardous to health and safety. Lacquer is made of cellulose nitrate and other synthetic compounds in a highly volatile solvent. The thinner used to clean lacquer off your paintbrushes is also highly volatile—not only will it dissolve the lacquer, but also most plastics, some synthetic cloths and other finishes.

Because lacquer doesn't have the oils found in other finishes, it doesn't bring out the color of the wood as well as oils or shellac. I use it to seal my wildlife carvings before painting them. I brush it on, or in some cases, just dip the carving into the can. Any drips and blemishes, such as dust and pet hairs, for example, can be trimmed off with a sharp knife after the lacquer has dried. Spray lacquer is also available in aerosol cans, and is handy for sealing woodcarvings that you want to look unfinished, yet keep protected from dirt and dust. I use Deft aerosol because it dries to a semimatte finish, and rubs out nicely with 0000 steel wool.

Paint—Paint is essentially finely ground color pigments mixed in liquid. I use artist's oil colors, thick mixtures of pigment in a linseed-oil base, which can be purchased in tubes from art-supply stores. Water-based paints, such as acrylics or latex, should not be used on raw wood because of their tendency to raise the grain.

Woodcarvings (particularly religious statues, ship figureheads and store signs) have traditionally been painted. However, paint is tricky to use on wood because it can easily make a nice carving look garish. I use oil paints in two ways. The first is a tinting or staining technique, used on European folk carvings, especially those from Tyrol, Bavaria and the Scandinavian countries. Put a small dab of artist's oil paint in a saucer or metal jar lid and thin it down with a few drops of turpentine at a time. The best way to do this is to dip a small camel's hair or sable paintbrush (No. 4 or No. 6) in the turpentine and shake out several drops on the saucer. Keep adding thinner to the paint until you have a weak stain. Test it on a piece of scrap wood for color intensity before actually applying it to the carving. Tinting works best with light-colored woods such as white pine, basswood or poplar. The color shows up better and the grain of the wood is allowed to show through.

The second oil-paint technique is one I use on wildlife carvings. First, I seal the wood with lacquer. Then I paint it with gesso, a thick, opaque, water-soluble, white paint—a procedure similar to preparing an artist's canvas for painting. The gesso provides a white background to help emphasize the colors. Next, I apply the oil paints, without thinning them at all. By using different paintbrushes, $\frac{1}{16}$ in. to $\frac{1}{2}$ in. wide, I can create textures in the thick paint to give the impression of fur or feathers. The paint is then allowed to dry for up to eight weeks.

I also use enamel, which is a opaque mixture of color pigments in a thick, protective, varnishlike solution. It ranges from matte to high gloss in a variety of colors. Apply one or two coats, and follow the manufacturer's directions for drying time.

Enamel is used on outdoor woodwork, such as house trim and lawn furniture. I use it on signs and other carvings that will be displayed outdoors. Enamel provides excellent protection because it blocks out ultraviolet light from the sun, which causes wood to change color and deteriorate. (I use pine for all outdoor carvings that will be painted with enamel—its porous texture allows the paint to penetrate deep into the wood fibers.)

Glazing—Glazing is a specialized finishing technique that works well on many woodcarvings. I use it on chip carvings or relief carvings made of light-colored wood and with a lot of small details I want to emphasize.

Glazing is done by brushing a dark stain over a surface that is already finished (preferably with an oil finish or stain) and then wiping it off. This leaves a darker color in the depressions of the carving, which creates artificial shadows.

First, I finish the carving with two coats of penetrating resin oil, such as clear Minwax. After the second coat has been wiped off and has dried, I brush on a layer of Minwax Special Walnut stain. The stain cannot penetrate the oil, but instead flows into the recessed areas. Make sure that you get the stain into every detail, then wipe it off with an absorbent, clean, dry cloth. Some of the stain will remain behind and darken shadow areas and details. You can easily control the degree of contrast by wiping more stain in one area than in another. As shown in the photos at right, a glaze defines details that would otherwise be difficult to see on light-colored woods.

Paste wax—Paste wax is a mixture of different natural and synthetic waxes, and has the consistency of butter. It can be used on raw wood as a finish itself or over another finish for added protection. I use the paste finishing wax made by Minwax.

Apply paste wax sparingly with a soft cloth. Let it dry for about 10 to 15 minutes, and then buff the wood to a mellow sheen with a soft, dry cloth or a horsehair shoebrush.

You can also make your own paste wax by mixing natural beeswax with turpentine. Homemade wax has a thicker consistency than most commercial paste waxes and so provides a little more protection, but it can be hazardous to make if you don't follow safety precautions. Carefully melt about 3 oz. of bleached or raw beeswax in a double boiler over low heat. Stir in 1 oz. to 2 oz. of turpentine, then let the mixture cool. Within an hour, the polish should set up to a butterlike consistency. If the paste is too soft, melt it again and add more beeswax. If it is too hard, dilute it with a little more turpentine. A small amount of melted rosin can also be added to harden and darken the wax, although I prefer the simpler mixture. Remember, this mixture is highly flammable in its liquid state. If the wax begins to smoke, it's too hot. Keep an airtight cover on hand to snuff out fires, just in case. When the mixture has cooled, seal it in an airtight container to preserve its freshness.

To use homemade paste wax, lightly rub or brush a thin layer on the wood, and let it stand for a day to let the turpentine evaporate. Then buff the carving with a clean cloth or a shoebrush.

To glaze a carving, apply two coats of penetrating resin oil, then carefully brush the stain into every detail (top). After wiping off the stain with a clean cloth (center), the shadows and details of the carving will be darkened and emphasized. Glazing works well on light-colored woods to define details that would otherwise be difficult to see.

1½ inch squares

Design

4

What makes something visually pleasing? For thousands
of years, people have been trying to answer this question. Artists
in every period of history, from the days of ancient Egypt to the
twentieth century, have formulated many theories of aesthetics,
though ideals of beauty often change from one culture to the next.
The only universal rule seems to be that a good design feels right
when you look at it. Whether it's a drawing, painting or
woodcarving, if the object is well designed, it will hold your
interest and be pleasing to look at. One of the learning plateaus
that separate an advanced woodcarver from a beginner is the
realization that pure technical expertise cannot compensate for a
weak or uninteresting design.

The word *design* can be confusing, because it is used to mean
several different things. A design can refer to the idea of how a
finished work will look. It also refers to the process of drawing out
the idea, as when making a pattern. Often, the word is used to
describe the particular style of a work—a Celtic design or a
geometric design, for example. In woodcarving, the word *design* is
used in all these ways. But before discussing any of these
definitions, it is important to understand what makes a design
interesting to look at.

Some Design Principles

The success of any carving depends on all of its visual elements
working together, but there are several basic principles that can
be applied to all successful designs.

The most successful carvings have strong outlines, only the
essential details and a feeling of balance. They do not look top-
heavy or weighted too strongly to one side. One way to prevent a

*Once you've planned a design for a
carving, make a scaled pattern to work
from, drawing in as many details as
you want in the final carving. Then
trace the pattern onto the wood.*

In this fifteenth-century French chest front (above), the constant repetition of the arches and curved shapes makes an uninteresting design. This could have been avoided by alternating three different panels in the chest front, or by using a different center panel as the focal point. This Italian panel (left), also carved in the fifteenth century, uses circles and arches successfully in a symmetrical design. (Photos courtesy of The Metropolitan Museum of Art, Rogers Fund, 1905.)

This headboard and footboard are examples of asymmetrical design. Although the right and left sides have different curves and shapes, the forms flow together in a harmonious pattern. (Designed and carved by Rick Gentile and Joan Columbus. Photo by Steve Chimento.)

carving from looking unbalanced is to make the design symmetrical, that is, one half a mirror image of the other. Many Gothic woodcarvers of the fifteenth and sixteenth centuries used circles and arcs in strongly symmetrical designs, as shown in the photos on the facing page. However, asymmetrical designs, that is, those having halves different from each other, can still appear balanced if the shapes are carefully arranged.

Sometimes the beauty of a design lies in the rhythm of repeating shapes and patterns. This is especially true of chip-carving designs, like the one shown in the photo at right. But too much repetition can sometimes become monotonous. For example, during the nineteenth-century Gothic revival in architecture, traditional patterns were often repeated without any attention to their arrangement or total effect.

A successful woodcarving must have good proportions, which means, an interesting variety of closely related shapes. This principle was applied effectively in the rococo style of the eighteenth century, when elaborate shells and mirror frames were carved in sweeping curves. No two shapes were identical and yet all the shapes blended together to make an attractive, balanced whole. Imitations of works from this period often look coarse and clumsy because they lack variety of shape and line. Notice that the curved lines in the photo at bottom left on p. 58 are not the same overall width, but instead taper from thick to thin. This is one of the secrets to a well-proportioned design: subtle variations in line and curve that make shapes interesting and pleasing to the eye.

Harmony is another important consideration in woodcarving design. As a general rule, you should place together only forms and motifs that are consistent in style and character. For example, the Gothic style of carving was based on geometric lines and curves. These could not be freely mixed with a later style, such as rococo, in which shapes were fluid and organic. Some of the worst examples of bad taste in our culture occur when styles from different periods are combined with no regard to their overall appearance. This is not to say that certain elements from each style could not be modified and arranged to be compatible, but this requires careful thought and discretion to be successful.

Creating an attractive, well-balanced design is really a matter of trial and error. Usually, you'll have to experiment with several pencil sketches, changing a line here and there before you arrive at a satisfactory solution. Don't be in a hurry to rush through this phase. Working out ideas on paper is the best way to ensure that your finished woodcarving will look the way you want it.

Developing a Sense of Design

Many people have difficulty translating the abstract design principles of symmetry, proportion and harmony into a pattern they can work from. If you find this to be true, the best way to develop a sense of good design is to learn to look at the world around you. Young children are good at this: Their environment is so new and fascinating that they see details and patterns that most adults miss. We must relearn the skill of viewing objects with a sharp eye and inquiring mind.

The beauty of this chip-carved design is enhanced by the repetition of the triangular cuts that form the geometric patterns. This is a Dutch mangle board carved around 1748. (Photo courtesy of The Metropolitan Museum of Art, Rogers Fund, 1911.)

The variety of sweeping curves in this rococo-style mirror frame (top) blend together for a balanced overall effect. (Carved by Rolf Tarldseth.) The curves in this acanthus-leaf carving (above) vary in width. They taper from thick to thin to create a fluid design. (Photos courtesy of Vesterheim, The Norwegian-American Museum, Decorah, Iowa.)

For example, we all know what a leaf looks like—it's green and it has a particular shape. But if you study it closely, you will notice subtle variations of color and complex shapes within delicate lacework patterns. Now if you can see this much in a single leaf, think how much richer the world would appear if you could view everything with a fresh eye.

This is really what learning design is all about—looking closely at everyday objects and the patterns they form, discovering what looks pleasing, and incorporating it into your work. I believe people can develop an intuitive sense of good design, and not even be aware of it. You can probably tell instinctively when something looks right—even though you can't explain the reasons why. For example, how many times have you noticed a picture hanging slightly crooked on a wall? It may be off-level by only a fraction of an inch, yet it makes you feel uncomfortable. Your eyes are capable of detecting very small details, which are then processed in your subconscious mind and communicated to you as a feeling. So learn to observe the world around you and trust your own sense of judgment.

Visualization—Another technique that is useful in planning a design and developing visual intuition is learning to see pictures of your ideas in your mind. Once again, this is something we all did as children in the form of daydreaming. It's a skill that many of us lose as adults, but it can be reacquired with a little practice. Simply close your eyes and imagine exactly how the finished design should appear. You will notice that at first it may take several minutes of concentration for your imagination to form a clear image. However, with practice, this visualization will require less time.

This technique not only helps you solve visual and technical problems in advance, it helps you while you are carving, too. It will seem as if your hands are shaping the wood without conscious effort. When you fix the image in your mind, your hands will be guided by subconscious mental processes that will ultimately develop into a woodcarver's instinct. If you consciously practice this exercise, you will quickly develop the ability to visualize, and the designing process, as well as your carving, will go along easily and be more successful.

Sketching—Two of the best tools you will find for helping develop your sense of design are a sketchbook and a pencil. The sketchbook should be your visual record of ideas—carvings you've seen in museums, interesting shapes found in nature, or anything else that catches your eye. Drawing is just a matter of practice, and keeping a sketchbook is a good way to improve your abilities. I have listed some books in the bibliography that might be helpful, too. I particularly recommend *The Zen of Seeing* by Frederick Franck, which is a good beginning or advanced book, and is helpful for breaking the ice and teaching you how to loosen up when drawing. Woodcarving and drawing are closely related. You will discover that as your sketching ability improves, so will your woodcarving skills.

PAGE OF A SKETCHBOOK

Broad-Winged Hawk

Iris- Dark Brown

Yellow

Dark Gray

— yellow

Bars - less distinct on young hawks

Red Maple

Blue bird and Nest

Barn Swallow

Keeping a sketchbook is a good way to improve your drawing skills. This page records things observed on a short hike.

Shaded areas show the contours
of areas that will be shaped
in this design.

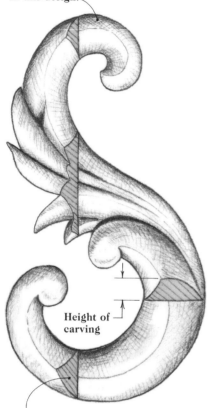

Height of
carving

Use section lines to determine the
height of a raised design and the
profiles of curves.

Working with Patterns and Clay

A sketch or pattern of a carving is like a road map, because it gives you a clear idea of where you're going before you actually start gouging wood. Patterns should be drawn full-size and show complete detail. Indicate the relative thickness of the wood by drawing cross sections of the design at several points on the pattern to get a better mental picture of the overall shape and varying thicknesses. Cross sections are defined in the drawing at left by the colored areas, but can also be indicated by dotted lines. Further indication of depth can be made by shading the design to show the contours of the areas to be shaped. Also, don't be afraid to sketch in lines and shadows directly on the wood as a guide while you are carving. This is especially valuable when carving in relief because it adds dimension to a flat surface. Pencil lines can be easily removed by carving them away, or erasing them when the carving is completed. (Don't use ink, because it soaks into the wood and is difficult to remove.)

Laying out patterns—Be sure to consider the structural strengths and weaknesses of the wood when laying out patterns. Wood is strongest along the length of its grain. Therefore, you have to carefully plan in advance how you will use the wood grain to its best advantage.

When carving sculpture, wildlife or other three-dimensional forms, align the thin, delicate shapes of your design parallel to the grain direction, or as close as possible. This will ensure maximum strength and prevent those parts from breaking off during carving or when the finished woodcarving is on display. Two-dimensional carvings with a lot of lines traveling in the same direction should also be aligned parallel to the grain. Although strength isn't as much of a concern with a relief carving as with a freestanding sculpture, proper alignment with the grain will make carving much easier and the splitting off of fine details less likely.

Thin parts of a carving
will break off if grain
runs across their width.

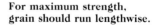

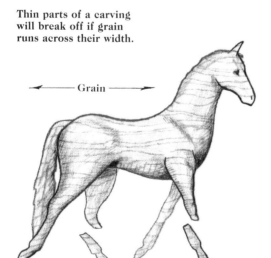

For maximum strength,
grain should run lengthwise.

Grain

Transferring patterns—In addition to drawing your own designs freehand, you can reproduce patterns from books using tracing paper and carbon paper. Lay a sheet of thin, strong tracing paper over the pattern and trace the outlines with a pencil. (You can buy tracing paper from art-supply stores, but I use whatever is handy, as long as it is tear-resistant and transparent. Medium-weight, white-bond typing paper works well.) Next, place a piece of carbon paper, inked side down, on the wood, and place the paper with the traced pattern on top of it. Transfer the pattern onto the wood by retracing over the outline. Press firmly, but not so hard that you tear the paper.

It's a good idea to secure one edge of the pattern to the wood with masking tape to prevent the paper from shifting. This way, you can lift up the untaped edge whenever you need to look at the wood to make sure the design is being transferred. (If it isn't, you're not pressing the pencil down hard enough.)

An alternate method is to make a cardboard template. Transfer the design onto a piece of cardboard with carbon paper, cut the pattern out, position it with a push pin or thumbtack on the wood and trace around it. Templates are especially useful for repeating designs, such as on borders and moldings. If you are using a small template on a large repeating pattern, make sure the template begins and ends at a logical break in the design, so that it will be easy to reposition it in the right spot as you work along.

Another way to transfer a pattern is to glue it directly to the wood with a little rubber cement, carving through the paper as you carve the wood. This is especially useful for chip-carving and relief-carving designs. When the carving is done, rub or sand off the remaining bits of paper and cement.

You can also draw your pattern directly onto the wood, another useful technique for chip and relief carving. But bear in mind that many of the pencil lines will remain after the carving has been completed, because they mark or cross high points in the design where little or no wood will be removed. Therefore, keep marks light to make cleanup easier. After carving, clean off any carbon paper or pencil lines with a little bit of solvent like Liquid Deglosser or Zip Sander on a wad of soft cloth. You can also sand off remaining lines using a fine grade of paper, like 220-grit garnet, as sparingly as possible. Wrap the paper around a flat block of scrap wood to prevent rounding off the crisp edges of the carving.

If you wish to enlarge or reduce the size of an existing pattern, the best way to do it is by using a grid. First, trace the original pattern on a piece of graph paper, or a grid of regularly spaced intersecting lines. Then make a second grid scaled to fit the project's final size. For example, if I want to double the size of a small drawing, I use a first grid with ½-in. squares, and a second grid with 1-in. squares. I sketch in the lines of the design where they pass through the squares of the first grid onto the corresponding squares of the second grid. This way, I am able to make a fairly accurate sketch with the dimensions I need. If I wanted an even larger pattern, I could redraw onto a grid of larger squares, and the design would still retain its proportions. In the drawing on p. 62, the design is being increased 100 percent by

To transfer a repeating design, trace a portion of the design onto a piece of cardboard to use as a template. Position the template with a thumbtack or push pin and draw the design onto the wood. Reposition the template to transfer the rest of the design.

sketching it from a ½-in. grid onto a 1-in. grid. This same technique can be used to reduce a design, too, as shown.

It's hard to find graph paper large enough to cover most of my final carvings, so I make my own grids on a piece of thin, but strong, artist's sketchbook paper. Also, most commercial graph paper has squares much smaller than I usually need, and working with them can make the process confusing. Grids with ½-in. squares are a good size for most projects. I try to work to even parts of an inch to make it easier to calculate the size and transfer the pattern.

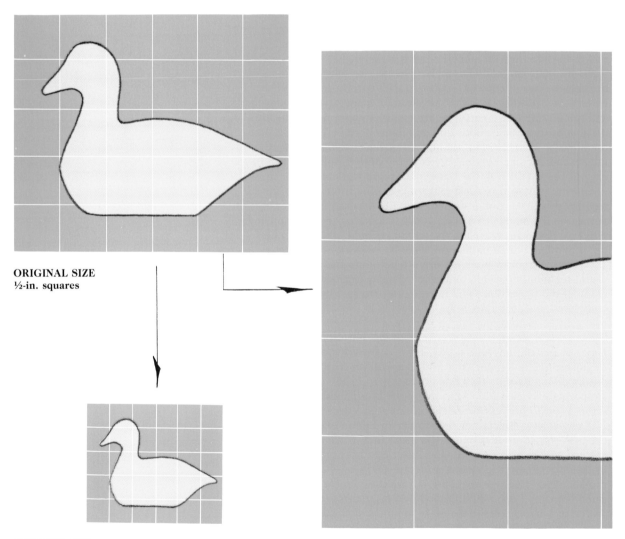

ORIGINAL SIZE
½-in. squares

REDUCED 50%
¼-in. squares

INCREASED 100%
1-in. squares

Using clay models–Sometimes, before beginning to carve a complex pattern in wood, it's helpful to model the design in clay. A clay model helps you see how the design will appear when carved in wood. This is especially useful if you are working with a three-dimensional design. I occasionally use a clay model for two-dimensional carvings with swirling and twisting leaves or other complex shapes that would be difficult to follow in a drawing.

I use ceramic potter's clay for modeling because it cleans up easily with water, and it's inexpensive. However, because it dries out quickly and becomes brittle, it must be stored in a plastic bag. (It's also a good idea to protect your models from drying out by covering them with plastic when you're not working on them.) There is an oil-based modeling clay called Plasticene that won't dry out and can be reused indefinitely, but I find it's hard to clean off my hands.

For modeling two-dimensional shapes in clay, you will also need a piece of plywood or Masonite to use as a workboard on which to shape the clay. (A piece about 14 in. square is a good size for most projects.) Place a copy of your pattern on the workboard to use as a guide, and build the model on top of it. For three-dimensional designs, you may need the additional support of a wire frame around which to build the model. Twist together a couple of pieces of coat-hanger wire to make the basic shape you need. To make a model of a horse, for example, you'll need a simple wire skeleton consisting of four legs, and perhaps a neck to support the weight of the clay that will be applied. Special tools and spatulas can be purchased for clay modeling. In the photo below, I am using wire-end tools to shape the clay, but a couple of teaspoons or table knives will do just as well.

Before beginning to carve a complex pattern, it's often helpful to model the design in clay.

Effects of Light and Shadow

Design doesn't end with the preliminary planning; some design considerations, such as the effect of light and shadow, have to be made while you are actually carving.

Though often overlooked, the effect of light and shadow is an important element in a woodcarving design. It is especially critical with relief carvings, because they are usually fastened to a wall and viewed only from certain angles. When light falls upon the surface of the carving, it is either reflected back to the viewer as a highlight, or absorbed into a shadowy area. The resulting patterns of light and shadow are what define the shapes seen by the viewer. The angle at which light strikes the carving can shift the location and intensity of highlight and shadow areas, and can either enhance or obscure certain details of the piece. This is why a woodcarver might sometimes have an excellent design on paper, and yet, when the carving is finished, it doesn't look right. The problem is often that the carver has overlooked the fact that carving is, in effect, drawing with light. The lighting always needs to be taken into account when planning a design.

The effect of light and shadow plays an important part in determining how a finished woodcarving will look. In this portrait, the carver designed the shapes so that the features of the face would be defined by light, even though the overall depth of the carving is shallow. The leaves of the wreath vary in depth to make them appear three-dimensional and freestanding. The contrasting effects focus the viewer's attention on the portrait, and add dramatic interest to the design. (Photo courtesy of The University of Texas, Institute of Texan Cultures at San Antonio.)

George Jack, the author of *Wood Carving: Design and Workmanship* originally published in 1903, describes the problem he had in carving a rose: "After taking infinite pains to reproduce…its numerous petals, and…its complicated foliage, I had not reckoned with the light which was to illuminate it, and that instead of displaying my work to advantage, it has blurred all its delicate forms into dusky and chaotic masses" (Jack 1978, pp. 85-86).

When an artist paints a picture, he works with one smooth, flat plane, and the light bounces off the entire surface evenly. A woodcarving, however, has three dimensions, and light will strike some parts of the wood more dramatically than others. By adjusting the relative heights in the carving, the position and intensity of highlights and shadows can be controlled.

Theoretically, the background of a relief carving is flat. Yet the old-time woodcarvers varied the depth of the background considerably, sometimes sinking it deeper behind one shape than another. This caused darker shadows and made the high sections stand out in greater contrast from the background, emphasizing details and drawing attention to a particular part of a carving.

If this sounds complicated, don't worry. You will eventually learn through practice how to compensate for the effects of light and shadow. And, with a little experience, lowering a background to make it appear darker will become as natural as using a pencil to shade an area on a drawing.

The best way to determine the effect light will have on your woodcarving is to think about this problem while you are carving. Step back occasionally to look at your work from a distance, to help you make sure your design will look right when completed. Look at it from several directions, at the same height at which it will eventually be displayed, and under the same lighting conditions. If the piece will be displayed in natural light, hang it on a wall near a window. For a large installation carving, like a statue or altarpiece, arrange a couple of spotlights in the studio to duplicate the final lighting the piece will have when it is installed.

You can see how the direction of light changes the feeling of a design in the fleur-de-lis shown in the photos at right. Historically, this design was used extensively to decorate public buildings and house interiors. Like many other standard architectural motifs, it was symmetrically designed to look balanced under a variety of lighting conditions—mostly because woodcarvers had very little control over the placement of windows in the building.

Notice how the changing directions of light emphasize certain shapes while obscuring others. When light is coming from the side, the oval decoration at the top of the fleur-de-lis shows a dramatic interplay of light and dark. Yet from other angles, this interesting shape has all but disappeared. Also notice how bulky the upper arms appear when the light is shining from below; the carving doesn't look as top-heavy when the light is coming from above. The important thing to remember is that, to a certain extent, you can control which shapes will be emphasized and which ones will be secondary through your design planning and an awareness of the effects of light.

Although the design is symmetrical, certain shapes of this fleur-de-lis stand out or recede as the direction of the light striking it changes. From top to bottom: light coming from the side, light coming from below, light coming from above.

With an asymmetrical design, the effects of changing light can be even more pronounced. For example, in the photos below, notice how the upper half of the curve appears to diminish in size as the light is moved from the left side of the carving to the right. You can compensate for this effect by lowering the height of a particular area to reduce the heaviness of the shadow it casts, or by widening the highlighted portion. You can also modify the design by increasing the size of certain parts in order to achieve a balanced feeling, although this must be planned well in advance before too much wood is removed.

The same lighting principles apply when you photograph woodcarvings. Whether you are taking the pictures indoors with floodlights or outdoors in natural light, you will notice that a carving usually looks best when the light is coming from an overhead angle of about 45° (unless you've designed it for specific lighting conditions). You may also want to use a piece of white cardboard positioned to reflect a little light into the shadow areas. The reflection will help reduce the contrast and illuminate details that might not otherwise be recorded on the film. Closely study how the light affects the carving and plan accordingly. Whatever you do, don't take a flashbulb or electronic flash and just blast away. Using a flash will obliterate most of the details by eliminating all shadows. More specific information on setting up lights and cameras can be found in any number of books and pamphlets available in a good camera shop.

On this asymmetrical design, the direction of the light has the effect of altering the relative sizes of shapes in the carving. Notice how the upper curved portion appears narrower with the light source at the left of the piece (left) than with the source at the right (right).

A Final Note

Woodcarvers today have a greater amount of freedom of design choice than any carvers in history. We have few artistic and stylistic restrictions, and are free to choose and adapt thousands of years of art styles in our work. However, there is danger in this freedom, too. You cannot just borrow a little here and there from the past, and then stick it all together and assume the design will look good.

In times past, an apprentice would be required to spend many years learning how to reproduce different traditional shapes. I don't think this type of intensive training is necessary today, but by studying and understanding past methods, we will have greater freedom and control in incorporating traditional techniques in our work. Like much of woodcarving, design is not difficult to learn, but it can take a lifetime to master.

In this oval box, or Tine, *carved by Ole Siengaard, curves and shapes are repeated on the surface and in the scroll work on the interlocking pieces connecting the top and bottom of the box. The repetition unites the piece rather than making the design monotonous. (Photo courtesy of Vesterheim, The Norwegian-American Museum, Decorah, Iowa.)*

This log chair, called a Kubbestol, provides a good example of symmetry and asymmetry working together in a design. All the strong visual elements are at the chair's center: the peak on the top edge of the chair, the design at the top of the framed area, the cutout section at the midpoint and the log cabin. This enhances the asymmetry of the landscape elements. The mountains and forest appear to recede, which adds dimension to the carving. (Carved by Halvor Landsverk, 1975. Photo courtesy of Vesterheim, The Norwegian-American Museum, Decorah, Iowa.)

How well repetition works in a design often depends on the shape of the object being carved. This Kubbestol is 42¾ in. high, and was carved by Halvor Lie Kristiansand in about 1900. Repeating shapes and patterns cover the surface and make up the border design around the back of the chair, the bottom of the seat and the base. Because the repeating shapes follow the irregular line of the chair, they're interesting to look at. (Photo courtesy of Vesterheim, The Norwegian-American Museum, Decorah, Iowa.)

The acanthus-leaf carvings on this wooden trunk (above) and cupboard door (right), both by Rolf Tarldseth, illustrate good proportion in design, as well as the successful blending of a variety of closely related, but different shapes. (Photos courtesy of Vesterheim, The Norwegian-American Museum, Decorah, Iowa.)

This is a reproduction of an Italian Renaissance chest once used in a Florentine monastery, carved by Peter Mansbendel. The chest is 32 in. high, 29 in. wide, 73 in. long and carved out of 4-in.-thick walnut. Despite the great variety of ornate shapes, there is still a good sense of balance and overall proportion. The design is symmetrical—the large oval shape below the keyhole marks the center—but the subtle differences in the faces and bodies of the figures keep the design varied and interesting (an important consideration on a carving of this size). The row of oval fan shapes on the front of the chest lid is the most repetitive area of the carving, but the large escutcheon design around the keyhole breaks up the repetition and also adds an interesting detail that engages the viewer's eye. (Photo courtesy of The University of Texas, Institute of Texan Cultures at San Antonio.)

Whittling

5

For most of my life, I've been carving wood in one form or another. I started learning when I was quite young and was fortunate to meet many helpful people who were willing to share their knowledge. My earliest childhood recollection is watching my father make toys for my brothers and me in the farmhouse where we grew up. I can still remember watching the fragrant pine shavings curl away from the knife's edge, and the rich, pungent smell of wood chips tossed into a crackling fireplace. During the long winter nights, we would sit around and watch as he carved tiny animals and figures for us. To a young child, it was like magic to see a tiny horse appear from a block of wood.

I think these memories are what make whittling so enjoyable for me. It's also fascinating to see just how many different types of woodcarvings can be made with a single knife. Because the knife is such a basic tool, it is often overlooked by beginners who are impatient to move on to the more sophisticated and intriguing carving gouges. This is unfortunate, because these carvers will never discover the potential of this simple tool. There is no better way to develop the delicate skill and coordination necessary for woodcarving than by learning how to work with a knife. For this reason, many woodcarvers believe that a good knife is the most important tool they own.

Knives

There are several types of knives that are suitable for whittling, and five different ones are shown in the photo on p. 72: a two-bladed jackknife, a three-bladed jackknife, a German-style chip-carving knife, a modified chip-carving knife and an X-acto knife. Just about any knife can be used for whittling, provided the blade

There's no better way to develop wood-carving skills than learning to whittle with a sharp knife.

is not too long. (You can use knives with curved blades, but I use straight-bladed knives because they're easier to control when cutting fine details.)

A two-bladed jackknife is one of the first knives I ever owned. The one in the photo below was given to me as a birthday gift over 20 years ago. The short blade is about 1½ in. long—just the right size for whittling. Even today, I always keep the knife with me and the edge razor-sharp, in case I find an interesting piece of wood to work when I'm out walking. This knife has given me a lot of enjoyment, but as with most pocketknives, the handle becomes uncomfortable to hold if I carve for too many hours at a time. (The long blade is 2½ in. long, too large for whittling, so I save it for doing those chores for which I shouldn't use a good knife—like cutting cardboard or wire—but have nothing else handy.)

For most of my whittling, I use an old German-style chip-carving knife. The best-quality steel is found in German or Swiss blades, and these knives are available from any good woodcarving-supply house at a reasonable cost. By reshaping the blade and handle, the knife becomes so comfortable I can use it all day long. I shorten the blade ¼ in. by grinding it on an emery wheel or electric grinder, making sure to work slowly and cool the blade in water frequently so as not to overheat the steel and draw out the temper. The steel should never be so hot that you cannot touch it. The finished blade is about 1½ in. long. Then, I reshape the handle slightly by filing a notch on the bottom about ½ in. behind the blade and about ¼ in. wide, or until the notch sits comfortably on my index finger. This gives my finger a place to curl around, and keeps it from slipping forward onto the cutting edge. The notch also makes it easier to carve fine details, because I have a comfortable leverage point close to the blade.

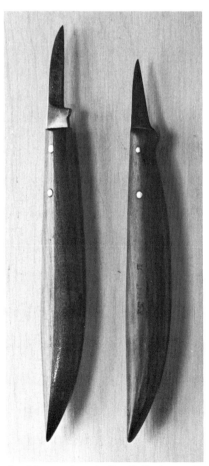

A chip-carving knife (left) is easily adapted for whittling by shortening the blade and by notching and slightly reshaping the handle (right).

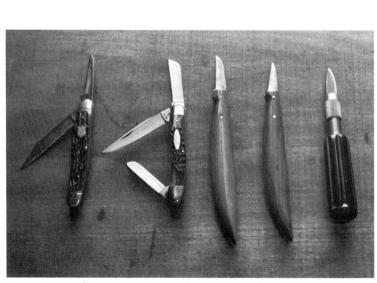

Several types of knives can be used for whittling: (from left to right) a two-bladed jackknife, a three-bladed jackknife, a German-style chip-carving knife, a modified chip-carving knife and an X-acto knife, available with interchangeable blades.

I also sand the varnish off the handle of the knife and seal the wood with a light coat of boiled linseed oil. This leaves a smooth, porous finish that absorbs moisture from my hand. The handle won't stick and cause blisters or calluses.

Although I seldom use one, an X-acto knife can also be a useful tool. It usually comes with a set of interchangeable blades of good-quality steel, and there are even small gouge attachments for scooping out wood, which are satisfactory for small projects. This set is good for beginners. I've found that the plastic and metal handles that come with these sets are not very comfortable to hold, but you can substitute wooden handles. The Warren Tool Company (Route 1, Box 14-A, Rhinebeck, NY 12572) makes rounded wooden handles, which can be purchased from most woodcarving-supply companies.

The knives I've discussed are the basic types available. Most woodcarvers develop a strong personal preference for one type. Try experimenting with different ones, and soon you will discover a knife that feels just right for your own hand.

Techniques

There are two basic shaping techniques in whittling. The method that you will probably use the most is called the paring cut, because it resembles the motion used to peel an apple. This method is good for removing large amounts of waste when roughing-out a block of wood, but it can also be used to remove fine shavings for details that need delicate control. Hold the knife with the edge facing you, as shown in the photo at top right. Brace the thumb of your hand on the end of the block and slowly close your hand toward your thumb. (Make sure your thumb is low enough to be out of the path of the knife.) This will pull the blade through the wood in a controlled movement. Always remember to pull the knife using just your hand muscles, and not the strength of your entire arm. If the knife were to slip with the full power of your arm behind it, you would not be able to stop it in time to prevent injury. Your thumb and hand will exert enough force to draw the blade through the wood safely. Still, it's not a bad idea to place a Band-Aid or a leather protector over your thumb for a little insurance, just in case.

The second whittling technique, the levering cut, is useful for getting into tight areas or for working difficult grain. I use it for shaping the tail and bill of the miniature duck, for rounding the profile of the Adirondack hermit (p. 78), or for working any area of a woodcarving where it is difficult to use the paring cut. Face the edge of the knife away from you, and place the thumb of the hand holding the wood against the back of the knife, as shown in the photo at bottom right. Using your thumb as a fulcrum, you can lever off chips of wood by pivoting the knife. With this method, you can nibble off stubborn wood, such as when you are cutting across end grain where the wood becomes tough to work. In the photo, it may look like the knife is being pushed away with the whole arm, as it would be when sharpening a pencil, but it's not. A pushing cut is dangerous and it doesn't provide you with the fine control needed for whittling.

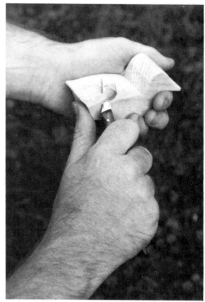

The paring cut can be used both for roughing-out a block of wood and for removing fine shavings for details. Brace your thumb against the wood and slowly close your hand to pull the blade toward you.

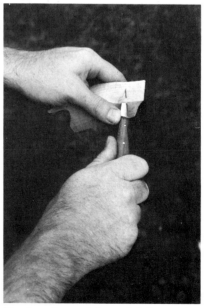

The levering cut is useful for getting into tight areas or working difficult grain. Use the thumb of one hand as a fulcrum and pivot the knife with the other to remove chips of wood.

Trace the pattern for the base of the duck onto the bottom of the wood.

Draw a line down the center of the duck, from bill to tail. Then sketch in lines ⅜ in. to either side of the center-line to indicate the width of the neck, head and bill.

A Miniature Decoy

This duck pattern is a scaled-down version of the basic decoy shape often found in antique collections. It's a good shape to begin with because it will give you experience in working with different directions of wood grain.

As discussed in Chapter 3, the direction of the grain determines the direction you move the tool when carving. If you carve with the grain, smooth, even shavings will curl away from your knife. If you reverse the direction and carve against the grain, the knife will catch between the fibers and split them apart, and the wood will splinter or split off in chunks—something you want to avoid.

In time, your understanding of carving with the grain will become instinctive and not require a lot of thought. It is a difficult concept to describe, but one that is easy to grasp when you are working. Once you achieve the feeling of working with the grain, your tools will seem to flow through the wood.

Carving the miniature decoy is fairly straightforward, but some of the areas around the head and neck are tricky and require some thought. Don't become discouraged—persevere and you'll discover that your hands have learned a lot by the time your duck is finished.

Trace the profile of the duck onto a piece of paper and then cut out the shape. Lay out the pattern on a piece of wood 4 in. long, 2 in. wide and 2½ in. thick. Basswood or pine is good to start with, but any straight-grained softwood will do. Align the pattern on the wood so the grain runs parallel to the duck's length—that is, from head to tail, as shown in the drawing on the facing page. Now cut the wood to shape with a bandsaw or small coping saw. (If you're using a coping saw, you'll need to draw the profiles on both sides of the wood for accuracy. This isn't necessary with a bandsaw because the blade cuts at a constant angle.) Make a pattern for the base and trace this onto the bottom of the block. This will serve as an guide for getting the correct shape. Now, as an old woodcarver would say, all you need to do is carve away everything that doesn't look like a duck.

Probably the easiest way to start is to fix the image of the completed duck in your mind. Study the photographs of different stages of the woodcarving, and picture yourself doing the work. This exercise will help you see the shapes and make it easier to carve a rounded shape from a rectangular block of wood.

I usually start by carving around the outline traced on the bottom of the wood. This will round off the chest and tail areas and help establish the basic shapes. On a large, full-sized decoy, this wood is usually cut away with a bandsaw, but on a small carving, it's faster to carve it away with the knife. The paring cut will work well for most of the base, although you may need to switch to the levering cut for working around the chest.

When you have the front and back rounded, pencil a line down the center of the duck from the bill to the tail. This centerline will help you keep both halves of the duck equal. On the head and neck, draw a line ⅜ in. away on each side of the centerline as a rough guide for the width. Carefully carve away the excess wood in these areas. Take out small chips when working around the

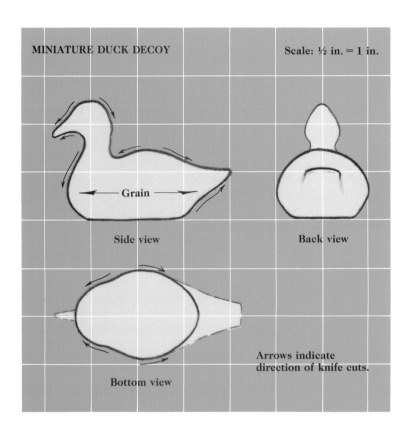

MINIATURE DUCK DECOY

Scale: ½ in. = 1 in.

Side view

Back view

← Grain →

Bottom view

Arrows indicate direction of knife cuts.

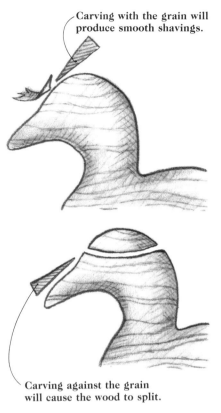

Carving with the grain will produce smooth shavings.

Carving against the grain will cause the wood to split.

When carving the head and neck, remove small chips so that the wood doesn't split off in chunks.

neck and side of the head; the knife will often be cutting parallel to the wood fibers, and it's easy for the wood to split off, removing more wood than you intended. It may be necessary to use a small piece of sandpaper to help with the final shaping around the sides of the head and under the neck.

After the head is shaped, use the paring and levering cuts to round off the body to an oval shape. Take your time. There's an old woodcarver's adage: "Three small chips are better than one big one." So go easy at first until the movements feel natural.

If you're new to whittling, you may find your hands become cramped or tired. Relax for a few minutes, and maybe walk around a bit. Or, if you encounter difficulties and carving no longer seems like fun, put your tools down and take a short break. Try to think through your problem. You may be working against the grain, the wood may have a hidden knot or irregular grain, or your knife might not be sharp enough. You will know when you are carving against the grain, because the wood will split and crack rather than shear away smoothly—if this happens, turn the piece around in your hand so you can change your carving direction. Switching to a different type of cut sometimes makes carving troublesome grain easier, because you can change the direction of your knife. In small pieces, knots are usually visible before you start carving, but if you happen to find one after you have started, don't scrap

Use the levering cut to shape the bill.

Shape the sides of the duck to match the shape of the base using the paring cut.

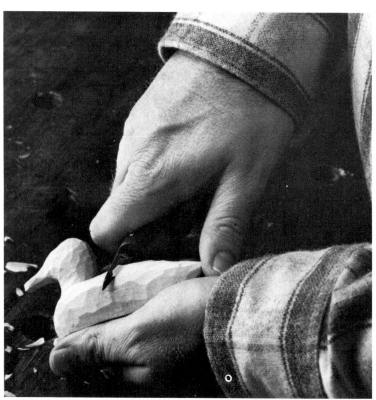

Use the paring cut to round off the back of the duck.

the piece. Carving around knots is a lot of work, because of the distortion they cause in the grain. But if you work slowly and carefully, it can be done.

A knife that isn't sharp enough can also cause problems. If you need to exert a lot of force in order to make a cut, the blade is probably dull. Another clue to a dull blade is that it crushes and tears when cutting across the end grain, instead of cutting cleanly—you can hear a slight crunching sound as you try to carve. Test for sharpness often by checking the knife against your thumbnail, as discussed on p. 29. The only solution to a dull blade is to sharpen it.

Remember, perfection is not important with this first project, but learning is. Encountering difficulties is part of the learning experience. So keep it enjoyable, and don't force your materials or yourself beyond a comfortable point.

When you have completed the duck, you can leave the wood natural, or color it with a wood stain or paint. Some woodcarvers like to sand their work smooth, but I prefer to leave the tool marks because they give the carving an interesting texture. If you have decided to leave the wood natural, seal it by applying a coat of boiled linseed oil or Minwax, and then wipe it dry. The finish will be slightly transparent and will show off the color and grain pattern of the wood.

Once you've completed the carving, you can leave the wood natural and seal it with linseed oil or Minwax, or color it with a wood stain or paint.

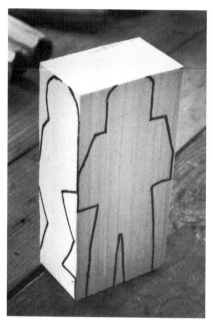

When transferring the pattern for the hermit, make sure the grain of the wood runs lengthwise.

An Adirondack Hermit

This character is one of my favorites. In real life, his name was Old Mountain Phelps, a hermit who lived in the Adirondack Mountains during the 1800s. He would guide people into the High Peaks wilderness, and some of his trails are still in use today. This pattern was drawn from old photographs taken around 1880.

Trace the heavy black lines of a full-size pattern on a piece of basswood or pine 5½ in. long by 3 in. wide by 2 in. thick. Make sure the grain runs from head to toe. Use a bandsaw or coping saw to rough out the side profile first, so that a flat surface will rest on the bandsaw table or workbench when cutting out the front. This will make it easier and safer to hold down the block. Redraw any front-view and back-view lines that have been sawn away and cut out the front profile with the bandsaw or coping saw.

Draw in guidelines for the head, beard and arms, as shown in the photo at left on the facing page, and then round off the sharp angles of the blank with the paring and levering cuts. I usually start with the legs and work my way up, saving the head for last. Carve until the legs and body take on a rounded shape.

To separate the back from the arms, cut a long notch from shoulder to waist on each side and round the contours of the back, arms and elbows. Use the same technique to separate the front of the head from the arms at the shoulders. (It might help to use a small V-tool to clear the more difficult areas.)

Cut out the side profile first. Then sketch in any lines that have been sawn away and rough out the front profile with a bandsaw or coping saw.

After cutting out the basic shape, draw in the head, beard and arms.

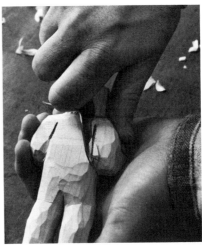

Separate the back from the arms with a long notch, and round the contours of the back, arms and elbows.

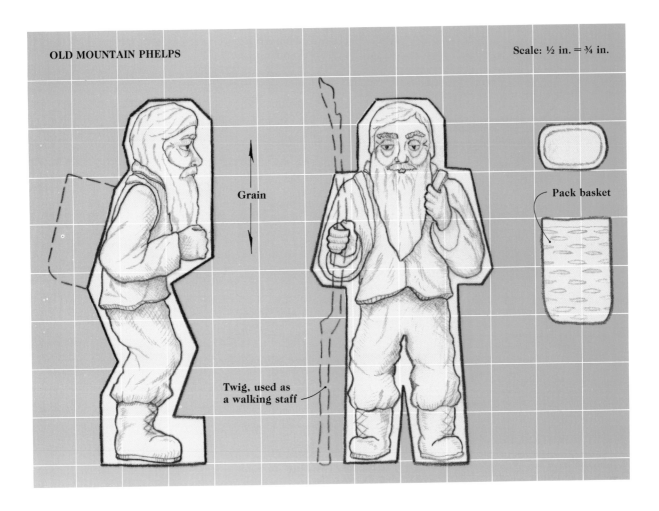

OLD MOUNTAIN PHELPS

Scale: ½ in. = ¾ in.

Grain

Twig, used as
a walking staff

Pack basket

The left arm will be shaped so that the hand appears to be holding the strap of a pack basket. Begin shaping the lower arm by carving out a triangular area between the arm and the beard. To do this, make two vertical cuts between the arm and beard and clean out the wood in between. Repeat these cuts until you have notched to a depth of about ¾ in. Use the same notching method between the left hand and shoulder to make a cut about ½ in. deep. Make a long notch to separate the upper and lower left arm, and then round the contours.

Use the same methods to shape the right arm, but be careful not to apply too much pressure—this section will be cross grain and may split off. One way to prevent splitting is to strop the knife for a few minutes to make sure that it's extra sharp and carve off a few small chips at a time.

You can carve the head and beard into a rounded shape now, but save carving the face until the rest of the body is done.

To shape the lower left arm, carve out a triangular area below the hand and between the arm and beard.

Use the tip of the knife to notch a ½-in.-deep area between the left hand and the shoulder.

Separate the upper and lower left arm with a notch (top), and then round them to shape. When shaping the right arm (bottom), be careful not to apply too much pressure—the wood can easily break off.

To form the hands, use a 6mm *V*-tool. Make short cuts to carve a line around each arm about ½ in. from the end. This line will form the cuff of the coat sleeve.

Next, carve the boots. Draw a pencil line about 1 in. above the sole of each boot, and cut a notch around this line with a knife or *V*-tool to a depth of about ⅛ in. Then carve away the excess wood around the boot to give the impression of pant legs tucked into the tops of the boots. Don't use too much pressure when carving around the toes of the boots; this area is cross grain and can split off easily.

Use a 6mm V-tool to form the sleeve cuff ½ in. from the end of each arm.

After marking the tops of the boots with a notch about ⅛ in. deep, carve away the excess wood around the boots to give the impression that the pant legs are tucked in.

Make a notch with the knife or 6mm V-tool to define the bottom edge of the hermit's coat. Then use the levering cut to taper the wood below the notch, to make it look as though the coat hangs over the pants.

Add laces to the boots with a sharp knife and make the fingers on the hands with a small V-tool.

Round out the waist area and, with a knife or a 6mm *V*-tool, make a ¹⁄₁₆-in. notch around the torso to mark the bottom edge of the coat. The notch should fall about halfway between the knees and the elbows. Trim away the excess wood below the line with the levering cut, and taper the pants up to the notch to make it look as though the coat is hanging down over them.

I add a few details now, such as *X*s on the boots for laces and fingers on the hands. Shape the hands with a sharp knife and use a 3mm *V*-tool to carve the fingers. (You can also carve fingers by making small notches with the knife.)

The most difficult part of this carving is detailing the face, because if you slip and take off too much wood, it will be hard to repair. You will need a very sharp knife with a pointed blade. (I use my modified chip-carving knife.) Strop it a few extra times to make sure it is razor-sharp. Then, rough-out the profile by making a notch to separate the eyebrow ridge and nose, and another notch to show the bottom of the cheeks and nose. I make the eye notch about ¾ in. down from the top of the head, about ⅛ in. deep and almost at a 90° angle. I make the notch for the cheeks and nose about ¼ in. below the eye notch. These measurements are difficult to measure precisely, and you can just estimate them. Part of the challenge of this hermit carving is that even the slightest change in the face proportions will give the carving a completely different feeling and character.

To shape the hair and beard, I use a 3mm *V*-tool to outline the forehead and cheek areas, and then I carve away some of the face to the depth of the outline cut. Using the knife point, incise a line on each side of the nose, extending from the eyes to the bottom of the nose, and gently carve away the excess wood over the cheeks.

Begin carving the face by making two notches, one to define the eye area and another to define the nose and cheeks.

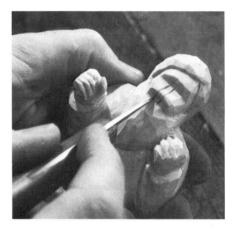

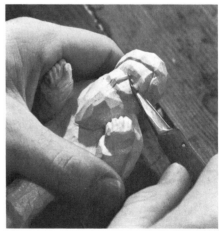

Outline the face with a 3mm V-tool and carve away wood to define the hairline and beard. Then incise a line on each side of the nose with the knife, and carve away the excess wood over the cheeks.

To set in the eyelids, hold the knife in your fingers the way you would grip a pencil, and incise the outline around the eyes with the knife point. Then carefully slice out a thin chip from above and below the center of the outlined area. Carve out two triangular chips on each side of the lower lid to define the pupil. (You could also take out one chip in the center of each lower lid to make a simpler eye.) Texture the hair and beard by making random lines with a 3mm *V*-tool. You can also suggest a few wrinkles in the face using this tool. Just carve two or three small lines near the outside corners of the eyes and one or two lines across the forehead. (Some people like to make a series of long cuts with a knife to get the same effect, but I think it's easier and faster to use the *V*-tool.) Use the same tool to outline the collar of the hermit's coat around the back of his neck, and then level the wood below it with a knife so that the collar appears to be raised above the coat.

You don't need a lot of detail in the finished carving. The accuracy of the basic shape and proportions are what give the carving its lifelike appearance. Other than some wrinkles in the clothes, few other details are necessary. Make these wrinkles by carving a couple of ¼-in. cuts with the 6mm *V*-tool behind the knees and in the crook of each elbow. You could notch these out with the knife, but the veiner gives a softer look—these old guides wore clothes woven from coarse wool, which didn't form sharp creases. This simplicity of detail gives the carving a rugged charm, characteristic of these Adirondack people.

To make Old Mountain Phelps's walking staff, drill a small hole through his right hand, and insert a twig trimmed to the length you want. Whittle out the pack basket from a piece of scrap and glue it to the center of the hermit's back with a drop of five-minute epoxy. These pack baskets were originally made of ash splints woven together. I create the texture with a few, evenly spaced lines made with the 3mm *V*-tool or notched in with a knife.

Use artist's oil colors to paint this carving. (Don't use a water-base paint because it will raise the grain and make the wood look fuzzy.) I use zinc white for the hair. The coat is ivory black, mixed with a little burnt umber. The pants are Prussian blue, mixed with burnt umber, and the boots and straps for the pack basket are burnt umber. These colors are often seen in the folk carvings of Bavaria, and are good for other types of woodcarvings, too, because they enhance the natural tones of the wood.

Thin the paints with turpentine to make a weak stain that will tint the wood, and enhance, rather than hide, its texture. Squeeze a little dab of paint out of the tube onto the edge of a clean saucer. Place several drops of turpentine in the center of the saucer and, with a small, natural-bristle paintbrush, mix a little of the paint with the turpentine. Test the color on a piece of scrap to make sure it's the shade you want before painting the carving. If it's too light, mix more paint into the turpentine; if too dark, thin it with a little more turpentine. You only need one coat of stain. Let it dry overnight. When the carving is dry, you can polish it with a little paste wax, and then buff with a soft, clean, lint-free cloth or horsehair shoebrush.

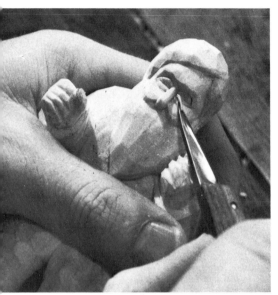

Outline the eyelids with a knife point. To define the pupil, carve out two tiny, triangular chips on each side of the lower lid, or one chip in the center of the lid.

Use a 3mm V-tool to texture the hair and beard.

Few details are needed—the posture and basic proportions give the carving a lifelike quality. Paint the wood with oil colors thinned with turpentine to let the grain show through.

A: Make two diagonal cuts on both faces, cutting about one third of the way into the wood. Look at the sides of the piece to check your depth of cut.

B: Use the point of the knife to cut into the center of the sides at a 45° angle, about ³⁄₁₆ in. away from the diagonal cuts you have already made.

A Whittler's Puzzle

No chapter on whittling would be complete without at least one of the old whittler's puzzles. So here is one of my favorites—a wooden pliers made from a single piece of wood with only twelve knife cuts. This project requires a long, thin-bladed knife to make the inside cuts. You can make a knife by grinding down a piece of thin steel and fitting it to a handle, or use a long, thin X-acto blade or something similar. I made the knife shown in these photos from a piece of a linoleum-knife blade.

Make a pattern from the drawing and trace it onto a piece of basswood, pine or cedar that has been shaped to the correct dimensions. Make the four diagonal cuts on the faces of the wood first (A). Make these cuts about one third of the way into the piece. Using the point of the knife, cut into the center of each side at a 45° angle until you have cut halfway into the piece (B). Begin these cuts ³⁄₁₆ in. from the ends of the diagonal face cuts.

To make the hinge, make two cuts in either one of the sides through the width of the piece (C). Start at the 45° side cuts and sever the wood all the way down to the diagonal face cuts, about ³⁄₁₆ in., as shown at far left in the drawing on the facing page. Gently rock the blade as you slice down through the wood. Be sure to keep the knife parallel to the face so that the cut will be straight through the piece. After cutting through, work the knife tip inside the piece from both sides of each cut to clear a hexagonal-shaped area, as shown at far right in the drawing. This is the secret to the puzzle. All the fibers in the hinge joint have to be severed, otherwise the pliers will break when you open them.

Next, make a straight cut halfway into each face from the diagonal cuts made in Step A to the ends of the piece (D). These cuts will form the jaws of the pliers and the handles. Now, hold the pliers by the handles, and very carefully split the jaws apart. If you are lucky, the pliers will open up without breaking. If not, then get another piece of wood and start over. If the wood is very dry, it helps to soak it in water for a few hours, and then let it air-dry overnight. This helps to control the splitting, although it may make the hinge joint harder to carve.

This is a fun puzzle to show your friends because it isn't seen much anymore, and it is impressive. Almost anyone can realize that it takes a delicate sense of touch and a bit of skill. However, just when you feel you have this trick mastered and you're starting to feel a little smug, be prepared to encounter some old whittler who will humbly show you how he used to make this puzzle in miniature—from a piece of wooden kitchen match.

C: For the hinge, make two through cuts in one side of the piece, joining the 45° side cut to the ends of the face cuts. Cut through the piece as you gently rock the blade down through the wood, and then sever the fibers from both sides to clear out a hexagonal area inside.

D: Make a cut on each face halfway through the piece between the jaws of the pliers and the handles. With gentle pressure, the pliers should open up without breaking. If not, try again.

WHITTLER'S PUZZLE

Transfer dotted lines to wood as part of pattern.

A: Two 45° diagonal cuts, made in the same position on each face of piece, ⅛ in. deep.

B: Two 45° interior cuts made from each side to center of piece. Cuts begin 3⁄16 in. away from ends of cuts made in Step A.

C: Two through cuts made from one side, connecting the cuts made in Steps A and B, and clearing a hexagonal interior shape.

D: Two straight cuts made in each face to separate the jaws and handles.

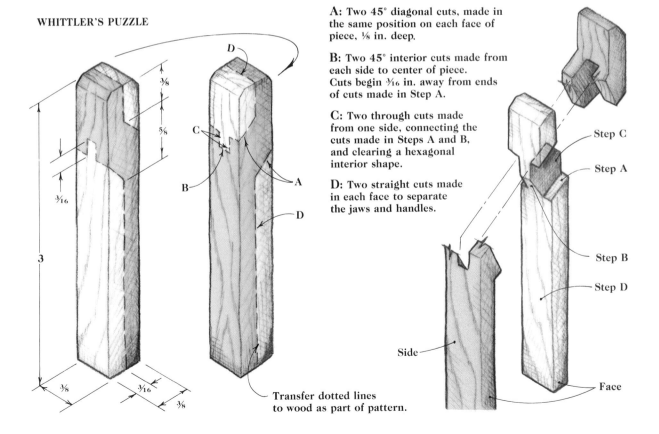

Step C

Step A

Step B

Step D

Side

Face

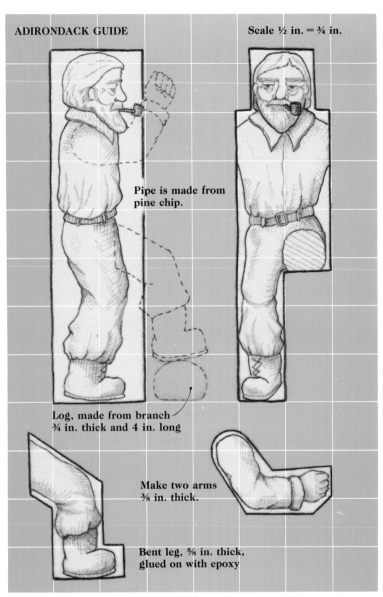

ADIRONDACK GUIDE

Scale ½ in. = ¾ in.

Pipe is made from pine chip.

Log, made from branch ¾ in. thick and 4 in. long

Make two arms ⅜ in. thick.

Bent leg, ⅝ in. thick, glued on with epoxy

The Adirondack guideboat was developed specifically for traveling the waterways of the Adirondack wilderness. It was a lapstrake construction, made of overlapping planks ³⁄₁₆ in. to ¼ in. thick, fastened together with thousands of copper tacks. The boat was extremely lightweight and could be carried easily. A pair of long, lightweight oars were stored above the carrying yoke.

Carve the guide as you did Old Mountain Phelps (pp. 78-85). Carve the bent leg separately and glue it on with epoxy. Whittle a pipe from a pine chip, drill a small hole in the mouth with a knife point and glue in the pipe. Fit the yoke into notches carved in the boat hull. Pare away wood from the center of the yoke so it fits closely around the guide's neck and shoulders. Put epoxy on the center and each end of the yoke, and on the guide's head where it will rest against the boat. Fit the pieces together and let them set.

Adjust the arms to make a good shoulder joint; the hands should reach the edge of the boat. Glue each arm to the guide and the boat, one at a time, and hold them in place while the glue is setting.

The trickiest part is fitting the log to the foot. Set the assembled carving on the log. If the carving tips backwards, carve away some of the bottom of the log. If it tips forward, get another branch and start again.

Tint the inside of the boat a light burnt umber and leave the rest of the guideboat natural with a coat of paste wax. Traditionally, these Adirondack guides wore blue-grey or brown wool pants, a red or green-checked wool shirt, and brown or black boots. When the paint has dried, fit the oars in over the yoke and secure them with a drop of glue.

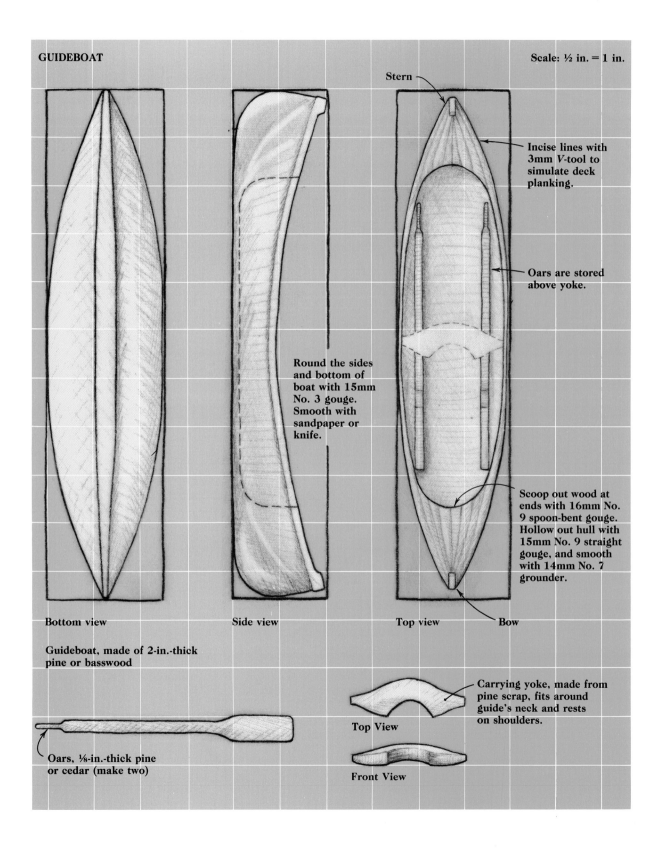

GUIDEBOAT

Scale: ½ in. = 1 in.

Stern

Incise lines with 3mm *V*-tool to simulate deck planking.

Oars are stored above yoke.

Round the sides and bottom of boat with 15mm No. 3 gouge. Smooth with sandpaper or knife.

Scoop out wood at ends with 16mm No. 9 spoon-bent gouge. Hollow out hull with 15mm No. 9 straight gouge, and smooth with 14mm No. 7 grounder.

Bottom view

Side view

Top view   Bow

Guideboat, made of 2-in.-thick pine or basswood

Oars, ⅛-in.-thick pine or cedar (make two)

Carrying yoke, made from pine scrap, fits around guide's neck and rests on shoulders.

Top View

Front View

Chip Carving

6

Chip carving is one of the oldest forms of decorative woodcarving and one of the simplest. Complex geometric patterns are formed by arranging dozens of small, triangular incisions made with just one knife. At first, this style of working may appear tedious and time-consuming, but once you have a little practice, you'll find it goes along quickly, and is quite enjoyable.

The simplicity of the techniques and the satisfaction derived from chip carving have made it a popular folk art for many centuries. Chip carving developed simultaneously among rural communities in many lands, including Scandinavia, Germany, Switzerland and Russia. It is believed to have been introduced in the British Isles by the Viking raiders who later settled along the coastal areas. As the centuries passed, many of the patterns and designs were freely exchanged between cultures, and in time, it became impossible to identify which motif was developed by a particular nationality.

As with most folk art, chip carving was used primarily to decorate household items. Wooden chests and boxes were carved with complex borders and rosettes, as were buckets, washboards, chairs, eating utensils and many other types of woodwork for the house—including beams, posts and shutters. During the long winter months, many elaborately decorated objects were carved and later given away as gifts for special occasions. Unfortunately, the slow pace of country life was hastened by the pressures of the industrial revolution, and fewer evening hours were spent carving by the hearth. Eventually chip carving faded into obscurity and was found only in remote parts of Switzerland and northern Europe. In America, the tradition was carried on by the German settlers in Pennsylvania, now known as the Pennsylvania Dutch.

Chip carving is a style of folk carving done with a single knife. (Carved by Wayne Barton.)

Throughout history, traditional chip carving was used as a training device for woodworking apprentices, and it still remains a good test of self-discipline and sharp tools. Mistakes and overcuts, once committed, are not easily corrected or concealed.

Chip-carved study in a country home in Austria. (Photo courtesy of The Tyrolean Folk Museum, Innsbruck.)

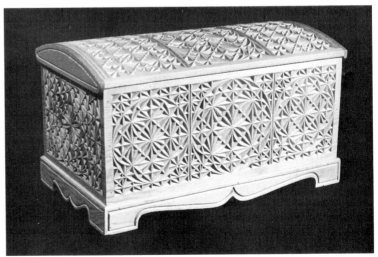

Dutch mangle boards were used with a roller to press water from laundry, but also used as decorative pieces. (Photo courtesy of The Metropolitan Museum of Art, Rogers Fund, 1911.)

Norwegian jewelry box, about 9 in. long, 14 in. wide and 8½ in. deep. (Carved by John Gundersen, 1972. Photo courtesy of Vesterheim, The Norwegian-American Museum, Decorah, Iowa.)

Materials

To start chip carving, all you really need is a knife. I usually use the straight-edged German-style knife I also use for whittling. Some carvers like knives with a skew blade, shown second from left in the photo below, or an angled Swiss-style blade, shown second from right. The knife you choose is a matter of personal preference, because these all work well for carving the stop cuts and slicing cuts used to make triangular chips. A knife with an offset blade, shown at far right in the photo, comes in handy for carving the long, sweeping curves sometimes used in chip carving.

Whatever knife you use, it must be razor-sharp. The beauty of a chip carving's final appearance is created by neat cuts and crisp, clean lines—an effect that a dull tool simply cannot produce. A sharp knife is also less likely to slip while you're carving, minimizing the risk of injury and the unnecessary frustration of spoiled work. I usually strop my knife on a piece of leather for five minutes or so, just to make sure it's extra-sharp. (For information on sharpening knives, see pp. 28-30.)

Just about any type of moderately soft, straight-grained wood can be used for chip carving, including pine, basswood, butternut, walnut, cherry and some types of cedar and mahogany. Centuries ago, the English even used a fine-grained oak, but most of the oak available these days is coarse and will not hold small details well unless the design is bold and simple. Stay away from fir; it splits easily and is almost impossible to carve.

The best method of holding the wood while carving is to brace it against a small bench hook. Your work will be held securely, but you'll still be able to turn it freely as you work without having to fumble around with clamps. A bench hook can be made from wood scraps, glue and a few screws, as shown in the drawing at right. I use a 12-in. by 12-in. bench hook because it makes a good work surface that can be used comfortably with pieces of wood of many sizes. The bench hook is simple to use. Just hook the bottom cross piece over the edge of the workbench, and brace the wood you are carving against the top cross piece.

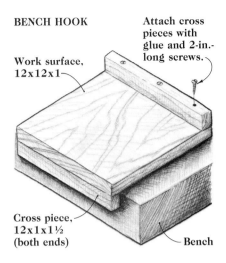

BENCH HOOK

Attach cross pieces with glue and 2-in.-long screws.

Work surface, 12x12x1

Cross piece, 12x1x1½ (both ends)

Bench

When carving, brace the wood against a small bench hook made from pieces of scrap wood.

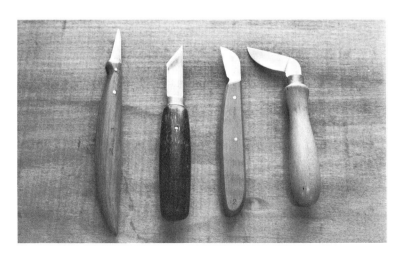

Four knives useful for chip carving. From left to right: A German-style straight-edged knife, a skew-bladed knife and a Swiss-style knife with an angled blade, all used to make triangular chips. A knife with an off-set blade is used for long, sweeping curves.

The Dreischnitt *(left) is made with two stop cuts and one slicing cut. The Sechsschnitt (right) is made with three stop cuts and three slicing cuts.*

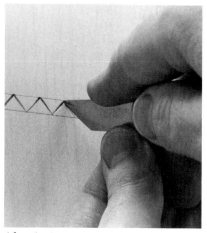

After laying out a series of triangles, press the tip of the knife into the wood at the apex and make two stop cuts down the sides of each triangle.

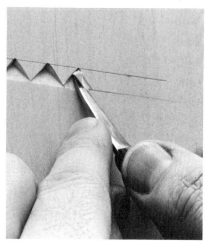

Carefully slice out the chip by pivoting the knife horizontally, at a 10° to 15° angle to the wood's surface.

Techniques

Most traditional chip-carving designs are made up of a series of simple triangular chips. By combining and arranging these triangles, a great variety of designs and patterns can be created. The chip is made with three cuts and is called the *Dreischnitt* (which in German means "three cuts"). Three *Dreischnitt* chips are often combined to form one large triangle, which requires six cuts and is called the *Sechsschnitt* ("six cuts"). The triangular chips are simple to make, and it takes less time to carve them than to describe the process. Practice on a piece of scrap wood until carving them becomes second nature, regardless of the direction of the wood grain. An hour of experimentation can save a lot of frustration later.

The *Dreischnitt*—The simple triangular chip, the *Dreischnitt*, is used for border designs. Each triangle is made with two vertical stop cuts to form the sides and a horizontal, slicing cut to remove the chip.

To lay out a row of *Dreischnitts*, draw two parallel guidelines about ⅜ in. apart (this distance can vary, depending on the size of the triangle you want). Set a compass to that distance and pivot it to mark off the points for each triangle. Continue marking off triangles, each time repositioning the compass leg on the farthest baseline mark. You can vary the proportions to get any size triangle, but simple, equilateral triangles are best to practice on.

To begin the *Dreischnitt*, make a stop cut by pressing the knife point 1/16 in. to ⅛ in. into the apex of the triangle, as shown in the photo at left. Hold the handle at about a 45° angle to the wood to ensure that the cut won't be too deep, then swing the handle down slowly. The cut should be deepest at the apex, and slope up to a very shallow depth where it intersects the baseline of the triangle. Make two of these stop cuts, one for each side of the triangle. (They're called stop cuts because they prevent splinters from running into the design when you make the slicing cut.)

To remove the chip, make a horizontal, slicing cut between the two stop cuts. Hold the knife blade at a 10° to 15° angle to the wood's surface and start the point into the left corner of the triangle. Slide and pivot the knife horizontally across to the opposite side of the triangle, as you push the blade with the index finger of your left hand toward the apex. Your right hand should be guiding and pivoting the knife and handle, not pushing. For a clean cut, make sure the slicing cut meets the two stop cuts. The secret to making these slicing cuts is to keep them shallow—no deeper than 1/16 in. to ⅛ in. at the apex.

When you're just starting out, the depths of the triangles can be slightly irregular and still look okay; getting uniform angles takes practice and patience. You can intentionally vary the depth of the cuts to get different effects, but I would suggest you practice making shallow cuts first. The deeper you go, the harder it is to remove wood fibers without leaving splinters, and you might have to make one or two additional cuts to clean them out.

When you are making the slicing cuts, watch the direction of the grain to avoid splitting the wood. If you notice splitting, reverse the direction of the cut and pull the knife blade toward you with your left index finger, using the same pivoting motion across the triangle to remove the chip.

Try to get in the habit of using the bench hook to secure the workpiece. This will make your work go smoothly and safely. It's also a good idea for beginners to keep both hands on the knife when making any of these cuts. Working this way provides greater control, but more important, it discourages the beginner's natural, but dangerous, tendency to hold the wood with one hand and cut with the other. Some experienced woodcarvers use this method of chip carving—making knife cuts with one hand and holding the wood in their laps with the other—but until you develop quite a bit of skill and control, I don't recommend trying it. With this method, the carver uses the same motions of the knife for stop cuts and slicing cuts as I've described, except the right hand does all the carving without the support of the left index finger. This method works well with softwoods and goes along quickly, but it's easy for the knife to slip.

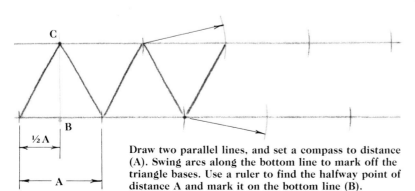

All of these traditional border designs can be made using the Dreischnitt, *or three-cut, chip.*

Next, draw a perpendicular line (B-C) to the top line. With the compass still set at A, begin at point C and swing arcs to find the triangle apexes.

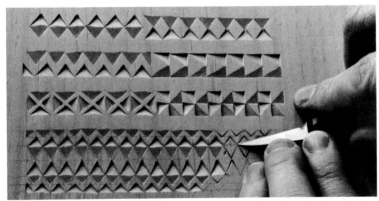

Draw two parallel lines, and set a compass to distance (A). Swing arcs along the bottom line to mark off the triangle bases. Use a ruler to find the halfway point of distance A and mark it on the bottom line (B).

To lay out a row of Dreischnitts, *draw two parallel lines and pivot a compass to mark off points of the triangles.*

The *Sechsschnitt*—The six-cut triangular chip is essentially three *Dreischnitts* combined to form one large triangle. To lay out a row to practice on, draw three parallel guidelines about ⅜ in. apart. The two outermost lines determine the height and the base of each triangle and the middle line indicates where the deepest, center point will be located. Using a ruler or compass, mark off the points of the triangles ¾ in. apart on the outermost guidelines, as you did for the *Dreischnitt* chips. Connect the points with a pencil line to form a row of triangles. Then draw lines connecting the points of each triangle to its center. These lines to the center will mark the location of the three stop cuts.

Place the point of the knife in the center of the triangle, and make three stop cuts out to the points of the triangle. Slope each cut so that its deepest part is at the triangle's center. Then carefully slice out three chips with the horizontal slicing cut. The finished *Sechsschnitt* will have three sloping sides meeting at its center and will look something like a reverse pyramid. (Again, be especially careful when making slicing cuts to avoid cutting against the wood grain.) This large triangular chip can be carved in a variety of shapes and proportions, with straight or curved sides. You can use a drafting compass to make curved sides, or draw them freehand. The technique for carving curved sides is the same as for carving straight ones.

The Sechsschnitt, or six-cut, chip is made by making three stop cuts from the triangle's center to its points, then slicing away three Dreischnitt chips.

These traditional border designs were made using Sechsschnitt triangles with straight and curved sides.

The sweeping cut—Another cut used in chip carving is a long sweeping cut that forms a deep *V* in the wood and tapers to a point at each end. Any of the standard chip-carving knives can be used, provided the cut isn't any longer than 2 in. to 3 in. For making a longer cut, I recommend using a knife with an offset blade. You'll have better control because you can steady your hand against the wood as you carve.

Mark the design on the wood with a pencil, and fasten the wood down with *C*-clamps or a large carver's screw. Incise a vertical stop cut down the center with the point of the knife, as shown in the photo at top right. Hold the knife in your right hand and slide it toward you in a steady, controlled cut. If you use the knife with the offset blade, you can rest your hand on the wood for extra support. (To make a large curve, hold the knife with both hands.) Work slowly and steadily, or it will be hard to follow the layout lines of your design. Make the cut about ⅛ in. to ½ in. deep, depending on the size of the design, with the ends tapering up to the surface. Then, using the same hand position and holding the blade at a 45° angle to the wood, slowly and carefully make a long slicing cut to meet the stop cut. Make another cut from the other side at the same angle, and you will have a long, sweeping *V*-cut. Be sure to watch the direction of the wood grain—at certain points in the curve, you might have to change the direction of the cut to avoid splitting the wood. If so, turn the piece of wood around and start the cut again from the opposite direction. The width of the chip can be controlled by changing the angle of the blade to the wood's surface when making the slicing cut—lowering the angle of the blade to the surface of the wood will make the cut wider without making it any deeper.

When you're just starting out, the sweeping cut can be the same depth throughout the curve, with only the ends tapering up to the surface. As you gain experience, you can vary the depth to make the cut deeper where the design is wide, and shallower where the design is narrow. This will make carving elaborate curves a bit easier as well as making them more interesting to look at. The sweeping curve is more advanced than the triangular chips, but it creates a graceful, flowing line. By incorporating all three of these chip-carving techniques into a single design, you can achieve some interesting effects.

For a large curve, make a stop cut down the center of the design (top) and an angled slicing cut along each side (bottom). Watch the direction of the wood grain—you may have to change direction to avoid splitting.

This design was made using several sweeping cuts and Dreischnitt triangles.

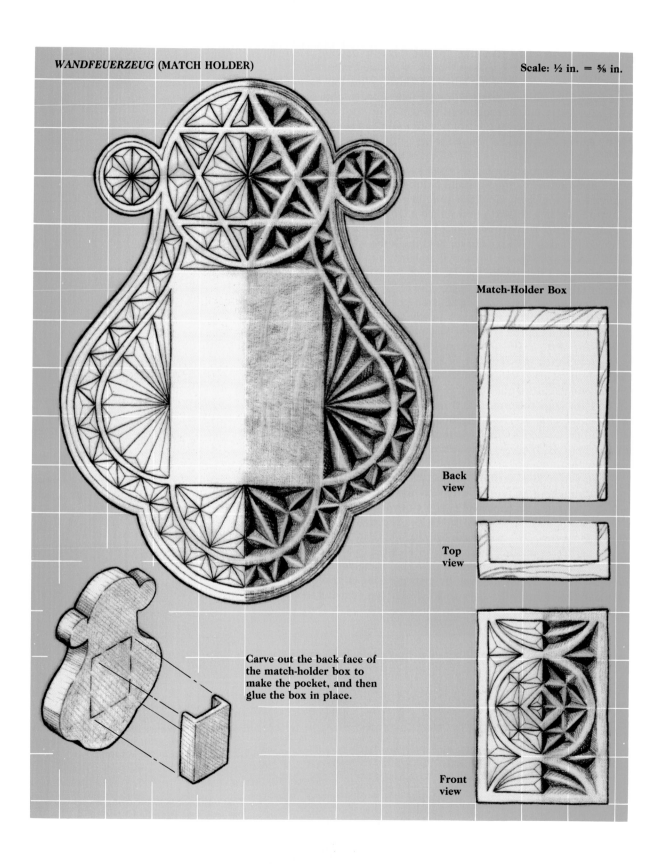

WANDFEUERZEUG (MATCH HOLDER)

Scale: ½ in. = ⅝ in.

Match-Holder Box

Back
view

Top
view

Front
view

Carve out the back face of
the match-holder box to
make the pocket, and then
glue the box in place.

A Match Holder

This match holder, or *Wandfeuerzeug,* is a German design that uses *Sechsschnitt* chips. I have one hanging on my fireplace, full of wooden matches. The pattern, dated 1908, was given to me by an old German woodcarver friend, who carved the match holder as part of his apprenticeship when he was a boy.

Once you've practiced and mastered both the *Dreischnitt* and *Sechsschnitt* chips, and sharpened your knives (pp. 28-30), you're ready to make the pattern. The match holder I carved is 6½ in. high by 5 in. wide. To make one that size, enlarge the pattern using the grid method, or a compass and ruler. To make the size shown here, trace the pattern on a strong, thin sheet of paper and then retrace it directly onto the wood using carbon paper, as discussed on p. 61. Although it's not really necessary, you can use a pencil to lightly shade the areas that will be cut away.

Transfer the pattern using a piece of carbon paper sandwiched between the wood and the pattern. While tracing, keep the paper in place with push pins or tacks.

This wooden match holder of German design is made up entirely of Dreischnitt *and* Sechsschnitt *triangles.*

I used a piece of ¾-in.-thick butternut for my match holder. I sometimes do all the carving before cutting the block to shape and to its finished size; a larger piece of wood is easier and safer to hold while working, especially if the carving is irregularly shaped. In these photos, I have bandsawn the wood to its shape first.

Where you begin carving is entirely up to you, but I start at the top of the border design and work my way around. First I make all the stop cuts, then I go back and remove all the chips. (I use the skew-bladed knife when I need to make a lot of stop cuts because I don't need to change my hand position as often as with a straight-bladed knife and the work goes much faster.) Remember to keep the chips shallow—1/16 in. deep is sufficient. You may have minor difficulties with the fan-shaped sections on each side of the match-holder box. The center stop cut on these is rather long, and may be hard to cut by just pressing the knife blade in. You may find it easier to hold the knife as you would hold a pencil. Then press the knife point into the center of the triangle and draw it along the line, making the cut deepest at the outer edge of the fan. Then cut out the remainder of the *Sechsschnitt* triangle as you normally would. The rest of the cuts shouldn't give you any problem, just work slowly and take your time. Although this design looks complicated, it takes only a couple of hours to carve.

You can cut a block to shape before or after carving, as shown here. First, make all the stop cuts for the straight-sided Sechsschnitts *in the border design.*

After making the stop cuts for the Sechsschnitts, go back and remove all the chips with slicing cuts made with a straight-edged knife. Keep the chips about 1/16 in. deep.

After the long center stop cut is made, make the short stop cuts and the slicing cuts of the Sechsschnitts in the fan.

To begin the fan-shaped design, it's easier to make the long center stop cuts by holding the knife in a pencil grip as you move the blade toward the outer edge of the fan.

Use the paring and levering cuts used in whittling to make the small chips on the face of the match-holder box.

The size of the match-holder box can vary, but I made mine about 2½ in. long, 1¾ in. wide and ¾ in. thick. To chip carve the face of the block, you can remove the chips with motions similar to the paring and levering cuts used in whittling (p. 73). (If you decide to try holding the wood in one hand and carving with the other, as I am doing in these photos, be sure to work carefully and keep your hand clear of the knife.)

After you have finished all of the carving, clean off any carbon smudges or pencil lines with a little Liquid Deglosser or Zip Sander applied to a wad of soft cloth. You can also sand marks lightly with a piece of fine sandpaper wrapped around a flat block of scrap wood.

I use a 10mm No. 8 gouge or a knife to carve out the back face of the block to form the pocket that holds the matches. The pocket is about 1¼ in. wide and ½ in. deep, large enough to hold about two dozen wooden matches. Square up the top edges and inside corners of the pocket with a knife, as shown in the photo below. I glued the box to the carving with Titebond, a yellow, aliphatic resin glue. You can also use a white glue, such as Elmer's Glue-All, but it will take a little longer to set.

After all of the work is done, you can give the carving a coat of finish. Many old chip-carved pieces were left unfinished, but you will find that a light coat of paste wax will help seal and protect the wood. The wax also helps emphasize the facets of the design by reflecting light. To apply the wax, lightly rub or brush on a thin layer, let it stand for 10 to 15 minutes, then buff with a clean, horsehair shoebrush. In time, the wood will acquire a warm, mellow patina.

Brace the block against the bench hook and use a gouge or knife to carve out a 1¼-in.-wide and ½-in.-deep pocket for the matches.

Square up the top edges and corners of the inside of the box with a knife before gluing it onto the carving.

Rosettes

Rosettes are circular designs frequently used in advanced chip-carving projects, and they can be a lot of fun to make. For centuries, they have been an important design element in chip carving, often the focal point of a decoration. I've seen them on a variety of old woodcarvings including Viking drinking mugs, Gothic chests and eighteenth-century mangle boards, which were used for washing clothes.

Drawing rosettes is not difficult. Basically, all you need to do is draw a circle, divide it into equal segments and subdivide these segments into triangles of any shape and size that you can carve. To lay out the proportions and major elements of the rosette, you'll need a drafting compass and a straightedge. (Consult a geometry textbook if you need help with some of the basics.) The trick is to divide the circle into equal segments—if they aren't exact, the design will look off-center. The best way to learn how to design and draw rosettes is to take the compass and paper and play around with them until it all falls into place.

Once you have a design, you can mark it directly on the wood using the compass, but it's easier to draw the design on paper and transfer it to the wood with carbon paper. Draw the straight or curved lines that mark the raised portions of the design, and subdivide the remaining areas into triangles. Then carve away the triangles using *Dreischnitt* or *Sechsschnitt* cuts. (The *Sechsschnitt* cut is more versatile because you can vary its proportions.) You may have to spend a little time thinking about how to plan the types of cuts and position them in your design, but after a little experimentation, it will come naturally.

The following rosettes are examples of typical designs that have been used by chip carvers for centuries. They are presented in order of degree of difficulty, beginning with the easiest. You can copy these patterns exactly, or once you understand how they are made, use one or more of their elements to create your own variations. (More examples of traditional patterns can be found in the books listed in the bibliography.)

Spiral—To make a spiral rosette, draw a circle to the diameter you need. With the compass still set to the radius, start at any point on the circle and swing an arc from the center of the circle to the circumference. Position the compass at the point where the arc intersects the circumference, and draw the next arc. Continue making arcs to the center of the circle from subsequent points of intersection (A-F).

From these six points, make small intersecting arcs outside the circle to the circumference, with the compass still set to the original radius. Lines drawn from the new points of intersection through the center of the circle will divide the circle into twelve sections. You don't need to draw these lines in—just mark the points where they intersect the circumference (G-L). From these points of intersection, make six more arcs from the circumference to the center to form a twelve-part, spiral rosette. To make the first design, mark out a curved *Sechsschnitt* on each spiral section. The deepest part of each *Sechsschnitt* should be close to the circumference of the circle. When carving, you will have to hold the knife in the pencil grip shown on p. 101 to incise the center lines of the chips.

To make the second design, add small freehand arcs to scallop the border of the spiral rosette. Draw lines to bisect these shapes as a guide for carving small sweeping cuts around the design.

THE SPIRAL

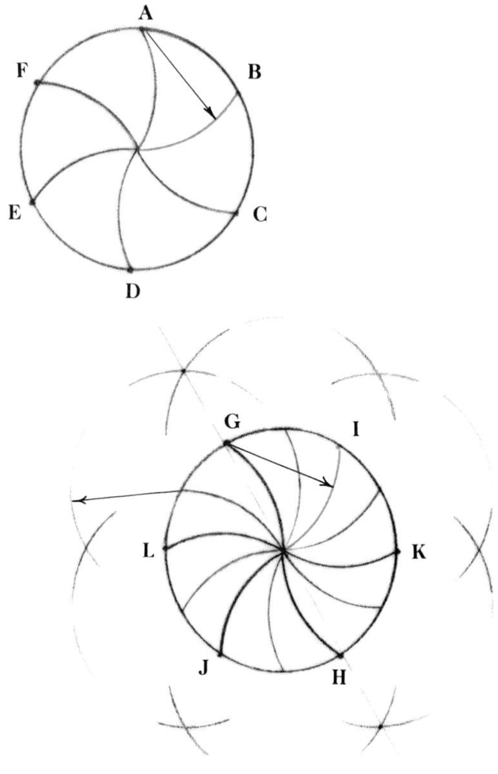

DESIGN 1

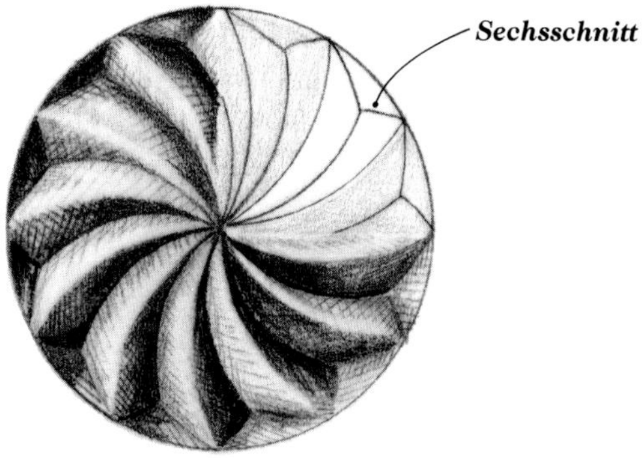

Sechsschnitt

DESIGN 2

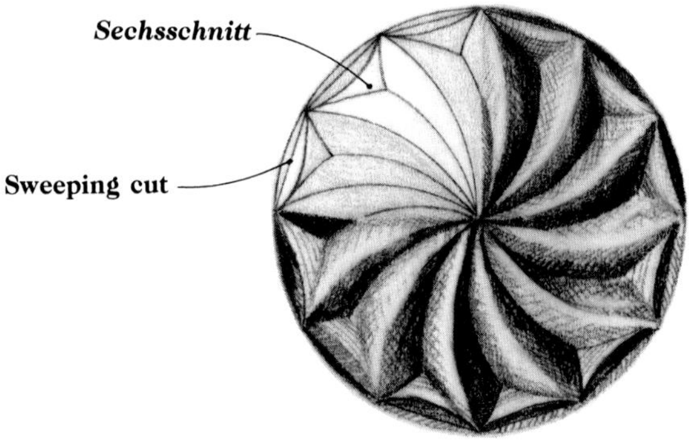

Sechsschnitt

Sweeping cut

Hexagon—To make a hexagonal rosette, draw a straight, horizontal line (A-B) and scribe a circle on it. Draw two more circles of the same diameter, using the first circle's two points of intersection with the line as the new centers (C,D). Then use each point where the circles overlap as the center of a new circle (E-H)—this will give you four additional circles. The original circle will now be divided into six equal petals.

To make the first rosette design, keep the compass set to the radius, and add decorative arcs inside the original circle from the outermost points of intersection of the six outer circles (I-N), as shown. The design is made entirely of sweeping cuts, so bisect each of the six petals and the scalloped border and use the centerlines as guidelines for the cuts.

For the second hexagonal rosette, start with the basic hexagonal shape and draw a circle inside it with a diameter equal to two-thirds the diameter of the large circle. (To do this, set the compass to two-thirds the radius of the large circle.) Next, draw three diagonal lines to bisect the spaces between the six petals. Use the lines and the small circle to locate the apexes and shared edge of two *Dreischnitt* chips between each petal. The petals are carved with a sweeping cut, so draw a line bisecting each one to use as a guideline.

THE HEXAGON

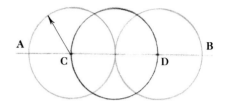

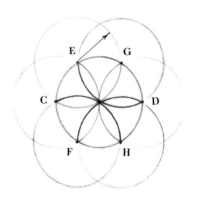

DESIGN 1

DESIGN 2

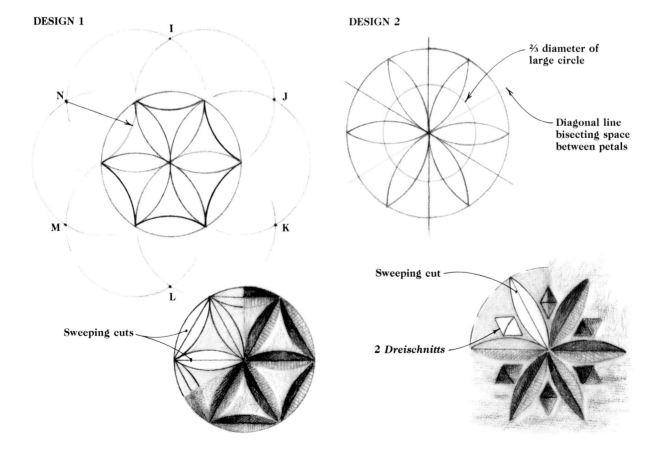

⅔ diameter of large circle

Diagonal line bisecting space between petals

Sweeping cuts

Sweeping cut

2 *Dreischnitts*

THE QUATREFOIL

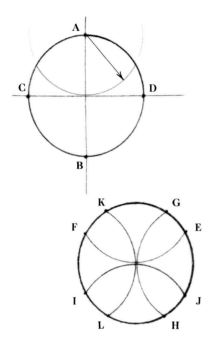

Quatrefoil—A quatrefoil is made up of four converging arcs. This is a popular rosette with Swiss chip carvers because it is easy to draw and resembles the flowers of high alpine meadows. To make a quatrefoil, draw two perpendicular lines, and then draw a circle using their point of intersection as its center. With your compass still set to the radius, scribe an arc through the circle from each of the points where the lines intersect the circumference (A,B,C,D). This will give you the basic quatrefoil shown at left. For the first design, draw diagonal lines connecting the points of intersection to form a square inside the circle. Then draw a small circle inside the square with the radius of the larger circle as its diameter. Lay out four *Sechsschnitt* chips between each wide petal, and three *Dreischnitt* chips at the tips and four on the surface of the petals, as shown below.

For the second design, start with the basic quatrefoil, and draw a small circle inside it with the radius of the larger circle as its diameter. From each of the points where the arcs intersect the circumference of the outer circle (E-L), draw additional arcs to the center to produce oval petals between the wide petals. Next, draw two 45° diagonal lines through the center of the circle to form an *X*. Use these lines to locate the shared edge of two *Sechsschnitts* at the base of each wide petal. Lay out two *Dreischnitts* at the tip of each wide petal, and large *Sechsschnitts* between the eight petals. Lay out two more *Dreischnitts* on each of the oval petals to create a diamond effect.

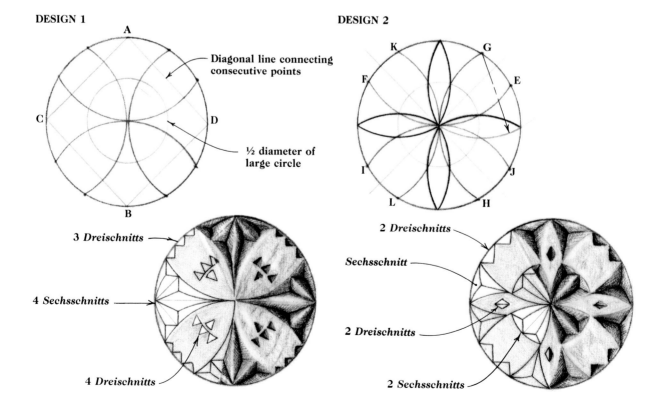

DESIGN 1

Diagonal line connecting consecutive points

½ diameter of large circle

3 *Dreischnitts*

4 *Sechsschnitts*

4 *Dreischnitts*

DESIGN 2

2 *Dreischnitts*

Sechsschnitt

2 *Dreischnitts*

2 *Sechsschnitts*

Double-hexagon—A double-hexagonal rosette can be easily made from the basic quatrefoil. Draw in the arcs to make the oval petals, as you did for the second quatrefoil design. Continue them through the circle rather than drawing them just to the center, so that they intersect the circumference at two points, not just one. You end up with a 12-pointed or double-hexagonal shape.

To make the first rosette design, start with the basic double-hexagonal shape. Draw a small circle inside the large circle, with the radius of the large circle as its diameter. Next, draw twelve lines from the circumference of the outer circle to that of the inner circle to bisect the space between the petals. These lines will mark the shared edge of two *Sechsschnitt* chips between each outer petal. Mark out a *Sechsschnitt* chip between each of the twelve inner petals, too. For extra detail, add a single *Dreischnitt* chip on each outer petal near the edge of the inner circle. The earliest example I've seen of this rosette is on a piece of Swiss woodenware carved in 1744. Designs of this complexity work best in large scale—about 3 in. to 4 in. in diameter. They're easier to carve at this size, and the details are large enough to be seen.

For the second rosette shown at bottom right, start with the double-hexagonal shape. Draw a small circle with the radius of the large circle as its diameter. At this point, you can erase the outer circle—you'll be left with a 12-pointed star. Mark out a *Sechsschnitt* cut to the full size of each outer petal. Draw guidelines for sweeping cuts on the inner petals and mark out a *Sechsschnitt* or *Dreischnitt* chip between each one. (*Dreischnitt* chips are easier to cut on rosettes 2 in. in diameter or less.)

THE DOUBLE HEXAGON

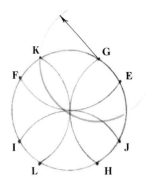

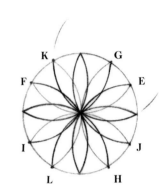

DESIGN 1

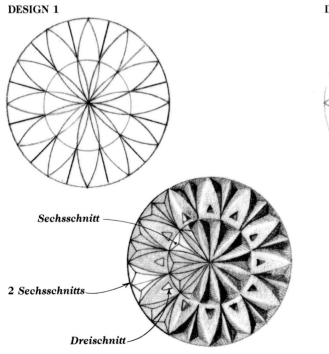

Sechsschnitt

2 Sechsschnitts

Dreischnitt

DESIGN 2

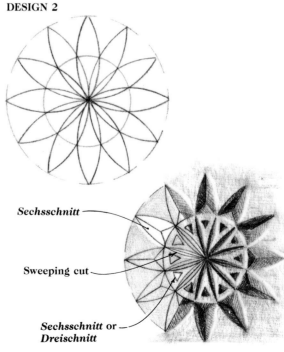

Sechsschnitt

Sweeping cut

Sechsschnitt or Dreischnitt

THE OCTAGON

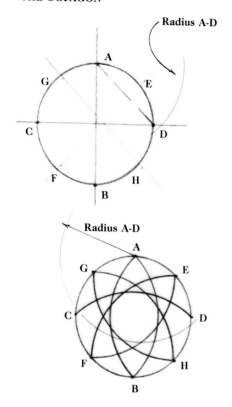

Radius A-D

Radius A-D

Octagon—Octagonal rosettes are well suited to chip carving because the layout lines form triangular shapes that are easy to translate into chips.

To construct an octagonal rosette, draw a circle to the diameter you want with its center at the intersection of two perpendicular lines. Draw two 45° diagonal lines through the center of the circle to form an *X*. Mark the points where these lines intersect the circumference (E-H). This will divide the circle into eight equal parts. Next, set the compass to the distance between two consecutive points where the original perpendicular lines intersect the circumference (A,D). Swing arcs of this radius from each of the eight points (A-H) on the circumference.

To make the first design, start with the basic octagon. Draw eight petals around the lines at the center of the circle freehand. These petals will be carved out with sweeping cuts. Mark out a *Sechsschnitt* cut between each of the eight outer petals to create the border, and erase any unnecessary interior lines. Then mark out a *Dreischnitt* between each of the large petals and around the center design, as shown in the drawing below.

For the second rosette design, start with the basic octagonal shape. Darken the two lines that mark the base of each petal tip. This will produce an eight-pointed star in the center of the circle. Erase the unnecessary interior lines, and draw new lines from the tips and bases of the star points to the center. Mark out *Sechsschnitts* in each of the sixteen triangles produced by these lines. Mark out large *Sechsschnitts* between the outer petals to make a border and pairs of *Dreischnitts* on each outer petal to create a diamond shape.

DESIGN 1

DESIGN 2

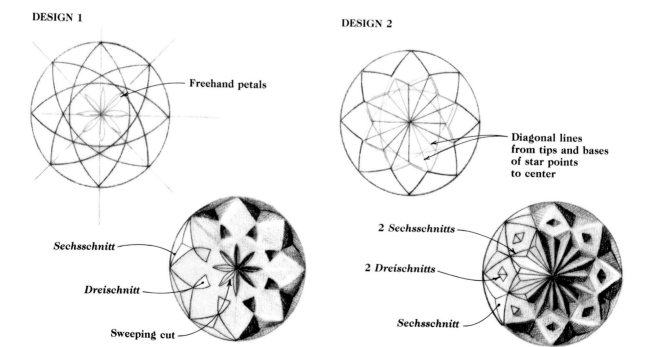

Freehand petals

Diagonal lines
from tips and bases
of star points
to center

Sechsschnitt

2 *Sechsschnitts*

Dreischnitt

2 *Dreischnitts*

Sweeping cut

Sechsschnitt

Heptagon—To make a seven-sided rosette, draw a straight, horizontal line and make a circle on it. With the compass still set to the radius, draw another circle, using one of the points where the first circle intersects the line as its center (A). Draw a straight line connecting the two points where the circles intersect (D-E). Use half of this distance (D-C) as the radius for a series of arcs drawn from points on the circle. Swing the first arc from a point of intersection of the two circles (D). Draw the next arc from one of the points where the first arc intersects the circumference (G). Continue until arcs intersect the circumference at seven points (F through K and D), and the circle is divided into seven sections. Use the distance between two alternate points on the circumference (G,I for example) as a radius, and draw partial arcs between the petals from the seven points on the circumference. This will add a scalloped border inside the circle's circumference.

The first rosette works well with a 2-in. diameter or less because of the large, simple shapes. Start with the heptagon and draw a line between the petals from circumference to center. Mark out large, curved *Sechsschnitts* in the areas between the petals. Next, draw a line bisecting the seven small petals within each large petal. These areas will be carved out with sweeping cuts. Finally, lay out a small *Dreischnitt* at the base of each small petal.

For the second design, start with the basic heptagon. Draw lines to bisect the small petals inside the larger ones as a guide for making sweeping cuts. The rest of the cuts in this rosette will be *Dreischnitts*. Mark out large, curved *Dreischnitts* between the petals along the outer border, and pairs of small ones between the small petals to create diamond shapes.

THE HEPTAGON

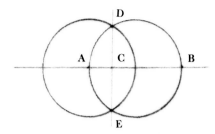

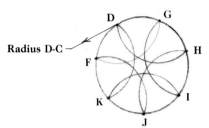

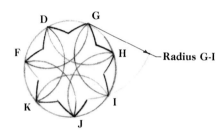

DESIGN 1

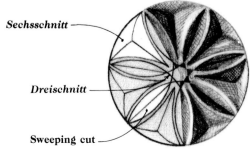

Lines drawn from circumference to center

DESIGN 2

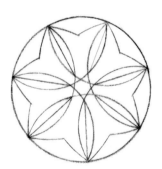

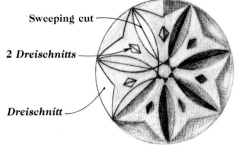

Sweeping cut

2 *Dreischnitts*

Dreischnitt

Sechsschnitt

Dreischnitt

Sweeping cut

Pentagon—This five-sided rosette is a bit more difficult to draw out than the others, but was often used by folk carvers because it is similar to the shape of many wildflowers. To divide a circle into five parts, scribe a circle around two perpendicular lines. With the compass still set to the radius, draw a circle from one of the points where the first circle intersects the horizontal line (D). Then draw a line connecting the two points where the circles overlap (E-G). Position one leg of the compass at the point where line E-G intersects the horizontal baseline (F). Position the other leg of the compass at the point where the first perpendicular line intersects the circumference of the original circle (A). Using that distance as the radius (A-F), swing an arc from point A to the horizontal baseline. Draw a straight line from the points where the arc intersects the circumference and the baseline (A-H) and set the compass to that distance. Using that distance as the radius, swing an arc from point A through the circle. Use each point of the arc's intersection with the circumference (I,J) to make two more arcs through the circle. Continue making arcs until the circle contains five petals.

THE PENTAGON

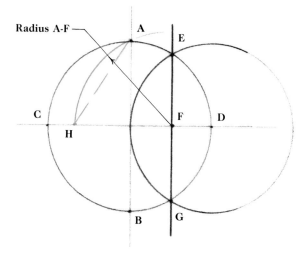

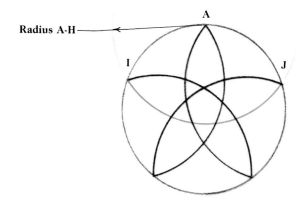

To make the first rosette design, start with the basic pentagonal shape. Draw a small circle inside the large one, with a diameter equal to two-thirds the diameter of the larger circle. (Use the same method used for determining the diameter of the small circle for the hexagonal rosette, p. 105.) Draw diagonal lines through the circle bisecting each of the five petals, then lay out two long *Sechsschnitts* within each petal. The deepest part of the *Sechsschnitt* should be close to the inner edge of the design. When carving these, you will have to hold the knife in a pencil grip, as for the spiral rosette on p. 104. Finally, use the small inner circle to position a pair of curved *Sechsschnitts* between each petal. The diagonal lines will mark their shared edge.

For the second design, start with the basic pentagonal shape. Draw a circle inside it with a diameter equal to three-quarters the diameter of the larger circle. Then draw another circle with a diameter equal to the radius of the larger circle. Draw in a border made up of *Dreischnitts* between the two outermost circles. Below the border and between each petal, lay out a pair of large *Sechsschnitts*. Next, draw in two sets of paired *Dreischnitts* on each petal, using the smallest circle as a guideline for their shared edges. Mark out five small *Dreischnitts* to make the star shape at the center of the design.

DESIGN 1

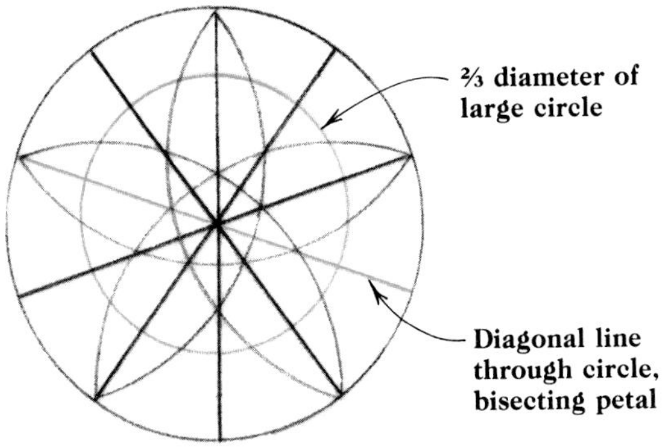

2/3 diameter of large circle

Diagonal line through circle, bisecting petal

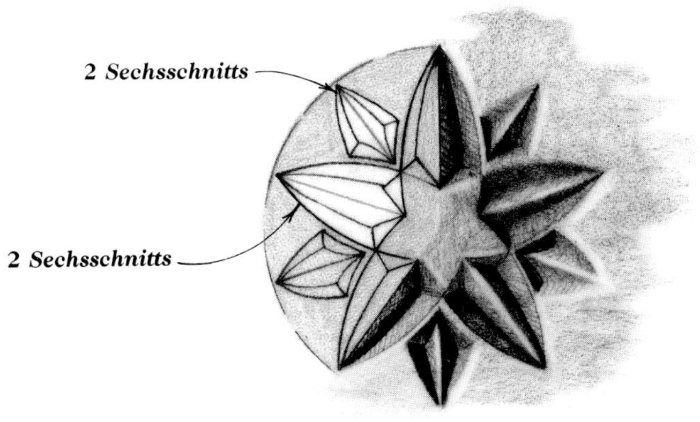

2 *Sechsschnitts*

2 *Sechsschnitts*

DESIGN 2

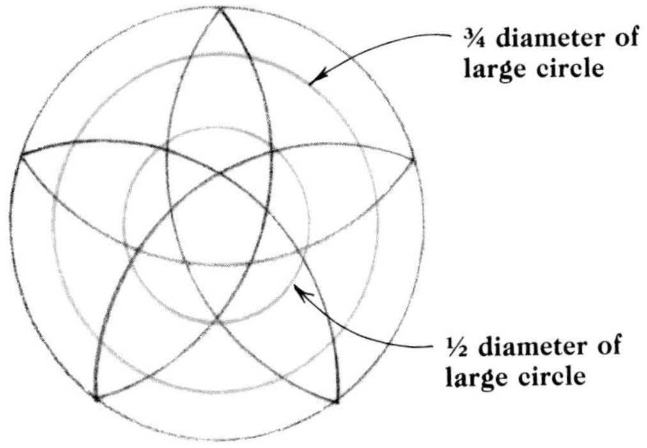

3/4 diameter of large circle

1/2 diameter of large circle

4 *Dreischnitts*

Dreischnitt

4 *Dreischnitts*

2 *Sechsschnitts*

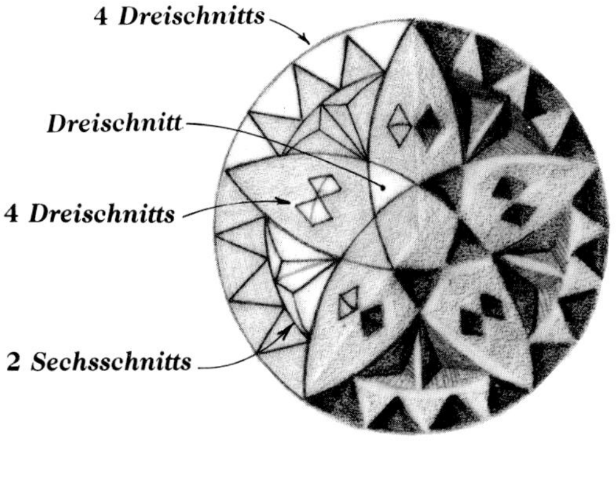

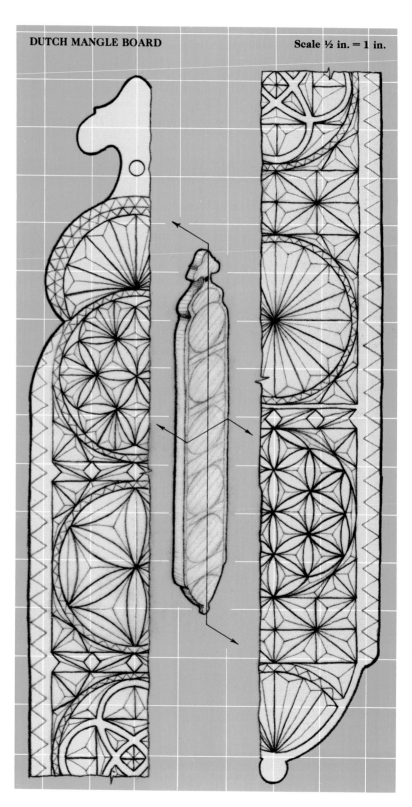

DUTCH MANGLE BOARD   **Scale ½ in. = 1 in.**

This mangle board was carved in 1776. Some of the original cuts have been simplified in the pattern. To carve the diamond shapes in the horizontal borders between the large rosettes, make Sechsschnitts with three stop cuts, but only two slicing cuts, to leave one side raised. The diamonds and triangles have been notched with small cuts.

This chip-carved gameboard is for an old European folk game called Fox and Geese, which is played much like Chinese checkers. The fox is the peg in the center of the board. Fifteen geese are placed in the holes as shown in the drawing below. The geese may move one hole in any direction except diagonally. The fox may do likewise, but may also jump pieces and the geese are then removed from the board. The geese win if they are able to block the fox so that he cannot move.

GAMEBOARD

Scale: ½ in. = ¾ in.

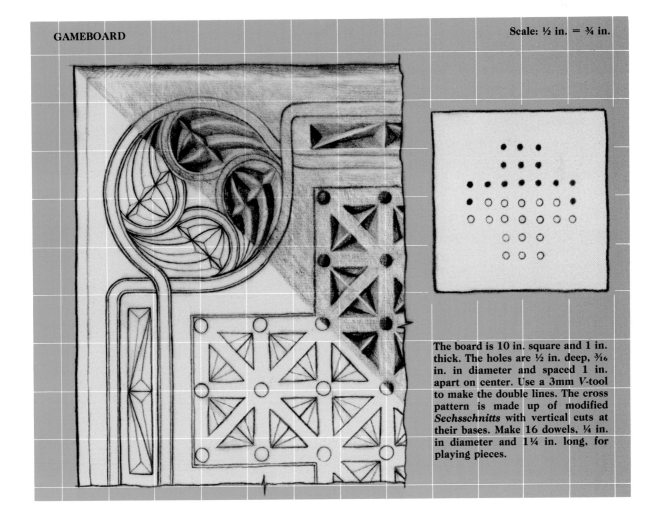

The board is 10 in. square and 1 in. thick. The holes are ½ in. deep, ³⁄₁₆ in. in diameter and spaced 1 in. apart on center. Use a 3mm *V*-tool to make the double lines. The cross pattern is made up of modified *Sechsschnitts* with vertical cuts at their bases. Make 16 dowels, ¼ in. in diameter and 1¼ in. long, for playing pieces.

Relief Carving

7

Relief carving is the method used to raise a design so that it stands away from its background. Relief carving has been an important technique since the days of ancient Egypt, and reached its peak during the seventeenth and eighteenth centuries, when European woodcarvers created works of such beauty and grace that they are standards of excellence today. Relief carving is still used to make two-dimensional designs for wall plaques, household decorations or furniture embellishment.

There are two basic styles of relief carving. If the design has been raised only slightly—about ⅜ in.—and appears to lie flat on the surface of the background, the carving is called a low relief. If the design has been raised more than ⅜ in., and appears to stand free of its background, the carving is called a high relief. Low-relief carving works best with simple designs, such as the Tudor rose on p. 126. High-relief carvings can be raised several inches above the background, and the technique works well with complex shapes to create the illusion of depth, such as in the baroque curve on p. 130 and the coat of arms on p. 136. Because of the extra height, the shapes can be molded, rounded and undercut so that they appear to stand completely away from the background or project out of it.

In low relief and high relief, the basic carving steps are the same. First, the background is carved away and smoothed, leaving a raised design and level background. Then, the design itself is shaped and smoothed. All background carving should be completed before any work is done on the freestanding design. Each step requires different techniques, but many inexperienced carvers switch back and forth between them—this creates a lot of frustration and extra work.

Relief carving is the method of creating a raised design by clearing away the background.

Plan your design on paper first, so that your ideas will be clear before you start to carve. This may sound confining, but planning allows greater flexibility in shaping the wood. If you solve the technical problems first, you will be free to concentrate on the creative work. Each one of the examples on these pages was planned out to the smallest detail before any carving was done.

This carved platter is a good example of low-relief carving. Stamps were used to decorate the background of the design. This piece is 13 in. in diameter, and is made of ¾-in.-thick basswood. (Carved by Thelma Rudser, 1954. Photo courtesy of Vesterheim, The Norwegian-American Museum, Decorah, Iowa.)

"The Hired Men—Ontario" by Fred Cogelow is a good example of high-relief carving. The piece is 26 in. high, 18 in. wide and 4½ in. deep. The face, lapels and hat of the seated figure are 2¼ in. above the rest of the background. The spacing of the beams adds to the illusion of great depth. (Photos by Michael Smith.)

This picture frame, carved in birch by Jacob Varnes in 1917, is 11¼ in. high, 7½ in. wide and ½ in. thick. (Photo courtesy of Vesterheim, The Norwegian-American Museum, Decorah, Iowa.)

This Norwegian mangle board, carved by Leif Melgaard in 1976, is 32½ in. long, 4 in. wide and 6 in. thick. (Photos courtesy of Vesterheim, The Norwegian-American Museum, Decorah, Iowa.)

Tools

I use gouges almost exclusively in relief carving. For the flower on p. 119, you'll need an 8mm No. 3 gouge, a 12mm No. 5 fishtail, a 12mm No. 7 gouge and a 6mm *V*-tool. For the Tudor rose, p. 126, you'll also need a 6mm No. 7 gouge, a 14mm No. 7 gouge or front-bent grounder and a 3mm *V*-tool. For the baroque curve, p. 130, you'll need an additional 15mm No. 3 gouge, an 18mm No. 5 spoon-bent gouge, a 20mm No. 5 fishtail gouge, a 10mm No. 8 gouge, a 14mm *V*-tool and a 12mm carver's chisel.

For the coat of arms, the most advanced project in this chapter, you'll also need an 18mm No. 7 gouge, a 25mm No. 7 gouge, a 10mm No. 7 spoon-bent gouge, 2mm and 7mm veiners and a keyhole saw.

A few gouges can do a surprising amount of work, because you can use them interchangeably. (For example, two small cuts made with a 12mm No. 5 gouge will look the same as one cut made with a 25mm No. 7 gouge.) A knife is useful for detailing and cleaning up the finished carving. You'll also need a solid workbench, some *C*-clamps, holdfasts or carver's screws to secure the piece to the bench, and a medium-weight mallet.

Techniques

Relief carving has four basic steps: outlining, setting-in, grounding-out and modeling. Carving the flower shown on the facing page is a good exercise for learning the techniques of relief carving, and it's interesting to carve another one every now and then, just to compare your progress. (You can change the size and shape of the petals to suit different gouges.) The design makes a nice decoration on furniture, doors or fireplace mantels.

The drawing on p. 119 shows how to carve with the grain, but you don't really need a pattern for this flower. Simply draw a circle about 3 in. in diameter on a block of pine or basswood about 8 in. square. Then draw a ¾-in.-diameter circle in the center and sketch five petals around it. To define the background, draw another circle whose circumference is 1 in. beyond the edges of the petals, and you're ready to begin carving.

Outlining—Outlining is the first step in isolating the raised portion of a carving, and is done by cutting around the design with a *V*-tool. Secure the block of wood with two *C*-clamps, holdfasts or a carver's screw. Use wood scraps under the clamps and holdfasts to keep the metal from damaging the wood. If you are carving too close to a clamp and the gouge slips, it will hit the piece of scrap instead of the metal, and the edge of the tool won't be damaged.

To carve the outline, guide the blade of a 6mm *V*-tool with the fingertips of one hand, while you firmly grip the handle and push the tool with the other. If the wood is too hard to push the gouge through, use a mallet. Hold the mallet by the head and top of the handle, and snap your wrist as you make a series of light tapping motions. If you're working with a hardwood like oak or mahogany, move your entire forearm to make heavier taps, but don't swing your arm in a sledge-hammer blow. This will tire you out quickly, and the force is difficult to control.

FLOWER

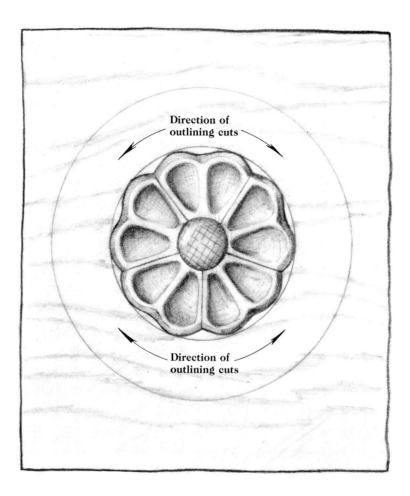

Direction of
outlining cuts

Direction of
outlining cuts

To work with the grain,
make outlining cuts in
directions shown.

Cross Section

Setting-in cuts are made vertically,
and the modeling cuts are made from the
outer edges toward the center, as shown,
in a downward direction.

*To draw a pattern for the flower, use a
compass to make three concentric circles—¾ in., 3 in. and 5 in. in
diameter—and sketch in five petals.*

*Begin by outlining the flower design
with a 6mm V-tool. If the wood is too
hard to push the tool through, make
light tapping motions with a medium-
weight mallet.*

Start the outline cut ¼ in. to ⅛ in. outside the design. Don't get too close to the petals—they'll be shaped later when there is less chance of their being damaged. Make four cuts, each going around a quarter of the circle, so that you are always working with the grain (turn the block when necessary). This is a good time to learn how to carve ambidextrously. Just reverse the position of your hands, still letting one hand guide the blade while the other pushes the handle. Being able to carve with both hands will save a lot of time, because you can change direction as you work without having to unclamp a piece and turn it around.

Be careful that the wood doesn't split into the design. As with all carving, the way to prevent splitting is to carve with the grain. However, in relief carving, you're working with a two-dimensional surface, and there are some other considerations. If you are making cuts that run either parallel or perpendicular to the wood grain, the gouge will carve from either direction without too much splitting. (The cleanest cuts are often those made perpendicular to the grain, so this a good direction to work in when putting the finishing tool marks on a background.) But when making cuts that are diagonal to the grain, one side of the gouge cuts with the grain, and the other cuts against it. Plan your cuts so splinters will run into the waste wood. When you need to carve a diagonal line, make two cuts from opposite directions, as shown in the drawing below, so that you are always working with the grain.

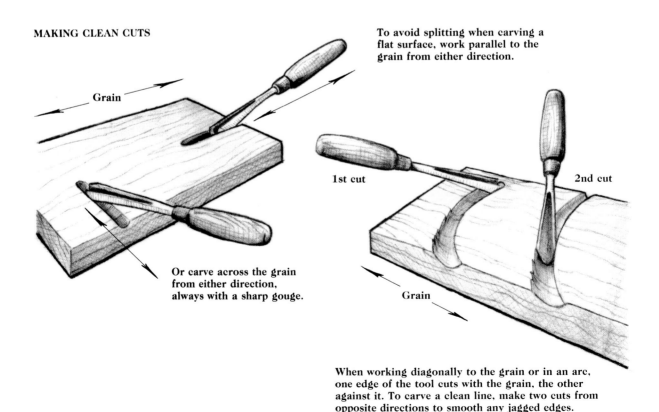

MAKING CLEAN CUTS

Grain

To avoid splitting when carving a flat surface, work parallel to the grain from either direction.

1st cut

2nd cut

Or carve across the grain from either direction, always with a sharp gouge.

Grain

When working diagonally to the grain or in an arc, one edge of the tool cuts with the grain, the other against it. To carve a clean line, make two cuts from opposite directions to smooth any jagged edges.

Setting-in—The next step, setting-in, is done by trimming the walls of the design vertically, and then enlarging the outline cut. By repeating these two steps, the background can be sunk as deep as you want.

To set-in, use a gouge whose sweep matches the curves of the design. (Position the cutting edge of the tool against the edge of your drawing to see if it matches.) I used a 12mm No. 7 gouge for this flower because its sweep matched the outside shape of the petals. It doesn't have to match exactly, just close enough to make a continuous line of vertical cuts around the design. For a complex, twisting curve, you'll need several different gouges to set in all the lines.

Lightly tap the gouge with a mallet to make vertical cuts around the design. Don't drive the edge any deeper than ⅛ in. in hardwoods or ¼ in. in softwoods, because you can break the tip of your gouge. This flower design doesn't need to be too deep—⅛ in. is sufficient.

Use the 12mm No. 7 gouge to set-in the curve around the outside edge of the petals by reversing the gouge so that the bevel faces the center of the flower. To make this vertical cut, tilt the gouge about 15° to 20° away from the center to compensate for the bevel angle.

Next, using a 12mm No. 7 gouge, make a series of horizontal, clearing cuts around the outline. Start the gouge about ⅛ in. to ¼ in. away from the edge of the design and work toward the outline to meet the vertical cuts. As you did when outlining, guide the blade with one hand, positioning your fingertips on top of the tool and your thumb underneath, and use your other hand to push the tool. You can also position your thumb on top of the blade and your fingers underneath to guide the tool, as shown in the photo below. (One position is sometimes more comfortable than the other, depending on the angle you're working in. I sometimes

To set-in, use a 12mm No. 7 gouge—its sweep matches the outside shape of the design (top). Tap the gouge with the mallet in a series of light motions rather than with a full swing. Don't drive the cutting edge too deep or you might break the tip of the gouge. For hollow curves on the edges of the petals, reverse the gouge so the bevel faces the flower's center, and tilt it slightly away from the design to compensate for the bevel angle (bottom).

After setting-in the flower, make a series of overlapping cuts around the design, toward and meeting the setting-in cut.

switch positions to keep my fingers or thumb from getting cramped if held in one position too long.) All forward movement is provided by the hand holding the tool handle; again, it's best if you can learn to work ambidextrously.

Keep the corners of the cutting edge above the surface of the wood. If you bury them, the tool will pry up splinters instead of carving smoothly. Also, the angle at which you hold the tool will vary, depending on the depth of cut you want to make and the angle of the bevel. For this flower, I used an angle of about 45°.

Alternate between enlarging the outline cut and deepening the vertical walls of the design until you have removed as much of the background as you want. I made the background on this flower ⅛ in. deep. The depth you use depends on how much shaping you want in the design. With a simple flower like this, you don't really need a lot of rounded shapes. However, if you were carving a rose or a chrysanthemum, and needed to shape several overlapping petals, you might want the design to stand ⅜ in. to 1 in. above the background.

After you have set-in the edges of the design, use the 12mm No. 7 gouge to set-in the center of the flower, using the same techniques you used to set-in the petals.

Set-in the center of the flower with a 12mm No. 7 gouge and a mallet (above), then widen the cut as you did around the outside of the design (right).

Grounding-out—Once the design has been set-in, you can begin grounding-out the background. In this third step, a series of cuts are made to remove waste from the background. For this flower, instead of clearing away the entire background, remove only the area 1 in. beyond the edge of the petals, indicated by the outer circle on the drawing.

I used a 12mm No. 5 fishtail gouge to ground-out the background; the corners of the cutting edge fit easily in the narrow spaces between the petals. Start at the edge of the outer circle and gradually taper the background down to the depth of the set-in petals. This tapered effect is called cushion relief, because the carving looks as though it's been pressed down into a soft surface. Cushion relief is a good way to make a carving blend into surrounding flat surfaces, such as on doors or furniture. Remove wood until the design is about ⅛ in. to ¼ in. above the background. Then make a series of smoothing cuts with the fishtail gouge. When smoothing the background, arrange your cuts so that the tool marks create a pleasing, even pattern around the flower.

Use a 12mm No. 5 fishtail gouge to ground-out the background.

Shape the contours of the petals by starting the cut at the edge of the flower and carving toward its center.

Bevel the edges of the petals with an 8mm No. 3 gouge (top). Finish modeling the flower by adding a crisscross design to the center and separating each of the petals with a 6mm V-tool (bottom).

Modeling—Once the background has been ground-out and smoothed, the design is completely raised and ready to be shaped. Use a 12mm No. 7 gouge to remove wood from the petal surfaces. Start each cut at the edge of the petal and carve toward the flower's center. Make a series of overlapping cuts to smooth the petals so they taper down to the center. Push the gouge or use a mallet, but be careful not to cut too fast and accidentally remove the center of the flower. Round the center with the 12mm No. 5 fishtail gouge. Hold the tool with the bevel up and gently carve from the top of the center to the outer edges to round off any sharp angles, as shown in the drawing on p. 119.

A nice effect can be made by finishing each petal with two scooping cuts. Start a 12mm No. 7 gouge at the outer edge of the petal at a nearly vertical angle (about 70°). Cut toward the flower's center, lowering the handle in a gentle scooping motion so that the cut becomes shallow near the center, or comes out of the wood completely. The deepest part of the cut, at the outer edge of the petal, should be about ⅛ in. or less. Make one of these teardrop-shaped cuts for both rounded lobes of each petal.

As a finishing touch, bevel the entire edge of the flower with an 8mm No. 3 gouge. The crisscross design in the center is carved with a 6mm V-tool, as are the lines separating the petals. You can leave the wood unfinished, or use paste wax to seal it and add a little shine.

Leave the wood unfinished, or use paste wax to seal it and add shine.

TUDOR ROSE

A Tudor Rose

This Tudor rose is an example of the decorative carvings that were popular in the fifteenth and sixteenth centuries. It combines the rose and the thistle, two Gothic motifs commonly used as religious or heraldic symbols. This design can be used on doors and furniture or made up as a panel to hang on the wall. It's also excellent practice for applying one of the most important principles of relief carving—make a few gouges do as much of the work as possible. If you can use a few tools efficiently, you won't have to spend a lot of time searching through dozens of gouges for just the right one. And you won't waste time constantly changing from one tool to another as you work.

I used oak for this traditional carving because it was commonly used in the fifteenth and sixteenth centuries, but you can use any good carving wood. Secure a 9½-in. by 12-in. piece of wood, ½ in. to 1 in. thick., to the bench with C-clamps, holdfasts or a carver's screw. Outline the design with a 6mm or 14mm V-tool. I made this design only about ⅛ in. high—just to show how much three-dimensional shaping you can create without carving deeply into the wood. Keep the outline cuts ⅛ in. or so away from the edges of the design, especially if you're working in oak, which can split easily along the grain. If you feel a split starting, stop the cut immediately and try carving from the opposite direction. Use the same V-tool to outline the border framing the design, but you can work a little closer to the line—about 1/16 in. away will be fine.

In spite of the different curved shapes in this design, a 12mm No. 5 fishtail gouge will do most of the work of setting-in the leaves, stems, buds, center and large petals of the rose. For the smaller curves on the tips of the leaves, the thorns and flower petals, use the 6mm No. 7 gouge. (Try to make as many of the setting-in cuts at one time with whatever gouge you are holding—this will help you work faster and more efficiently.) Use these same gouges for widening the outline cuts. Don't set-in the border—plane a vertical edge around it with one side of a V-tool after the background has been ground-out.

Ground-out the background with a 14mm No. 7 gouge or a front-bent grounder. I prefer the grounder because it's easier to control the cutting angle. Use the 12mm No. 5 fishtail gouge to get into the tight corners around the leaves, stems and flowers.

Outline the entire design with a 6mm or 14mm V-tool. Use a mallet if you're carving a hardwood.

Use a 14mm No. 7 gouge or front-bent grounder to carve away the background. Use a 12mm No. 5 fishtail gouge to get into tight areas.

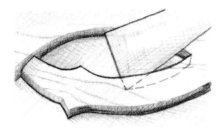

1st cut

2nd cut

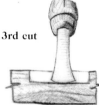

Front views

Carve out the excess in the middle by carving across the area to meet the other cuts.

Hold the fishtail gouge so that the corners meet the setting-in cut on both sides.

3rd cut

Side view

The enclosed sections where the branches intertwine near the base of the stem will be a little tricky to clean out. Tilt one corner of the fishtail gouge into the area at a 30° angle and slice along the stem to meet the bottom of the setting-in cut. Repeat this cut on the other side of the area with the other corner of the gouge. Then carve away the raised section that remains in the center by cutting across the grain, as shown in the drawing at left. In small places, where it's difficult to fit the entire cutting edge, hold the tool vertically and gently scrape the edge across the wood to clean out the area.

When the background has been ground-out and smoothed, begin shaping the rose, using the same techniques used for the flower on p. 125. Set-in each small petal, using the 12mm No. 5 fishtail gouge for the top of the petal, the 6mm No. 7 gouge for the sides and a 14mm No. 7 gouge for the center. The small, pointed petals between the large petals are set-in with a 6mm No. 7 gouge. Shape the contours of each rose petal with the 6mm No. 7 gouge, using the scooping technique used on the petals of the flower (p. 125). Use a 12mm No. 7 gouge, with the bevel up, to round over the edges of the rose center, then crisscross the inside with a 3mm V-tool. Use the same method to shape the two thistle buds in the lower half of the design.

Carve a vein down the center of each leaf with the 6mm V-tool. Then, use the 6mm No. 7 gouge to make a series of overlapping cuts from the edge of the leaves to the center. Make the cuts shallow at the edge of the leaf and deepest at the vein. (The 6mm No. 7 gouge gives more variation and texture to the leaves than a flat, wide tool would.)

After the background has been cleared, plane the vertical edge of the border with a V-tool.

Invert a 12mm No. 7 gouge to round over the edges of the flower center.

To separate the thorns from the stem, incise a line between them with a 6mm *V*-tool. Then make another cut with one side of the *V* parallel to the background or angled down slightly to trim wood off the surface of the thorns—they should be about 1/16 in. above the background. (Watch the grain direction or the thorn can split off the stem.) This detailing will make the thorns appear to protrude from the lower part of the stem. Create a ragged effect on the leaves and thorns by nicking the edges with a 3mm *V*-tool or notch them with a knife. Bevel each side of the stem at a 45° angle with a cut about 1/16 in. deep (or less), using a 12mm No. 5 fishtail gouge, or better yet, a 12mm carver's chisel. The bevel will catch light and help define the shape.

Because this relief carving is quite low, I finished it with the glazing technique to bring out the details and create the illusion of depth. As discussed in Chapter 3, glazing is an easy way to finish a carving. Just brush on a layer of boiled linseed oil or clear Minwax, let it soak in for a few hours, then wipe it down with a clean, dry cloth. After letting it set for 24 hours, brush on a coat of Minwax Special Walnut stain, and quickly wipe it off. Some stain will remain in the recesses and details to make them show up better. Let the carving dry overnight, polish it with paste wax and buff with a horsehair shoebrush for added luster.

DETAILING THE THORNS

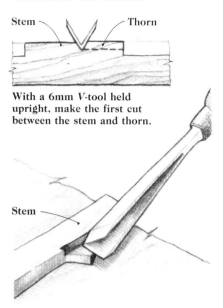

With a 6mm *V*-tool held upright, make the first cut between the stem and thorn.

Make the second cut with one side of the *V* flat on the thorn to trim off about 1/16 in. of the surface.

Bevel each side of the stems at a 45° angle with a 12mm No. 5 fishtail or a 12mm carver's chisel.

Glaze the carving with boiled linseed oil and stain to bring out the details and create the illusion of depth.

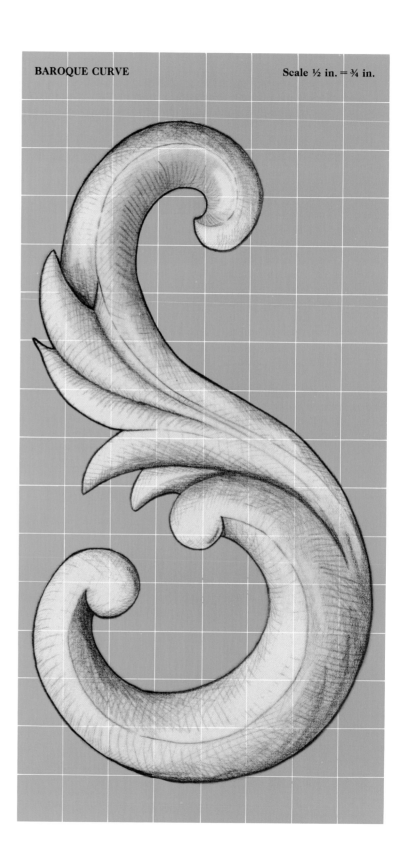

BAROQUE CURVE   Scale ½ in. = ¾ in.

A Baroque Curve

This traditional design was taken from an old family table. Curves of this type were, and still are, frequently used in furniture and interiors or carved on a panel to hang on the wall. The size can be modified to fit cabinets, headboards, tables and large chairs. This curve can also be grouped with two or more others to form a repeating design on shutters or doorway pediments. Other applications are limited only by the carver's imagination. The varying thicknesses along the curve make this a strong and attractive design.

This project is a high-relief carving. The method used for grounding-out the background is a very efficient way to remove a lot of wood quickly. The sweep cut used in this project is a good technique for making smooth, controlled finishing cuts on irregularly shaped surfaces.

Secure a piece of 2-in.-thick butternut, 15 in. by 8 in., to the bench with a carver's screw—the surface has to be free of clamps, because the entire background will be ground-out. Trace the pattern onto the wood, and outline the design, using a 14mm V-tool and a medium-weight mallet. Keep the cuts ¼ in. to ⅛ in. outside the edges of the design, and don't try to outline the delicate leaf sections or the inside curves at each end. These will be shaped during setting-in, when there's less chance of damage.

Because butternut is fairly soft, set-in the carving to an initial depth of ⅜ in. A 20mm No. 5 fishtail gouge, a 14mm No. 7 gouge and a 15mm No. 3 gouge will match all of the curves in the design. Enlarge the outline cut with the 14mm No. 7 gouge. Then repeat these setting-in steps to make the total depth ¾ in. (The extra height is needed for modeling the design.) Smooth the vertical walls by paring the wood away carefully with a fishtail gouge.

Begin by outlining the design with a 14mm V-tool. Don't try to outline the delicate leaf sections or curved ends.

Then enlarge the outline cut by cutting around and toward the curve with a 14mm No. 7 gouge.

Use a fishtail gouge to trim the walls of the design vertically.

To ground-out the background in a high-relief carving, you need to remove a lot of wood. Grounding-out can be done with an electric router, but a good woodcarver can clear a background in less time than most people need to set up a power tool. You'll need a carver's chisel, or an 18mm No. 7 gouge, and a medium-weight mallet. Make a series of parallel cuts in the background, one behind the other, and about ⅜ in. deep. Space the cuts in rows about ¼ in. apart, running across the grain. Each time you drive the gouge into the wood behind the previous line of cut, the waste will chip and break away. Because this design will be raised about ¾ in., grounding-out should be done in two stages, each time to a depth of ⅜ in. (If you are working with a hardwood, ground-out in four stages, each to a depth of 3/16 in.) When carving the final layer, be careful not to drive the chisel too deep, or the background will be uneven, and you'll need to do some extra smoothing to remove the marks.

Use a carver's chisel, or an 18mm No. 7 gouge, and a mallet to clear the waste from the background using rows of vertical cuts, spaced about ¼ in. apart.

When the background has been completely ground-out, smooth it with a 20mm No. 5 fishtail gouge, a front-bent grounder or any straight gouge with shallow sweep. Smoothing is sometimes easier with the front-bent grounder, especially where lateral clearance is restricted. In very tight places, where working room is cramped, such as the inside curves, you'll need a spoon-bent gouge. Spoon-bent gouges are available in a great assortment of sweeps and widths, and are indispensable for complicated designs. The spoon-bent gouge is probably used less than any other tool in a woodcarving set. Part of the reason for this is the natural tendency to use the spoon shape in a scooping motion, which greatly restricts its usefulness. For smoothing backgrounds, the spoon-bent gouge should be positioned at the angle where it just begins to cut, then, carefully but firmly, it should be pushed across the wood without changing the angle, as discussed on p. 8. This produces the same cut a straight gouge would make, but instead of starting the cut 15° to 30° to the work, the tool can be held at almost 90° to the work. This angle allows you to carve areas inside deep recesses that would otherwise be impossible to reach.

Make all the smoothing cuts the same length, short or long, and all in the same direction, either parallel or perpendicular to the grain. Don't let them become a jumbled, chaotic pattern—they form your finished background, so you'll want them to look neat.

After grounding-out the waste wood, smooth down the background with a fishtail gouge or front-bent grounder.

A spoon-bent gouge is useful for grounding-out inside curves or other hard-to-reach areas.

Make all the smoothing cuts the same length and in the same direction to give the carving a crisp, even background.

At this point, the raised portion of the carving will be standing free and clear from the smooth, level background. Rough-shape the contours by carefully rounding off sharp angles, cutting from the top surface of the design downward. For the outside of the curve, use a 12mm carver's chisel or a 15mm No. 3 straight gouge. For the inside, use a gouge of greater sweep, like a 10mm No. 8, so that the corners of the gouge won't dig into the edges of the tight curves and split the wood. Cut the lines that form the valleys between the leaves with a 14mm V-tool, and round them with a 14mm No. 7 gouge.

These roughly shaped surfaces can be finished off with long, smoothing cuts. These finishing cuts, which distinguished the professional works of old, are best made with a sweep cut to follow the contours of the curve. If you are right-handed, make a sweep cut by steadying the blade of the tool in the fingers of your left hand, with the palm resting firmly on the surface of the carving. Push the tool with your right hand while you pivot the palm of your left on the wood. In this way, the edge of the gouge can be made to follow a well-controlled curve. By changing the way the tool is held in your left hand, and by pivoting on a different area of your palm, a variety of arcs can be made. If you hold the blade in your thumb and fingertips, with your fingers stretched out as far as is comfortable, and then pivot on the inner heel of your palm, the tool will move in an arc of about 5 in. in radius. If you curl your fingers around the blade and hold it in a fist, and then pivot on the outer heel of your palm, you can move the tool in an arc with a 2-in. radius. This requires a bit of practice, and like all woodcarving techniques, should be able to be done with either hand. Sweep cuts are very useful, and can be used to create a smooth finish both on the inside and outside surfaces of curves.

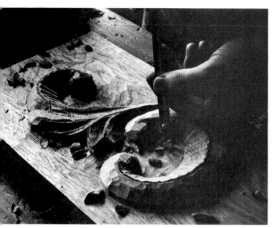

Rough-shape the curve by cutting down from the top surface of the design to round off sharp angles.

Pivot your palm on the wood to make sweep cuts. Use a spoon-bent or curved gouge on inside curves (above), and a chisel on outside curves (right).

On the inside curve of this design, make sweep cuts with a 18mm No. 5 spoon-bent gouge, or another gouge that is about the same size. The gouge should be wide enough to cover the inside curve in one cut, if possible. For the outside curve, use a carver's chisel to maintain the convex shape.

Watch the direction of the grain so that the cuts will be smooth and polished, not fuzzy. Well-made finishing cuts eliminate the need for smoothing with sandpaper. Never substitute sandpaper for good technique.

Use any clear finish on this carving. I used a clear Minwax to bring out the color and grain pattern in this piece of butternut. After it dried for 24 hours, I polished it with a light coat of paste wax and buffed it.

Finish the carving with Minwax or another clear finish.

Scale ½ in. = 1 in.

A Coat of Arms

Heraldic crests and coats of arms have been an important tradition—and important woodcarving subject—since the early thirteenth century. Originally a coat of arms was painted on the shield carried by a medieval knight, or woven into the surcoat that covered his armor, as a means of indentifying friend from foe on the battlefield. The word *heraldry* comes from the medieval herald, who announced the contestants at jousting tournaments. The term eventually became associated with the recording of family coats of arms and lineage.

Coats of arms make interesting and challenging woodcarving projects because of the great variety of figures and symbols. They usually have a shield displaying an emblem, and a scroll with the family motto or name below it. Above the shield is a helmet, which traditionally indicated a knight's nationality and rank. The crest is the emblem fastened to the top of the helmet and was another means of identification during battles and tournaments.

This coat of arms is for the Bütz family, as described in *Armorial General Precede d'un Dictionnaire des Termes du Blason* (Reitstat 1934), which lists European coats of arms and crests. There are several other books with examples of shields, crests and foliage decorations listed in the bibliography. *Heraldry* (Boutell 1970) contains a large assortment of motifs as well as interesting accounts of their historical origins. Professional and fraternal orders also have their own designs, some of which date back to the early trade guilds. All of these sources of information provide a rich assortment of designs for a woodcarver to choose from, or you can design your own. You can easily modify the pattern shown on the facing page—use the basic outline, but change the shield and crest. The twists and curls in the foliage can be altered or omitted altogether.

This project is fairly difficult to carve. A full-sized clay model will help you work out the relative depths of the wood and the contours of the foliage before carving. As discussed on p. 63, I use water-based pottery clay because it cleans up easily. Pile a layer of clay on a piece of plywood or Masonite the size of the design you'll be making, and smooth the clay to an overall thickness of about 1 in. Make two patterns. Set one aside (to be transferred to the wood later) and cut the other out and place it on the clay. Outline the carving with a table knife and then remove all the excess clay. Add small pieces of clay to build up the foliage, helmet, shield and scroll to a thickness of about ½ in. Smooth and shape the raised portions with clay-modeling tools or with a kitchen spoon and knife, until you have the contours you want. Refer to the clay model as you carve the wood to check shapes and thicknesses.

For this carving, use a soft, fine-textured wood like pine, butternut or basswood. I chose butternut because of its attractive grain patterns. You can use a hardwood like walnut, mahogany, black cherry or oak, but you'll have to work quite a bit with a mallet. Don't use maple or birch or any wood with wavy or irregular grain patterns because it will be hard to carve the curves in the foliage.

Transfer the pattern onto a piece of wood 14 in. long, 10 in. wide and 1¾ in. to 2 in. thick, and cut out the basic shape with a bandsaw or coping saw. Some areas within the design are completely cut out (this is called pierced carving). Secure the wood to the bench with a C-clamp, use a drill to start the holes and clear out the enclosed spaces in the foliage and at the bottom of the shield with a keyhole saw.

Outline and set-in the rest of the shapes, starting with the helmet, the highest section of the carving. Set-in the helmet with a 15mm No. 3 and a 10mm No. 8 gouge to a depth of about ½ in., and remove wood from the shield and foliage around it with a 25mm No. 7 gouge. Lower the scroll about ¼ in. below the shield (the scroll will be about 1¼ in. thick). Sketch in the shield emblem and set it in about ¼ in. Smooth the background of the shield and the scroll with a 12mm No. 5 fishtail gouge. You may need a knife to clean out small corners and details where the leaves overlap the shield. Detail the shield and the arms on the top of the helmet with a 3mm V-tool, a 12mm chisel and a knife.

After bandsawing out the design, clear internal areas with a keyhole saw.

Outline and set-in the design, making the shield area about ½ in. lower than the leaves, and the scroll about ¼ in. below the shield.

Next, smooth and round the foliage with a 20mm No. 5 fishtail gouge to reduce the amount of wood you'll have to cut through to set-in the leaves. Use an 18mm No. 7 gouge to set-in the large outside curves, the 10mm No. 8 for the inside curves and the small curves at the tips, and a 2mm veiner for the clefts between the leaves, as shown in the drawing below.

Begin modeling the leaf clusters on either side of the helmet. Use the 20mm No. 5 fishtail gouge to taper the leaf surfaces to a thickness of ½ in. at their tips. Then cut an arc across the leaf surfaces and clefts with a 10mm No. 8 gouge, as shown in the drawing. (Watch the direction of the wood grain to avoid splitting.) This cut will create an undulating surface on the leaves, and will establish the height of the clefts. (These clefts will later be shaped to appear as folds in the leaf.)

Use a 10mm No. 8 gouge to model the stem with angled cuts.

DETAILING THE LEAVES

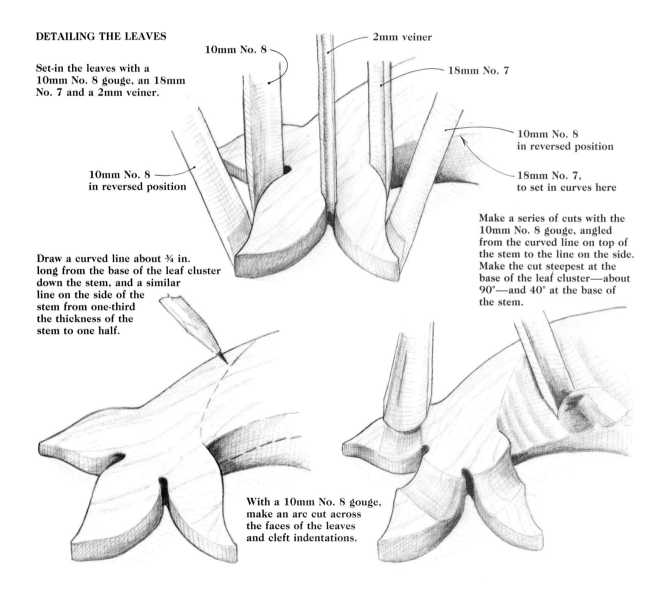

Set-in the leaves with a 10mm No. 8 gouge, an 18mm No. 7 and a 2mm veiner.

10mm No. 8

2mm veiner

18mm No. 7

10mm No. 8 in reversed position

10mm No. 8 in reversed position

18mm No. 7, to set in curves here

Make a series of cuts with the 10mm No. 8 gouge, angled from the curved line on top of the stem to the line on the side. Make the cut steepest at the base of the leaf cluster—about 90°—and 40° at the base of the stem.

Draw a curved line about ¾ in. long from the base of the leaf cluster down the stem, and a similar line on the side of the stem from one-third the thickness of the stem to one half.

With a 10mm No. 8 gouge, make an arc cut across the faces of the leaves and cleft indentations.

Before carving the stems of the leaf clusters, draw a curved line about ¾ in. long from the base of the lowest leaf in the cluster down the stem, as shown in the drawing on p. 139. Draw a similar guideline on the side of the stem, curving up from one-third the thickness at the base of the lowest leaf to one-half the thickness at the base of the stem. Model the stem by making a series of cuts with a 10mm No. 8 gouge, connecting the two curved lines. To make the stem look twisted, you need to change the angle of these cuts. Start with a 40° cut at the base of the stem, and increase the angle gradually, until the cut is almost vertical at the base of the cluster. Smooth the inside curve with sweep cuts, as on the baroque curve (p. 134). Use an 18mm No. 5 spoon-bent gouge, and twist the handle while pushing the tool, so that the cutting edge follows the changing angles of the curve.

Model the outside of the curve with a 12mm No. 5 fishtail gouge. Start at the base of the stem, and carve away the sharp edge, holding the tool at 80° to the wood. As you work along the curve, turn the tool gradually so that it flattens out to an almost horizontal position—about a 10° angle—on the face of the leaf. (When working the surface of the leaf, be careful not to remove wood from the cleft.) This cut should not remove more than half the thickness of the leaves.

Use an 18mm No. 5 spoon-bent gouge in an angled sweep cut to smooth the inside curves of the stem.

Use a 7mm veiner to shape the surfaces of the leaves in the clusters. Rough-out and smooth hollows around the clefts, leaving a slight vein in the center of each leaf about $\frac{1}{32}$ to $\frac{1}{16}$ in. high. Don't make the vein straight—it should follow the contour of one edge of the leaf. Complete the modeling and smoothing of each leaf in the two clusters with a 6mm No. 7 gouge. Use the scooping cut used for the flower on p. 125 to give the face of each leaf a gentle, curved shape and smooth off any sharp ridges left by the veiner. Be careful not to cut off the vein.

Bevel the edges of the leaves slightly with an 8mm No. 3 gouge or a carver's chisel. This bevel should be about 45° to the face of the leaf and about $\frac{1}{16}$ in. wide.

You can use the same techniques to model the other leaves in the carving, or you can simply round them with a 10mm or 12mm gouge. Make sweep cuts with a 10mm No. 7 spoon-bent gouge to smooth the deep curves on the leaves around the shield. Be sure not to make the edges of the leaves too thin—no less than $\frac{1}{4}$ in. at the edges.

The secret to having the leaves appear thin and yet be strong is to undercut the edges from the back of the carving. With a 6mm No. 7 gouge or a 7mm veiner, taper the back edges at an angle of about 45°. Keep the edges about $\frac{1}{16}$ in. thick so that the leaves won't be too fragile. Then smooth the cuts with a 12mm No. 5 fishtail gouge.

Start the tool at an 80° angle on the stem and finish at a 10° angle on the face of the leaf.

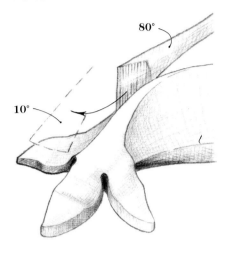

Use a 6mm veiner to smooth hollows around and between the clefts.

Smooth each leaf with a 6mm No. 7 gouge.

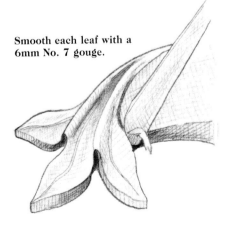

Turn the woodcarving over, and taper the edges of the leaves to about $\frac{1}{16}$ in. They will appear thin and delicate, but will still be strong.

Bevel the edges slightly with a 8mm No. 3 gouge or a chisel.

SCROLL ENDS AND FOLD

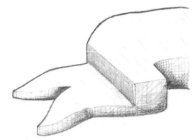

Set in the large fold with a 20mm
No. 5 gouge.

Bevel the *S* section so that the large fold
slopes to the short ends.

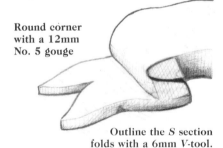

Round corner
with a 12mm
No. 5 gouge

Outline the *S* section
folds with a 6mm *V*-tool.

Set in the edges
and carve out waste
from the sides.

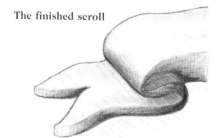

The finished scroll

Next, shape the folds of the scroll. Round the scroll off so that it tapers gradually from the center thickness of about 1¼ in. down to about ½ in. at the ends of the large fold. Draw in the short ends with a pencil on both sides and set-in the large fold that separates them from the top of the scroll to a depth of ½ in. with a 20mm No. 5 fishtail gouge. Round off the corner of the large fold with a 12mm No. 5 fishtail gouge. Taper the background of the scroll ends to the depth of this setting-in cut—start about ¾ in. away from the ends and angle the cuts downward.

Start the *S* folds by sloping the wood from the surface of the large scroll to the surface of the short ends, as shown in the drawing at left. Then draw the lines of the *S* fold and outline it with a 6mm *V*-tool. Set-in the edges with a 12mm No. 5 fishtail gouge, and clear away the excess wood with a 6mm No. 7 gouge. The two levels of the *S* will create the illusion of cloth folded over upon itself. Finish up by tapering the short ends to a thickness of no less than ¼ in. Undercut the back of the scroll edges with a 45° bevel, as you did for the leaves.

Before putting your tools away, check the entire carving for splits or rough edges that need to be smoothed. Use the 12mm fishtail gouge to clean out any of the tight areas around the shield. You may need to use a little 220-grit sandpaper to smooth rough spots in the deep folds of the leaves around the shield.

When the coat of arms is complete, you can finish it with any one of several finishes. Seal dark woods like walnut, mahogany or butternut with a clear finish, preferably a penetrating resin oil like Minwax. Varnishes, lacquer or French polish are difficult to apply to as intricate a carving as this.

Use the 12mm No. 5 fishtail gouge to smooth tight areas around and between the shield and leaves.

If you used a light-colored wood like pine or basswood, you may want to darken it with a stain before sealing it, or better still, use a penetrating oil finish that has stain in it. You can also tint light-colored wood with artist's oil paints that are thinned with turpentine (p. 52). Traditionally, coats of arms were painted, because the colors of the shield and crest were an important identifying mark. (Check to see if there are historically significant colors for the design you carved.) After the paint has dried, apply a light coat of paste wax. Whatever finish you choose, you'll have a handsome woodcarving to display or present as a gift.

Finish this carving with a clear finish or a stain. You can also tint it, using oil colors thinned with turpentine.

This carving of St. George and the dragon is a French design from the fifteenth century. The pattern at right has been modified slightly. (Photo courtesy of The Metropolitan Museum of Art, Bashford Dean Memorial Collection, Purchase, 1929.)

ST. GEORGE AND THE DRAGON   Scale ½ in. = 2in.

ACANTHUS LEAVES Scale ½ in. = 2 in.

Model the inside curves with a 14mm No. 5, 14mm No. 7 and 10mm No. 8 gouge. For the outside curves, use a 15mm No. 3 and 14mm No. 5. Incise the veins with a 3mm *V-tool*.

This 13-in.-high wall panel is decorated with a Norwegian acanthus-leaf design. (Carved by Phillip Odden. Photo courtesy of Vesterheim, The Norwegian-American Museum, Decorah, Iowa.)

Wildlife Carving

8

Wildlife has been a popular carving subject for thousands of years. Prehistoric people, whose lives were closely linked to the natural world, carved the creatures that were important to their existence. Ancient ivory and soapstone carvings, and the woodcarvings preserved in the tombs of the Egyptian pharaohs, reveal that our ancestors regarded nature as a collection of supernatural beings on whom their lives depended.

Today, we have a more realistic interpretation of nature, and as a result, there is an increasing effort to duplicate natural details in wildlife carvings. This is especially true in the United States, where wildlife carving ranges from the folk art of decoy making to a sophisticated science—there are carvers who spend years perfecting a single wildfowl.

Wildlife carving presents great opportunities for mastering the challenges of working in three dimensions. But it is more than just a technical exercise; it's a relaxing and refreshing way to observe and understand the world around us. When I first developed an interest in wildlife carving, I saw things I hadn't noticed before—the closer I looked, the more I learned. I became aware of the personality of each bird and animal.

Recreating this personality in wood is the greatest challenge of wildlife carving and its greatest reward. Whether or not you successfully capture the spirit of the creature you are carving depends on how closely you study the behavior of your subject. Through observation, you'll discover that the gracefulness of a flying bird or a leaping deer is actually created by a series of flowing movements. Through these motions, each creature expresses its unique personality. The more time spent studying a bird or animal, the more strongly its movements and attitudes

Wildlife carving presents the challenges of working in three dimensions, and of capturing personality in wood.

become impressed in your memory. These recollections will guide you while you are carving.

No matter where you live in this country, there are wildlife preserves close by, and these provide the opportunity to study live subjects. (Stuffed specimens don't have the same feeling living wildlife has, and photographs often distort shapes.) I live in the heart of the Adirondack forest, and a great variety of large and small animals—foxes, bobcats, bears, squirrels and chipmunks—live in the woods around our cabin. It's not unusual for a deer to walk up and look in the windows. I also keep several bird feeders filled with sunflower and thistle seeds, which attract many species of birds all year round—chickadees, nuthatches, grosbeaks, blue jays and a variety of finches. They provide me with plenty of models for close study.

Birds and animals present a great variety of shapes and sizes to carve. The beak of the hummingbird and the flower (top left) are both made of brass. The ruffed grouse (center) is 12 in. high, the bobcats (bottom left) are 17½ in. high and the eastern coyote (above) is about 6 in. high.

Tools and Materials

To carve the chickadee on p. 151, you need a knife, a 5mm No. 3 gouge, a 5mm No. 8 gouge and a 3mm *V*-tool for detailing. I also use a small, hooked knife, made for me by James Roth of Arizona, for scooping out wood underneath the tail section of small bird carvings that would be difficult to reach with a gouge.

For the loon on p. 158, you'll need several large gouges: a 12mm No. 5 fishtail, an 18mm and 25mm No. 7, a 6mm No. 8 and 3mm and 6mm *V*-tools. Large carvings, like the loon, have to be secured to the bench, so you'll need clamps or a vise, too. For the river otter on p. 166, you'll need a knife and a 4mm No. 8 gouge.

The osprey is the most advanced project in the chapter, and you'll need a knife, a 15mm No. 3 gouge, a 12mm No. 5 fishtail, an 18mm No. 7 gouge, a 3mm No. 8 gouge, a 12mm macaroni tool, 3mm and 6mm *V*-tools and a 12mm carver's chisel.

To simulate the texture of feathers or fur, you can use a small gouge, or you can burn thin lines into the wood with a woodburning tool. This tool has a small metal point fitted to a handle and heated by electric current, and is designed for woodcarvers. I use a Hot Tool, which has interchangeable tips and a rheostat for controlling the temperature. (There are several types available. The more sophisticated versions have delicate heat control and razor-sharp tips, but the Hot Tool is good for general use.) Texture lines should be very fine and close together, so I wear a pair of 3X magnifying lenses that fit over my glasses.

For wildlife, the best paints are artist's oil colors, available in small tubes. They dry more slowly than acrylics, which allows more time for blending the colors, but they may take anywhere from two to eight weeks to dry completely. (Alkyd paints, made by Winsor & Newton of London, are similar to oil colors, but they dry faster because they contain alkyd resins.) I use acrylic paints for the eyes, noses, beaks and legs, because they have more shine than oil paints.

This hooked knife was custom-made for scooping out wood underneath the tail sections of small birds, areas that would be difficult to work with a straight gouge or knife.

You'll need No. 1, No. 2 and No. 6 sable paintbrushes. I also use a No. 2 badger-hair fan blender, an artist's brush with long, stiff, fan-shaped bristles.

To make the legs of bird carvings, you need 18-gauge and 24-gauge copper or brass wire, wire cutters, needlenose pliers, and an electric hand drill. You also need branches or pieces of driftwood if you want to mount your carvings on a perch.

I use a quick-setting epoxy adhesive called E-POX-E 5. This glue comes in two tubes—one for resin, one for hardener. The glue sets up in about five to ten minutes and forms a strong, waterproof bond. (Some epoxies require 24 hours to harden, which is too long to wait if you're holding the pieces together until the glue sets.)

Another useful adhesive is epoxy putty. It's made by several manufacturers, but the best one I've used is available from the Brookstone Company (127 Vose Farm Rd., Peterborough, NH 03458). I use it to glue in the glass eyes of wildlife carvings because it can be molded easily, hardens in a couple of hours and is stronger than wood. This epoxy putty is also useful for shaping feet or smoothing sections where pieces of wood have been joined together; it can be thinned with water and easily shaped, but it's waterproof after it hardens.

To achieve lifelike realism in wildlife carvings, glass eyes are a necessity. These are available from several woodcarving-supply companies, come in a variety of sizes, and are sold in pairs. The eyes I use are crystal and handmade in West Germany. I keep an assortment of sizes in stock, ranging from 4mm to 14mm in diameter. You can buy eyes with colored irises or clear with black pupils. I use clear eyes and paint the backs with acrylic colors to match the right color for the bird or animal I'm carving. Chickadees, for example, have a dark-brown iris, loons bright red, otters brown, and ospreys yellow or red.

For the carvings in this chapter, I used white pine, because it's easy to carve, strong, and has smooth, fine grain that holds details well. Basswood is also good to use.

For painting wildlife, you'll need (from left to right) a No. 1, No. 2 and No. 6 sable paintbrush and a No. 2 badger-hair fan blender.

Here are some of the tools and materials you'll also need: (clockwise from top) a woodburning tool, a hardwood branch to use as a perch, copper or brass wire, needlenose pliers, wire cutters and a hooked knife.

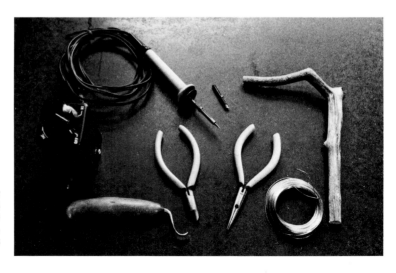

Techniques

Wildlife carving uses the same tools and techniques as whittling, but details, such as eyes, legs and feather or fur textures are added for a realistic effect. This chickadee project is a good introduction to the techniques used to add these details.

Chickadees are one of my favorite birds. They travel in flocks with other small birds, such as nuthatches, woodpeckers and kinglets. They are common throughout most of the United States, although they vary slightly in color in different regions. This black-capped chickadee is one of the few birds that stay around the Adirondacks through our long winters.

I've provided a pattern for a chickadee, but you can draw your own. If you're able to observe these tame birds (they are easily attracted to bird feeders and are fond of sunflower seeds), make some quick sketches and make patterns from the drawings. You'll need two patterns to carve this chickadee, one for the top view and one for the profile.

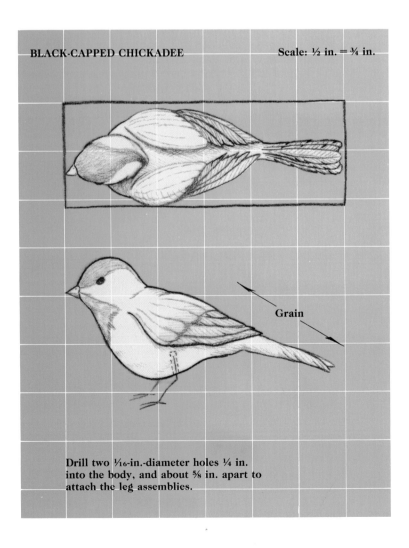

BLACK-CAPPED CHICKADEE   Scale: ½ in. = ¾ in.

Grain

Drill two ¹⁄₁₆-in.-diameter holes ¼ in. into the body, and about ⅝ in. apart to attach the leg assemblies.

When transferring the pattern, be sure the grain runs along the length of the tail. Cut out the profiles with a bandsaw or coping saw. Then using whittling techniques (p. 73) and a sharp knife, round the angles off the blank to shape the tail and head. Use the paring cut to round the head and back and the levering cut to round the neck. To remove wood from the underside of the tail, I make paring cuts with the hooked knife, adding a scooping motion from the wrist.

Pencil in the edge of the wing to separate it from the side of the bird. Then incise the pencil line with a 3mm V-tool, and use the levering cut to remove wood from the side, so that the wing is raised slightly above the body. Sketch the arrangement of feathers on the wings and tail as shown in the pattern, and incise the lines for each feather with the 3mm V-tool. Use the levering cut to slice away wood on the feathers so that they step up gradually from the back to the front of the bird and appear to overlap.

After the details are carved, brush or spray a coat of lacquer on the carving. The lacquer seals the pores of the wood to prepare it for painting, and hardens any thin, delicate feather details. I hold the bird on a stick of wood while applying the lacquer. Glue a 1½-in. No. 6 wood screw to a stick of wood. Drill two leg holes in the body 1⁄16 in. in diameter, ¼ in. deep, and about 5⁄8 in. apart for the legs, then twist the wood screw into one of the leg holes. Holding the bird on the stick, prime the surface with two coats of gesso. (You don't have to paint the bird now, but you need to apply the gesso before setting in the eyes, because it's difficult to remove if any gets on the glass.)

Use a knife to remove sharp angles from the bandsawn blank. Use the paring cut to round off the head and back, and the levering cut to round the neck.

The hooked knife is used with a paring cut to scoop out wood from the underside of the chickadee's tail. A 5mm No. 3 gouge could also be used.

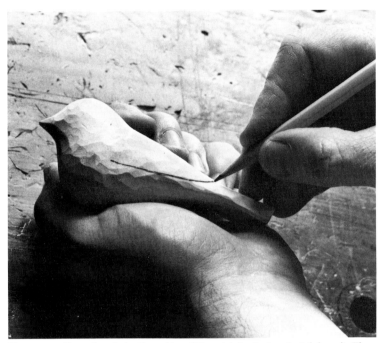

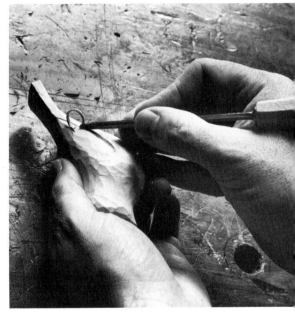

Use a pencil to sketch in the edge of the chickadee's wing (above). Then incise the line with a 3mm V-tool (right).

Next, pencil in the feathers for the wings and tail, and incise each one with the 3mm V-tool.

Lever off a slice from each feather to create the effect of overlapping.

Setting-in eyes—The exact placement of the eyes on a wildlife carving is very important because it determines the expression of the bird or animal. For example, the eyes of a hawk or osprey are set slightly forward, which gives them an alert, fierce look. Ducks' eyes are set back, which gives them a gentle look. Loon eyes are positioned somewhere in between, which gives them a wild-eyed, slightly crazy look. Moving the eyes a tiny bit one way or another will create subtle changes of expression. Always draw the eye locations in pencil before carving to make sure they're correct.

To make sockets for the eyes, use a 5mm No. 8 gouge. (You can find tiny gouges in linoleum-carving kits that also work very well. Don't use a drill because it can split the wood—a sharp gouge makes a cleaner cut.) Paint the back of 5mm eyes with burnt-umber acrylic paint. Check the size of each hole you carved by inserting a glass eye into it. The hole should be ⅛ in. deep, and about ¼ in. in diameter, large enough for the eye to fit in, with a little room to spare. Place a small piece of epoxy putty in the hole, cut the glass eye off its wire stem with wire cutters, and press the eye into the hole. Shape the excess putty that squeezes out around the eye with a toothpick to form a lid. On birds, the eyelid is round; on most animals, the lid shape is oval.

Use a 5mm No. 8 gouge to carve out the eye sockets.

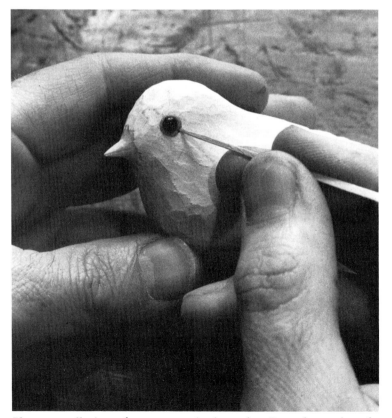

Place a small piece of epoxy putty in the socket. Press the eye into the putty and shape the excess with a toothpick to form a round eyelid.

Making legs and claws—To make each claw, you need four 2-in. pieces of 24-gauge copper or brass wire. Hold each end of the wire with a pair of wire cutters or needlenose pliers, and bend it into an *L*-shape. Bend one end of the wire into a loop, then twist the loop together with the pliers to form a claw about ½ in. long. Do this for all four pieces. For the leg, use a 1½-in. piece of 18-gauge copper or brass wire. Position the four claws around the leg, leaving about ⅜ in. of the thicker wire extending below the claws. With a piece of thread, tie a single loop around the base of the leg and another around the top of the leg, as shown in the drawing below, and coat the entire assembly with five-minute epoxy. (Cast-lead claws and legs are available from woodcarving suppliers, but they're brittle and can break easily.) Don't put any glue on the ⅜ in. of wire extending below the claws; this piece will support the carving on its mount. Repeat the process for the other leg and let the glue dry.

Paint the leg assemblies with burnt-umber acrylic paint, and glue them into the leg holes of the chickadee with epoxy.

After the leg assemblies have been epoxied and painted, they are ready to be glued in place.

MAKING LEGS AND CLAWS

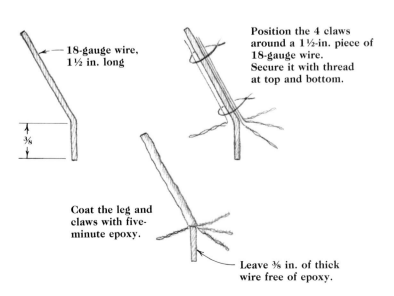

Bend four pieces of 2-in.-long, 24-gauge wire into an *L*-shape with a loop.

½

Twist the loop together with needlenose pliers.

18-gauge wire, 1½ in. long

⅜

Position the 4 claws around a 1½-in. piece of 18-gauge wire. Secure it with thread at top and bottom.

Coat the leg and claws with five-minute epoxy.

Leave ⅜ in. of thick wire free of epoxy.

Blend and texture the paint with a No. 2 badger-hair fan blender.

Painting and texturing—For painting the chickadee, you need ivory-black paint for the top of the head and bib, and titanium white for the cheeks. Mix burnt umber with titanium white and ultramarine blue to make grey for the back, wings and tail feathers. Mix titanium white with a little yellow ochre for the breast, sides and bottom. Pictures and photographs from bird books will help you mix the right shades of color and guide you in their placement. A sheet of glass about 12 in. square makes a good palette for mixing the paints.

Apply grey paint to the tail feathers with a No. 6 paintbrush, working up the back and over the wings. Wipe excess paint off the brush onto a paper towel and rinse the brush off in paint thinner. Next apply the white and ochre paint to the breast, sides and bottom of the body with the same brush. Apply white paint to the cheeks with a No. 2 brush, then clean it and apply black paint to the head and bib. To simulate the appearance of feathers, make short strokes with a No. 1 brush to blend the paint where the colors meet.

You can leave the bird painted as it is, or you can add shading and texture for more realism. (Practice this next technique on a piece of scrap wood or a clean corner of your palette before working on the carving.) Use a No. 1 brush to add a dark-grey outline around each tail feather and wing feather. Blend the dark-grey lines with the light-grey surfaces of the tail and wings by stippling with a clean, No. 2 brush. Hold the brush vertically and dab it up and down lightly in the dark-grey outlines. Don't stipple too hard or too long—three or four dabs is enough. Use this technique to soften all the dark-grey lines around the feathers.

Lightly drag the No. 2 fan blender through the wet paint in the direction of the barbs of the feathers. (The barbs are the fine branches along both sides of the shaft.) Start the brush at the shaft of the feather and drag it in a diagonal direction towards the outer edge. This dry-brush technique will produce a fine texture in the paint that closely resembles that of real feathers. (Be sure to wipe the brush clean after each stroke to prevent muddying the colors.)

After cleaning the fan blender thoroughly, texture the paint on the body and breast in the same way, starting near the tail and working towards the head. Finish by blending the black paint of the head and bib into the nearby areas. As a final touch, paint a very thin layer of burnt-umber acrylic on the beak with the No. 2 brush, and let the carving dry.

Mounting—To make the base, cut out a 3½-in.-diameter circle of ½-in.-thick wood on the bandsaw. I use butternut, cherry or walnut. Round the top edge of the circle slightly with 180-grit sandpaper and smooth the entire piece with 220-grit paper. Finish the wood with French polish or a clear penetrating resin oil.

Find a forked branch for the chickadee to sit on, about 4 in. long. Any hardwood or a piece of driftwood will make a strong perch. Glue the branch into a hole drilled in the base. Position the chickadee and mark two holes ¾ in. apart or less on the branch. Then drill a 1⁄16-in.-diameter hole at each mark, about ¼ in. deep, and glue the extra ⅜ in. of wire at the base of each leg into it.

Make the base out of a 3½-in.-diameter circle of ½-in.-thick hardwood. Drill a hole in the center of the base and glue a forked hardwood or drift-wood branch into it for the chickadee to stand on. Drill two ¹/₁₆-in.-diameter holes in the branch and glue the extra ⅜ in. of wire at the base of each leg into them. Bend the legs to about a 60° angle to the body of the bird, and the carving is finished.

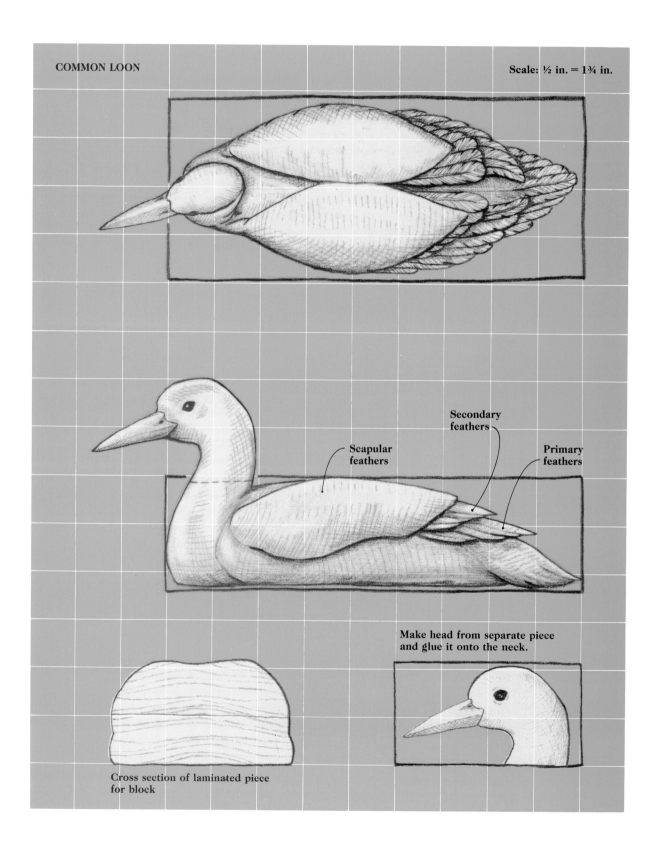

COMMON LOON

Scale: ½ in. = 1¾ in.

Scapular feathers

Secondary feathers

Primary feathers

Make head from separate piece and glue it onto the neck.

Cross section of laminated piece for block

A Loon

Few birds symbolize the rugged wilderness of our northern forests better than loons. They're large birds found in quiet lakes and ponds, submerging easily and swimming great distances underwater in search of fish. In the spring, loons can be seen swimming with one or two chicks riding on their backs. On quiet summer nights, their call, a wild, yodelling laughter, echoes throughout the wooded hills and mountains—not a sound that is easily forgotten.

Although you can scale this pattern down to fit smaller pieces of wood, I laminate two pieces of 2-in., air-dried pine for the 4-in.-thick body. Carving a solid block thicker than 3 in. frees internal stresses in the wood, and the piece may check weeks, or even months, after the carving is finished.

Lamination requires that the grain of the pieces be parallel. If the grain is not aligned, the boards may tear apart when a severe change in humidity occurs. When wood warps, the heartwood cups away from the pith as it absorbs moisture, and shifts back as it dries. If the grain is properly aligned, the laminated pieces will move in the same direction. Correct grain alignment will also make the block easier to carve, because you won't have to continually change direction to avoid splits.

To laminate a 4-in.-thick block for the loon, place two 2-in.-thick boards so that the annual rings on the end grain are traveling in the same direction. The grain of both pieces should run along the length of the blocks. Before gluing, make sure the surfaces to be joined fit together without gaps. Have the rough wood planed at a lumberyard, or level it yourself with a jack plane. Don't sand the surfaces—sanding clogs the wood pores and keeps the glue from penetrating. Wood glues such as Elmer's or Titebond work well for laminating wood for indoor projects. However, if the wood is going to be exposed to extreme moisture changes, use a waterproof glue. (Decoys to be used in the water or displayed outdoors should also be sealed with marine varnish.)

Apply a liberal amount of glue to each planed surface and use C-clamps to hold the pieces together while the glue dries. Wipe away any glue that squeezes out while it is still wet. (Smeared glue seals wood and prevents it from taking stains, but because most of this block will be carved away, it is not a problem.)

LAMINATION

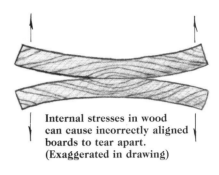

Internal stresses in wood can cause incorrectly aligned boards to tear apart. (Exaggerated in drawing)

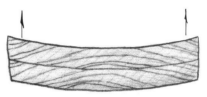

Boards with the grain correctly aligned will move in the same direction. (Exaggerated in drawing)

Laminate two pieces of 2-in.-thick pine, 15 in. long and 6 in. wide, to make a 4-in.-thick blank. Use C-clamps to hold the wood while the glue is drying.

When the laminated block has dried for 24 hours, cut the loon out on the bandsaw. Cut the profile first, so that there will be a flat side of wood to rest on the bandsaw table when you cut out the top view. Cut the head out of 2-in.-thick pine, and shape it with a whittling knife. Turn the head slightly to one side to give the carving an alert pose, glue the head to the body with epoxy, and let it dry.

Because this piece is large, it needs to be secured while you're carving, but it also needs to be turned easily in order to be worked from several angles. You can screw a hardwood block to the bottom of the carving and hold the block in a vise, or screw a large, square piece of plywood to the bottom of the carving and clamp the board to the workbench with two or more C-clamps. You could also secure the block with a carver's screw through a hole in the workbench. If you use the carver's screw, drill a hole through a piece of wood to use as a spacer between the carving blank and the bench. The spacer will allow clearance for the gouges when you're carving the sides of the loon.

Cut out the body on the bandsaw, then cut the head out of 2-in.-thick pine, carve it to shape with a knife, and glue it on with epoxy.

METHODS OF SECURING LARGE CARVINGS

Screw a hardwood block to the bottom of the blank, and secure the block in a vise.

Put a spacer block between the carving blank and the workbench. Use a carver's screw through the bench to secure the blank.

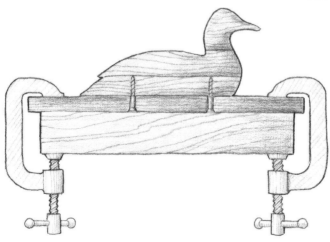

Screw a large piece of plywood to the blank, and clamp the plywood to the bench with C-clamps.

To rough-shape the body, use 18mm and 25mm No. 7 gouges and a mallet. Round off the sharp angles, and the stepped area for the wing feathers with the 25mm gouge. The primaries are the large flight feathers along the end of the wing. The secondaries are the smaller feathers, and the scapulars are the feathers at the shoulder of the wing. Loons have large scapular feathers, which they use when diving to help propel them underwater. Shape the curves of these feathers with the 18mm No. 7 gouge. Smooth off any ridges left by the large gouges with a 12mm No. 5 fishtail.

To separate the scapulars from the primaries and secondaries, incise around them with the 6mm V-tool and pare away the excess on either side of the cut with the fishtail gouge. Hold the knife in a pencil grip and incise the outlines of each of the tail and flight feathers, as shown in the drawing below. Make the cuts about ¹⁄₁₆ in. deep. Next, slice out the curved, triangular section at the end of each feather. Then make a beveled cut on each surface to create a series of overlapping feathers. Clean up any rough areas by sanding each feather lightly with 220-grit sandpaper.

Secure the loon to the bench and define the stepped areas between the feathers with a 25mm No. 7 gouge.

CARVING THE FEATHERS

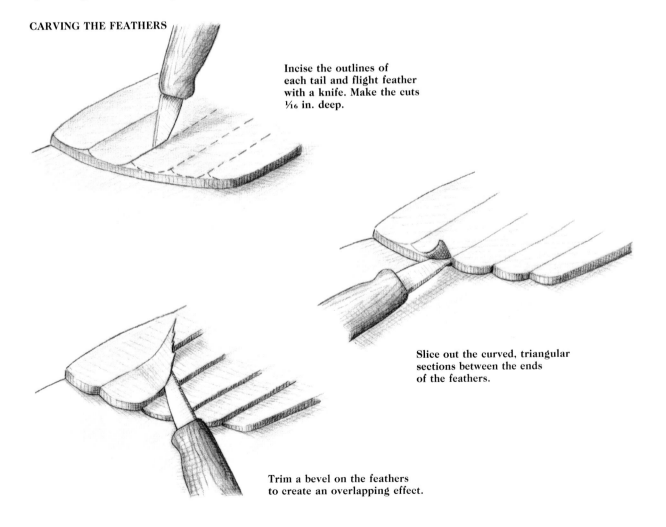

Incise the outlines of each tail and flight feather with a knife. Make the cuts ¹⁄₁₆ in. deep.

Slice out the curved, triangular sections between the ends of the feathers.

Trim a bevel on the feathers to create an overlapping effect.

Once the back of the body has been carved, shape the front of the loon. Pare down the beak with a knife and incise a line with a 6mm *V*-tool between the upper and lower beak to form the mouth opening. Use the *V*-tool and a knife to gouge out two small openings for the nostrils at the base of the beak.

Trim away the excess wood around the neck and breast with the fishtail gouge. Pay attention to the changing grain direction between the body and the turned head and alter the direction of your cuts as necessary to avoid splitting out the wood. The feathers on the neck and breast of a real loon are smooth, so I use a rasp or file to shape the wood and finish it with 180-grit and 220-grit sandpaper. Use the 220-grit paper to smooth any other rough areas on the woodcarving, brush away the sawdust and seal the carving with lacquer.

Mark the positions of the eyes on each side of the head, and look at the loon from the front to make sure they're at the same height. The eyes of a common loon are bright red, which gives the bird a wild-eyed appearance. Paint the backs of two 10mm glass eyes, if you have used the pattern to make a loon two-thirds life-size. Carve the eye sockets with a 6mm No. 8 gouge, and check the fit. Glue the eyes in and form a round eyelid in the epoxy putty, as described for the chickadee (p. 154).

Burning-in is an effective way to duplicate the texture of the large flight feathers on waterfowl. I apply lacquer to the wood before I use the Hot Tool. It seems as though less heat is needed to create the textured effect after the lacquer penetrates the wood. Practice burning-in on a piece of scrap wood before actually trying it on the carving. The texturing on feathers is very subtle, so it's important not to make the lines too bold or deep. Experiment with the temperature control on whatever woodburning tool you're using to get the correct temperature. I set the temperature medium-high, although this will vary with the hardness of the wood. At the correct temperature, the Hot Tool will scorch brown lines and produce some smoke. If the tool is too hot, the wood will turn dark brown or black, there will be a lot of smoke, and the texturing will be very coarse and deep.

I burn-in the tail feathers and the primary and secondary feathers on the wing. The rest of the feathers on a loon are very smooth and show very little texture.

Draw the shaft and the angled barbs on each feather that will be textured. (Because the feathers overlap, not all of the shafts will be visible.) Don't make the arrangement of the feathers too regular. The feathers on a living bird are not perfect—they overlap slightly and haphazardly, like shingles on a wooden roof, so the exposed width of each feather should vary. I use the standard Hot Tool tip, which resembles a skew chisel, to shape the shaft that runs down the center of each feather. To burn-in the shaft, hold the tool vertically and make two parallel lines, about ⅟₁₆ in. apart, bringing them together gradually so they meet at the tip of the feather. Next, hold the tool as you would hold a pencil, but at a 45° angle to the wood—the chisel edge should be almost flat against the surface. Then run the tool over the first set of lines to widen them, and make the shaft appear slightly raised.

When the shafts have been burned-in, unplug the pen and let it cool before changing tips. Use a needle-point tip to burn-in the curved lines of the barbs. Press the tool lightly at the shaft and draw it out to the edge of the feather. Gradually increase the pressure to vary the depth and darkness of the lines. Continue burning-in the barbs, making the lines as close together as you can. At random intervals, burn-in one to three very thick lines at the edge of each feather to indicate breaks. (Breaks occur where the barbs have separated slightly, and a bird smooths them back together when it preens.) When burning-in the feather details, ash and residue will build up on the tip of the tool. Keep a piece of 000 steel wool handy to wipe the tip clean every few mintues. When you've finished detailing all the feathers, clean any charred residue off the bird with 000 steel wool or a small, fine, wire brush (I use a brush made for cleaning suede).

Hold the woodburning tool like a pencil, and burn-in the barbs on the tail and wing feathers. Then burn-in one to three thick lines at the edge of each feather to indicate breaks.

The loon is painted with only two colors—black and white. Paint the head, neck, sides and back with ivory-black oil paint and a No. 6 brush. Apply black paint liberally to the back. When painting the burned-in feathers, be sure to move the brush in the direction of the barbs so that paint will flow into the grooves. Then make ½-in.-long strokes with the dry fan blender to create the impression of smooth feathers. Work from the front of the carving to the back.

Let the paint dry thoroughly for several days or longer (drying time will vary with the temperature and humidity). Then paint the white chest with a No. 6 brush, and the neck patches with a No. 2 brush. Blend the colors with the fan blender, dragging a few lines of white paint about ⅛ in. over the black.

Paint the rectangular spots on the scapular feathers with a No. 6 brush. The best way to duplicate them is with a dry-brush technique. Dip the brush into titanium-white paint that has been thinned with a drop or two of turpentine. Brush most of the paint onto a piece of scrap paper or cardboard. The first few strokes will leave a thick glob of paint; when most of the paint is off the brush, you'll see brush marks in the paint, especially toward the end of the stroke. Now, paint the spots on the back—the dry brush will leave a feathery texture. You can paint three to five spots before you need to dip the brush in the paint and start over. Use the same dry-brush technique with a No. 2 brush for the small spots on the sides and the wing and tail feathers.

When the white paint has dried completely, paint the black streaks on the chest and neck with oil paint. Then paint the beak with ivory-black acrylic paint. Gently scrape off any paint that may have gotten on the glass eyes with a knife point, and the loon is finished. I don't mount this carving. I leave it as is so it appears to be swimming on the water.

Use a No. 6 brush that is almost dry to make the rectangular white spots on the scapular areas.

When the white paint has dried completely, paint black streaks on the chest and neck. Paint the beak with black acrylic, and the loon is finished. I leave this carving unmounted so it appears to be swimming on the water.

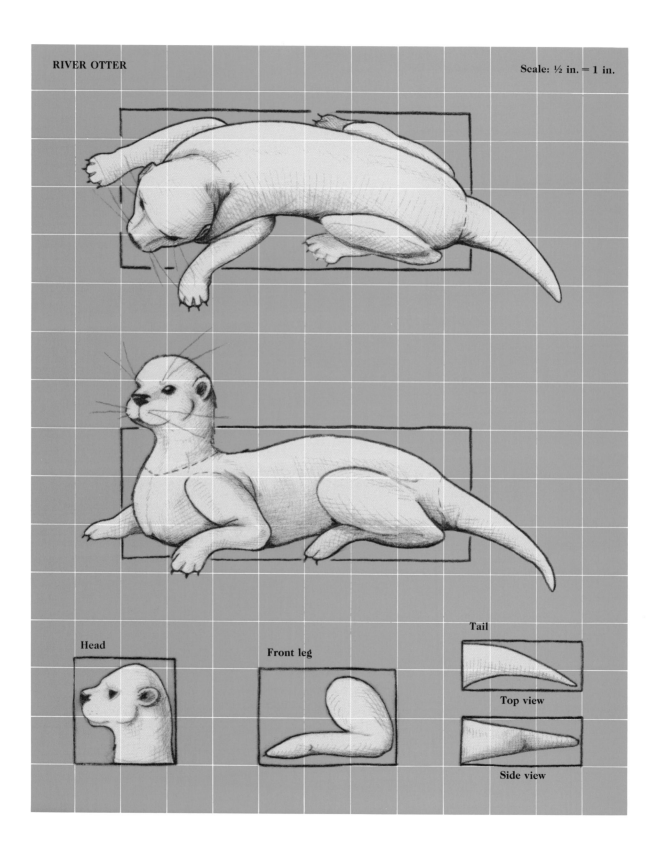

RIVER OTTER

Scale: ½ in. = 1 in.

Head

Front leg

Tail

Top view

Side view

A River Otter

One of the major differences between bird carvings and animal carvings has to do with the way the carvings are mounted. A bird carving should have a feeling of weightlessness, achieved partly by the pose and partly by the thin legs that support the body. In carving and mounting an animal, we are dealing with the opposite problem. The finished piece should give the impression of having weight and mass. Before you begin carving, you should have a good understanding of the anatomy of the animal, and how its flesh and muscles flex and extend as the animal moves. You should also mount the carving so that the wood fits closely to the base to make it appear that the animal has relaxed weight.

To carve this otter, I cut out pieces of white pine and fit them together, instead of cutting out the blank from a single piece of wood (although you can do that, too). The individual pieces make it easier to adjust the position of the front paws and tail so they rest on the driftwood and give the illusion of mass. This technique works well with complex shapes mounted on irregular bases.

Bandsaw the rough shapes, and arrange the pieces on the mount to get an idea of their final positioning. Round the front legs, tail and head with a whittling knife. Glue each of the front legs to the body, one at a time, with five-minute epoxy, and hold them in position until the glue sets. Then glue on the head and tail. (Don't glue the body to the base just yet.) Apply small pieces of epoxy putty around the glue joints. Then dip your fingers in water and blend the joined pieces to the body. Trim the excess putty off with a knife and, when it hardens, sand it smooth with 220-grit paper.

Cut out the individual pieces for the head, body, tail and front legs and arrange them on the mount to get an idea of their final positioning.

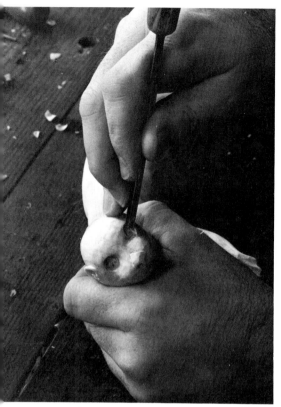

Carve the assembled otter to rough shape with a knife. As you're carving, continually check the fit of the front legs to the base. Carefully carve away the excess wood until the bottom of the carving conforms to irregularities in the surface of the base.

Use a 4mm No. 8 gouge to hollow out the insides of the ears, thin down the webbed area between the toes and shape the muzzle. Use the same gouge to carve the eye sockets about ³⁄₁₆ in. deep and about ¼ in. in diameter. Paint the backs of 6mm eyes with light-brown acrylic paint (I use Van Dyke brown mixed with a tiny bit of titanium white) and glue them in place. Unlike the chickadee and loon, which have round eyelids, the otter has almond-shaped lids. As discussed earlier, adding eyes is one of the most important steps in wildlife carving, because they give the creature its lifelike facial expression. Subtle changes in the shapes of the eyelids will change the appearance and personality of the otter. Push the putty around with a flat toothpick until you find an expression you like.

Texture the fur with the 3mm *V*-tool or with a woodburning pen before painting. I burn-in the fur for animal carvings because it creates a very fine, realistic texture. The basic techniques are exactly the same as for texturing the barbs of the feathers on the loon, except the lines follow the direction of the animal's fur. Start at the tail, and burn-in short lines about ¼ in. long (otter fur is short and fine). Make the lines as close together as you can. Around the face and muzzle, the fur gets shorter, so the lines should be about ⅛ in. long. Study photographs to determine the direction of the fur around the body.

Carve out sockets for the eyes about ³⁄₁₆ in. deep and ¼ in. in diameter with a 4mm No. 8 gouge. Paint the backs of 6mm glass eyes with light-brown acrylic and glue the eyes in place.

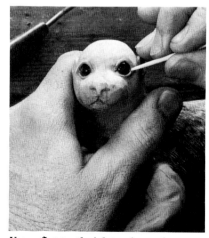

Use a flat toothpick to shape the epoxy putty to form the eyelids. Subtle changes in the shapes will change the expression of the otter.

Burn-in lines ¼ in. long on the body, and about ⅛ in. long around the face and muzzle.

To paint the body, lighten burnt-umber oil paint with a little white and yellow ochre. The colors on a real otter vary with the time of year and can range from light brown to dark grey. The chest is almost white. Paint directly onto the textured wood (you don't need a priming coat), making sure to follow the lines of fur with the brush. Let the paint dry, then glaze the entire carving with a thin wash of burnt-umber acrylic. Thin a dab of paint with water in a saucer, as described on p. 84. Paint on the tint with a No. 6 brush, covering only a few inches at a time, and then wipe the paint off with a clean, dry rag. This will leave a thin layer of dark paint in the burned-in grooves, creating the illusion of thick, soft fur. Use the No. 1 brush to paint the nose with ivory-black acrylic, and paint a tiny black line at the end of each toe to color the claws. Glue the otter to the mount with epoxy or secure it with a wood screw.

I made the whiskers from 1½-in.-long paintbrush bristles, taken from a natural-bristle sash brush. Glue the whiskers into five or six small pinholes on each side of the nose along the muzzle, and three over each eye, to make a jaunty little beastie.

Glaze the carving with an acrylic wash after burning-in the fur. Paint the nose and claws and secure the otter to the mount. Add whiskers made from 1½-in.-long paintbrush bristles around the nose and eyes for a finishing touch.

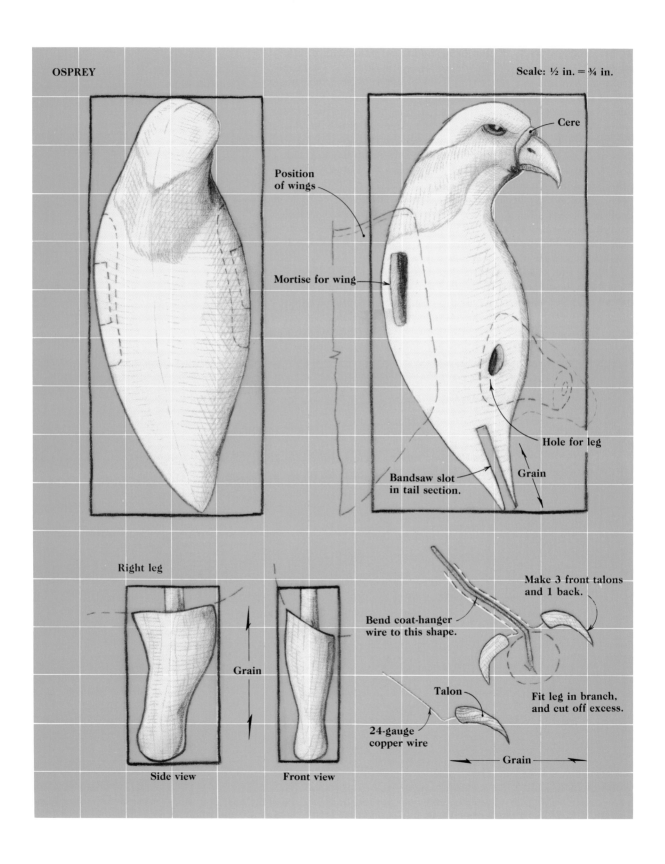

OSPREY

Scale: ½ in. = ¾ in.

Position of wings

Mortise for wing

Cere

Hole for leg

Grain

Bandsaw slot in tail section.

Right leg

Grain

Side view

Front view

Bend coat-hanger wire to this shape.

Make 3 front talons and 1 back.

Talon

Fit leg in branch, and cut off excess.

24-gauge copper wire

Grain

An Osprey

The osprey, or fish hawk, is a large bird with a wing span of over 4 ft. It builds its nests in the tops of pine or balsam trees. The osprey can be found near freshwater lakes and streams, where it soars in wide circles searching for fish. Its keen eyes can see from hundreds of feet away, and once its prey is spotted, the osprey hovers briefly, then dives towards the water. I've seen an osprey dive completely underwater, and then struggle back into the air with strong beats of its wings, clutching a large fish in its long, curved talons.

In this carving, the osprey is positioned as if touching down on a branch. The wings are outstretched to slow its descent, with the tips of the primary feathers on the wings carved as if bending back under the pressure of the braking downstroke. This challenging project uses whittling and relief-carving techniques.

Lay the pattern on a piece of wood 7 in. long, 4 in. wide and 3 in. thick so the grain runs parallel to the slot for the tail. Bandsaw the profiles and the tail slot. Whittle off the sharp angles on the body to shape the bird. When detailing the beak, make sure your knife is razor-sharp to avoid splitting off the curved hook, which will be cross grain. Pencil in the upper base of the beak, called the cere. Incise a line on both sides of the cere with a 3mm *V*-tool, and round the cere with a sharp knife. Then smooth it with 220-grit sandpaper to blend it into the beak. Incise a line for the mouth opening with the *V*-tool.

Bandsaw the slot in the body for the tail. Rough out the shape of the osprey with a knife using whittling techniques.

Incise a line on both sides of the cere with a 3mm V-tool. Round the cere with a knife and then sand it to blend it into the beak.

Cut out the tail from a piece of wood 3¾ in. long, 5 in. wide and ¼ in. thick. Lay out the pattern so the grain runs from front to back. Fit the tail into the bandsawn slot in the body, trimming away excess wood with a knife. The tail should fit snugly, but not be too tight. Assemble the pieces and make a pencil line where the body overlaps the tail, then take the pieces apart. This guideline will prevent you from removing too much wood when detailing the feathers, which would loosen the fit of the tail to the body.

Secure the tail, top side down, to the bench with a C-clamp, fastening the clamp inside the pencil line where no wood will be removed. Use a 15mm No. 3 gouge to remove about ⅛ in. from the center of the underside of the tail. Smooth and taper the wood up to the sides of the tail to form a gentle hollow. Turn the tail over, reclamp it and round off the top. With the same 15mm gouge, thin down the sides of the blank to about ⅛ in., until the top side of the tail is also curved. Don't apply too much pressure, or the piece will split and you'll have to start over.

Draw the feathers on the top side of the tail. The center tail feather is uppermost, overlapping the feathers on either side of it. Outline each feather with a 12mm macaroni tool. The square shape of the tool will leave a stepped effect, which creates the illusion of overlapping feathers. Be careful not to press too hard. Remove the tail from the clamp and use a knife to round the ends of the feathers and blend the curves into the outline cuts made by the macaroni tool.

Turn the tail over and pencil in the feather outlines on the underside so they line up with the feathers on the top. Clamp the tail to the bench and carve the feathers on the underside with the macaroni tool. Begin with the two uppermost, outside feathers and work toward the center. Smooth any rough spots and thin the edges with 220-grit sandpaper. Set the tail aside in a safe place.

Outline the feathers with a 12mm macaroni tool. The square shape of the tool will leave a stepped effect, creating the illusion of overlapping feathers.

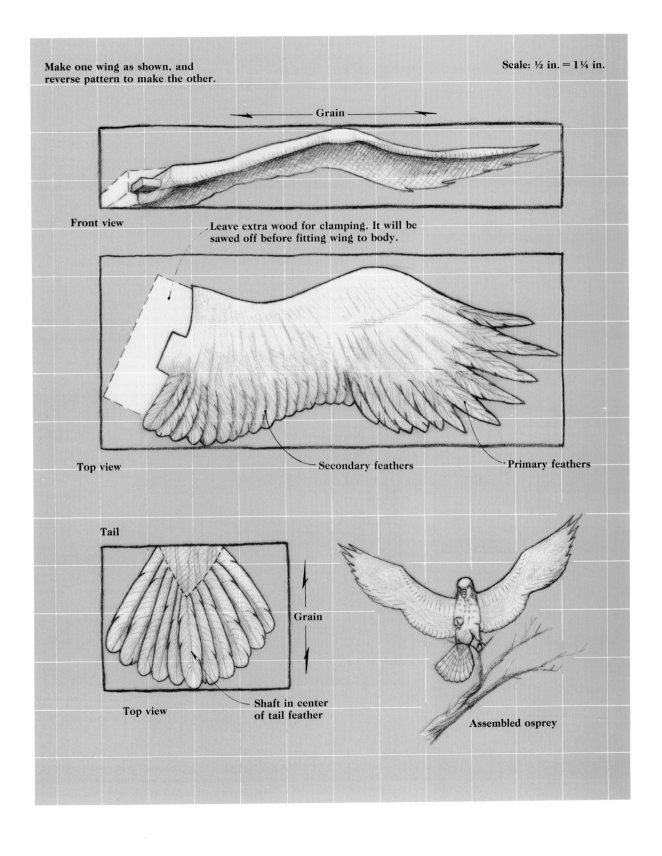

Make one wing as shown, and
reverse pattern to make the other.

Scale: ½ in. = 1¼ in.

Grain

Front view

Leave extra wood for clamping. It will be
sawed off before fitting wing to body.

Top view

Secondary feathers

Primary feathers

Tail

Grain

Top view

Shaft in center
of tail feather

Assembled osprey

Trace the top view of the wings on the edge of a 2-in.-thick piece of wood 12 in. long and 5 in. wide. Cut out this shape on the bandsaw, then trace and cut out the front view. Double-check the positions of the patterns as you are tracing so you don't end up with two wings for the same side. Clamp the wings to the workbench and hollow out the underside as you did for the tail. Rough-out both sides with an 18mm No. 7 gouge and smooth them with a 12mm No. 5 fishtail or 15mm No. 3 gouge. Draw in and outline the feathers with the 12mm macaroni tool. (The uppermost feather on the top side of the wing will be the one closest to the body, overlapping the others.)

The primary feathers on the tips of the wings require special attention to the wood grain to avoid splitting. On the top side of the wing, work the gouge from the tips to the base of the feathers. On the underside, start carving at the middle of the feathers and work in both directions—toward the base of the feathers and toward their tips. Smooth any rough spots on the primaries and secondaries with 220-grit sandpaper, but leave the tool marks on the rest of the wing. Use a knife and the paring cut to bevel the ends of the primaries at about a 45° angle, and the levering cut to bevel the secondaries. Clear away any wood remaining between the feathers, as well as the ridges left by the macaroni tool.

The wings are joined to the body with a mortise-and-tenon joint. Each tenon should be about ⅜ in. long, 1¼ in. wide and ¼ in. thick.

Use a knife and the levering cut to bevel the secondaries so that they appear to overlap (top left). Use the paring cut to bevel the ends of the primaries at a 45° angle (bottom left), taking special care to avoid splitting out the delicate grain at the tips. Smooth off rough spots with 220-grit sandpaper, but leave tool marks on the rest of the wing.

The wings are attached to the body with a mortise-and-tenon joint. Mark the mortises on both sides of the body, as shown on the pattern. Cut out each mortise by drilling two ¼-in. holes, ½ in. deep, at each end of the marked area with the drill angled 45° to the back of the bird. Clean out the wood between the holes with a 12mm carver's chisel. Grip the chisel about 1½ in. from its edge and press it along the sides of each mortise. Split out the waste in the middle, carefully removing the wood a little bit at a time, and smooth the walls.

Next, saw off the excess wood used for clamping the wings to the bench. Leave a ⅜-in.-long tenon at the base of each wing. Use a 6mm V-tool to incise a line ⅛ in. deep along the base of the tenons. Pare the tenons down with a knife until they are about ¼ in. thick and fit into the mortises. Then glue both wings and the tail in place with epoxy.

Cut out each mortise by drilling two ¼-in. holes, ½ in. deep, at each end (above left). Angle the drill 45° to the back of the bird. Clean out the waste between the holes with a 12mm carver's chisel (above right). Press the chisel straight down the sides of the mortise, carefully splitting out wood towards the center, and smooth the walls.

Incise a ⅛-in.-deep line along the base of each tenon with a 6mm V-tool. Pare the tenons down to about ¼ in. thick to fit the mortises in the body.

Bandsaw the upper legs out of ½-in.-thick pine. Place them upside down in a vise and drill a ⅛-in.-diameter hole about 1 in. down the center of each one. Whittle the upper legs with a knife to round them to shape. Then carve a ¼-in.-diameter dowel at the top of each leg to fit into the body. Drill two ¼-in.-diameter holes 1¼ in. apart and about 1¾ in. from the rear end of the body to take the upper-leg dowels. Test-fit the dowels in the holes, then remove them and trim the top of each leg with the knife so it is angled to fit snugly against the curve of the body. Glue the legs in place with five-minute epoxy.

When the epoxy has set, seal the carving with lacquer. When the lacquer has dried, roll out a thin rope of epoxy putty, about ¼ in. in diameter, between the palms of your hands. Press it around the joints of the wings, tail and legs. Dip your fingers in water and work the putty into any gaps in the joints. Blend it into the sides of the body to round the joined parts, and to make them appear to be a solid piece. The putty will harden and make a very strong joint. After the putty has cured for 24 hours, smooth any rough spots with 220-grit sandpaper.

Carve a ¼-in. diameter dowel at the top of each upper leg. Trim the area around the dowels so that the legs fit snugly against the curve of the body.

Drill ¼-in.-diameter holes in the body and test-fit the dowels before gluing the upper legs in place with epoxy.

Next, paint the bird with two coats of white gesso. (If you want to burn-in feathers, do this before applying the gesso.) When the gesso is dry, carve eye sockets with the 3mm No. 8 gouge. Paint the backs of a pair of 8mm glass eyes with yellow acrylic paint, and glue in the eyes with epoxy putty.

Roll out a thin rope of epoxy putty, dip your fingers in water, and blend the putty into the body to round the joints of the wings, legs and tail.

Painting a carving this size takes a bit of time. Lay the osprey on its back and paint the underside of the body, wings and tail first. These should be white, mixed with a tiny bit of burnt umber and burnt sienna; the bands are light brown. When the paint has dried, hold the carving by the legs and paint the head and top surfaces. The head is white with a black stripe through the eyes, blending into the neck and a dark-brown crown. The back and the tops of the wings and tail are the same light-brown color as the underside, but a slightly darker shade. The dark bands on the tail, primary and secondary feathers are also brown, darkened with a little black. Lay down the basic colors, stipple shading along the flight-feather edges, then blend and texture the paint with a dry fan blender. Paint the cere grey and the beak grey or ivory black.

Lay the osprey on its back and paint the underside of the body, wings and tail with white oil paint, mixed with burnt umber and burnt sienna. The bands are light brown, and the head is white with a black stripe through the eyes. Stipple shading along the edges of the flight feathers, then blend and texture the paint with a dry fan blender.

You can mount this carving in two ways, as shown on pp. 180-181. To make a wall mount, cut an oval 9 in. long and about 5½ in. wide out of ¾-in.-thick hardwood. (I used butternut, but walnut or cherry are also good to use.) Sand the piece smooth and round or bevel the edge with 220-grit sandpaper. From the back of the piece, drill a ⅛-in.-diameter hole near the top, angled upward, through the front so the mount can be hung on the wall. Select a weathered, hardwood branch with a fork to mount the osprey as if it were landing. Cut the thick end of the branch off and sand it smooth. (The branch should be about 8 in. long from the thick end to the point where the osprey will grip the fork.) Drill a ¹⁄₁₆-in. pilot hole 1 in. into the end of the branch and a ⅛-in.-diameter hole through the mount about 2 in. up from the bottom. Fasten a 1½-in. No. 10 wood screw through the back of the mount and into the end of the branch. The carving can be hung on a finishing nail or screwed into the wall.

This osprey can also be mounted on a freestanding base for display on a shelf or fireplace mantel. For stability, the base is slightly larger than the piece used for the wall mount, but the carving is mounted in the same way. Use a 1½-in.-thick oval piece of wood 10 in. long and 6 in. wide. You can use a thick branch or piece of driftwood for the osprey to land on instead of the forked branch, if you prefer.

Make the claws by whittling a set of eight talons from ⅛-in.-thick pieces of pine, then sand them smooth. (These are very fragile, so be careful when shaping them.) Make a hole about ³⁄₁₆ in. deep in each talon with a large sewing needle, and glue a 3¼-in.-long piece of 18-gauge copper wire into each of the holes with epoxy. When this has cured, bend each wire ¼ in. from the thick end of the talon into an *L*-shape, as for the chickadee. Dip each talon into lacquer to seal the wood. Next, sand the paint off a 6-in. piece of coat-hanger wire with 180-grit sandpaper. (This will clean and roughen the surface so the glue will adhere better.) Cut two, 3-in.-long pieces of this wire and bend them as shown in the pattern to make the legs.

No two branches are identical, so each leg has to be adjusted and bent slightly to get the osprey into the right pose on the branch. Test-fitting the carving at this stage is important, because once the talons have been glued on, it's very difficult to bend the wires without damaging the leg assemblies. Drill two ¹⁄₁₆-in.-diameter holes into the branch, about 2 in. apart and three quarters of the distance through the diameter of the branch. Place the leg wires into each of these holes. (The bend in the wire should just touch the surface of the branch. If the wire is too long, cut away the extra with wire cutters.) Then fit the other end of each wire into the holes in the upper legs of the osprey. Have someone hold the bird steady while you check the angles for the correct position. It might be necessary to bend the wires a bit to make the carving look right. There should be about 1 in. of leg wire between the bottom of the upper leg and the branch. (If you made a freestanding base, now is a good time to check the balance of the carving. If the carving tends to fall over, adjust the bend of the wires so that the weight is evenly distributed.)

Whittle a set of eight talons from ⅛-in.-thick pine, then sand them smooth.

Glue a 3¼-in.-long piece of copper wire into a small hole made in each talon. When the glue has set, bend each wire ¼ in. from the talon into an L-shape, then seal the talon with lacquer.

When the coat-hanger wires are adjusted, take them out of the branch. Then fasten the four talons to each leg wire, placing the bends of all five wires together. Wrap the assembly at top and bottom with 24-gauge wire, and coat the leg with epoxy. When the glue has set, glue both leg assemblies into the branch and the upper legs. Bend the talons so they grip the branch.

Let the carving stand overnight, then detail the legs. Cover the wires of each leg assembly with a thin layer of epoxy putty, and blend it into the upper leg. Texture the scales on the claws with a small palette knife or a flat toothpick. Dip the detailing tool in water frequently as you work so the putty doesn't stick to it.

When the putty sets, paint the legs with white acrylic mixed with burnt umber and burnt sienna, using a No. 6 brush. Paint the talons with a thin coat of ivory-black acrylic using a No. 2 brush (and a No. 1 for hard-to-reach places). The finished osprey is an impressive and dramatic woodcarving to add to any collection.

Fasten the four talons to each wire leg, placing the bends of all five wires together. Wrap the assembly with 24-gauge wire and coat the leg with epoxy.

Glue the leg assemblies into the branch and the upper legs. Cover the legs with epoxy putty, then texture the putty to make scales on the claws. Bend the talons so they grip the branch.

Use driftwood and an oval base to mount the osprey on the wall.

In this variation, the osprey has been mounted on a freestanding base. This mount is made in the same way as the wall mount, but the legs of the osprey have been positioned so that the bird appears to be landing on the branch.

Sometimes called "The Tiger of the Air," the Great Horned Owl is a powerful hunter. Shape, assemble and finish the owl using the same techniques as for the osprey. Drill holes in the tail feathers and the piece of driftwood, pack them with epoxy putty and work ends of a thick wire into the holes to mount the owl. Use yellow, 14mm eyes. The body is painted with burnt sienna, burnt umber and white. The beak can be carved separately, glued on with epoxy, then painted dark grey or black.

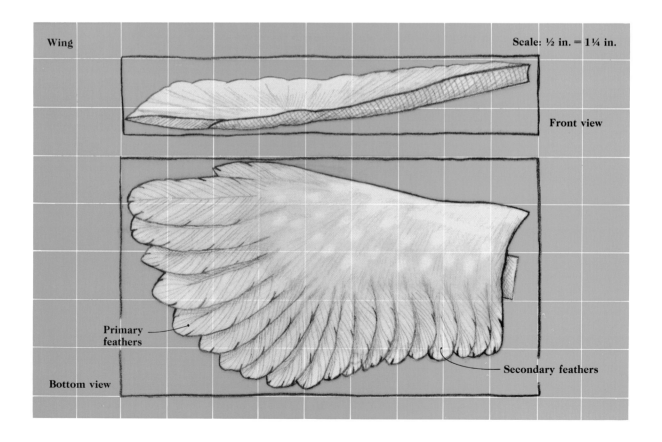

Wing

Scale: ½ in. = 1¼ in.

Front view

Primary feathers

Secondary feathers

Bottom view

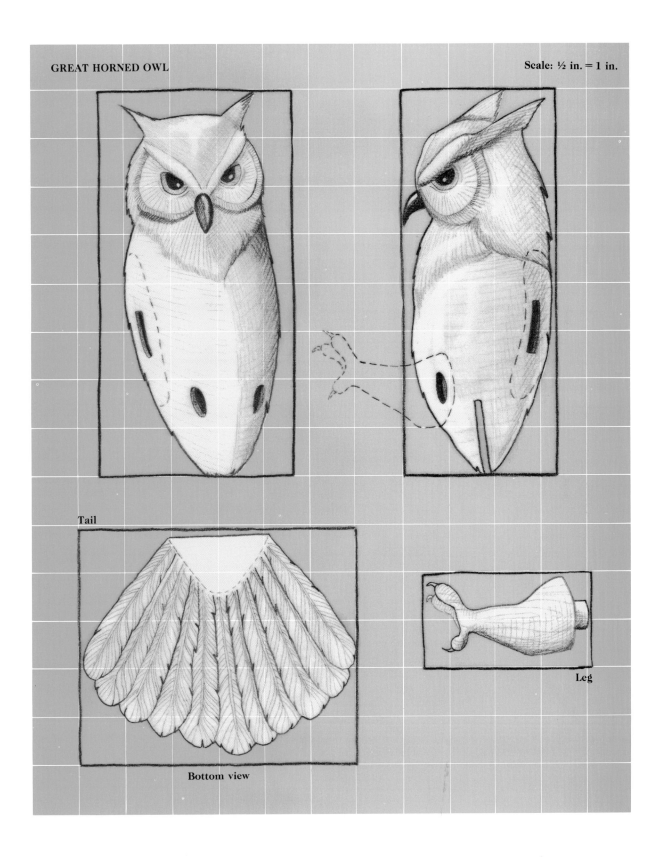

GREAT HORNED OWL

Tail

Bottom view

Leg

Lettering 9

Letters carved in wood have a warmth and lasting beauty that can't be matched in other mediums. You can focus attention on a message in a dramatic way or personalize your home with carvings in fireplace mantels, doors or wall plaques.

Carving existed long before paper was invented and could be considered one of the earliest forms of writing. (Incised bone and tortoise shell 4000 years old have been found in China.) Historical inscriptions can provide carvers today with ideas and inspiration.

Lettering is one of the few types of carving that can seem like work. It requires a high level of concentration and control that can be tedious. But when the tools are put away, it's easy to forget the difficulty as you look back on your workmanship with pride.

Materials

For the projects in this chapter, I used 6mm and 18mm No. 7 gouges, a 4mm No. 8 gouge, a 3mm *V*-tool, a 4mm spoon-bent skew chisel and 6mm and 12mm chisels. For the sign on p. 192, you'll need a 20mm No. 3 gouge and 14mm No. 5 and No. 7 gouges. The flat side of a 30mm carpenter's chisel makes it easy to pare wood from the sides of incised letters and shape edges, and a 15mm No. 13 *V*-tool is good for outlining and cleaning up. A 10mm and 12mm fishtail gouge are useful for carving serifs, which are the angled or rounded stems on the ends of some letter styles.

Use woods with smooth, even grain; curved grain causes a lot of frustration when you're trying to carve straight lines. The wood can be ¼-in. to several inches thick, depending on the size and depth of the letters. Don't carve deeper than one third into the wood or it will be too fragile. For outdoor carvings, use a weather-resistant wood or a marine-varnish finish to avoid checking.

Letters carved in wood have a feeling of permanence, and can focus attention in a dramatic way.

A traditional Scottish saying was carved on this butternut fireplace mantel in Modified German lettering. The tool marks add texture to the background of the shallow-relief letters.

A cipher intertwines the initial letters of a name to make them into a puzzle. (Carved by Fred M. DiGiovanni.)

Incised Roman letters were used to carve this slogan from the War of 1812.

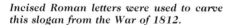

OLD ENGLISH

ABCDEFGHIJKLM
NOPQRSTUVWXYZ

Recessed Letters

There are two methods of carving letters—you can recess them into the wood or raise them from the background—and each method can be done in three different ways. The three types of recessed lettering are outlined, incised and intaglio. (The projects on pp. 187-191 are made from 3½-in.-square blocks of butternut or basswood, secured to the bench with a carver's screw.)

Outlined–Outlined letters are the easiest style to carve, and work best with complex typefaces, such as Old English.

Prepare the wood by smoothing the background with a jack plane, or texture a planed surface with a 15mm No. 3 gouge. Then outline the letter with a 3mm V-tool. The cut doesn't have to be deep—about ¹⁄₁₆ in. in a ¼-in.-thick board. To finish this basswood letter, I used the glazing technique (p. 53), which darkened the outline and emphasized the letter. You can also texture letters by stamping inside the outlines or in the background.

Outline the letter with a 3mm V-tool. Then glaze the wood to make the letter stand out clearly from the background. Use a stamp to add more texture.

Incised–In incised lettering, the sides of the letters slope to form a *V*-shaped valley at the center. I stained the wood first, then carved the letter to expose the natural wood beneath. The sloped sides make it easy to paint the letters, so this is a good style to use for signs that will be hung outdoors.

Draw in the centerline of each letter. To incise letters up to 1 in. high, use a knife in a sweeping cut (p. 97). For larger or ornate letters, use a 15mm No. 13 *V*-tool to incise the letter. Make the cut deeper to widen the lines where necessary. If you're carving serifs, touch them up with a straight-edged knife. With practice, you can carve straight and curved lines, as well as italics, with the *V*-tool.

You can also incise letters with gouges, chisels and a mallet. Make stop cuts at the centerlines and remove wood at the sides, as described on p. 193. You can use this method on letters over 5 in. high, or on small letters in hardwood or wood with irregular grain, where it would be difficult to make clean cuts with the *V*-tool.

Use a 15mm No. 13 V-tool to incise the letter. Cut deeper to widen the lines.

ROUND HAND SCRIPT

$$ABCDEFGHIJKLMN$$

$$OPQRSTUVWXYZ$$

$$abcdefghijklmnopqrstuvwxyz$$

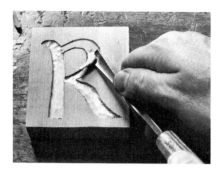

Use a fishtail gouge to carve out the interior of this Celtic letter, and a 4mm spoon-bent skew chisel to clean out the ridges left by the gouge.

Intaglio—Recessed letters with vertical sides and carved-out interiors are called intaglio. This style is more difficult to carve than other recessed-letter styles because extra work is required to smooth the interior. However, intaglio letters cast deep shadows, which make them dramatic and easy to read. This style is good for letters 6 in. to 12 in. high, because they'll show up well from a distance. The interior of a large letter is also easier to carve out because there is more clearance between the sides. The inside of an intaglio letter can be painted or it can be stamped and stained for emphasis. Don't use this style for outdoor lettering—rainwater will sit inside the shapes and cause the wood to rot.

Set-in the letter to a depth of about ⅛ in. using tools with sweeps that match the edges of the shapes. To set-in the Celtic letter shown in the photos at left, I used a 10mm No. 5 fishtail, a 6mm No. 7 gouge and 6mm and 12mm chisels. To carve out the inside of the letter, I used a 5mm No. 3 gouge and a 10mm No. 5 fishtail. Angle the gouge to cut along the set-in edges, as you did when carving the enclosed sections on the Tudor rose (p. 128). Use a 4mm spoon-bent skew chisel to ground-out the area inside the letter and to smooth the ridges left by the gouge.

The letter should not be carved any deeper than the width of the shapes—and only half this distance is better. For example, a 2-in.-high letter will have stems and curves about ¼ in. wide, so the letter doesn't need to be carved any deeper than ⅛ in. to ¼ in. You can make the letter deeper, but grounding-out the inside becomes more difficult, and it's easier to break off delicate parts of the letter. Besides, deepening the letter does not improve its visibility very much.

CELTIC

ÁBCDEFGHIJKLɑɒN

OPQRSTUVWXYZ

abcdefghijklmnopqrstu

vwxyz

Relief Letters

There are three styles of relief letters: raised, rounded and beveled. The techniques for carving these letters are the same as those used for relief carving (pp. 118-125). Wood is removed around each letter so that the letter appears to be raised from the background. Relief styles work best with letters that are 1 in. to 6 in. in height. If the letter is any smaller, it is difficult to ground-out the areas inside and between the letters. When the letters are too large, grounding-out becomes slow and tedious work, because so much wood has to be removed from the background.

One way to make large relief letters (6 in. to 12 in. high) is to cut out each shape with a bandsaw. Then remove the wood from the enclosed spaces of letters like *A*, *B*, *D*, *O*, *P* and *Q* with a drill and coping saw. Drill a hole in the space to be cleared. Loosen the tension on the coping saw and unhook the blade. Then insert the blade through the hole, reassemble the saw and cut away the interior wood. Secure the letters to the background with glue and screws. They can be left raised, or they can be rounded and beveled using the same techniques used on small letters.

Raised—Relief lettering can be shallow or deep. Shallow relief letters are less than ¼ in. above the background. They're simple and quick to carve—a good style to use for long inscriptions.

For the 3-in.-high letter shown in the photos at right, outline the letter with a 3mm *V*-tool to a depth of about ⅟₁₆ in., as for the outlined letter on p. 187. Then clear away the background by making shallow scoops with a 4mm No. 8 gouge. Don't remove too much wood, just enough to lightly texture the background. This works well in softwoods, with all styles of letters, and is good to use in thin wood where you can't carve too deep.

Shallow raised are the easiest relief letters to carve. Outline the letter ⅟₁₆ in. deep and clear away a small amount of the background to texture the wood.

MODIFIED GERMAN

ABBCDDEEFFGHHIJKKLLMM
NOPPRRSSTTUUVWXYYZ

ROMAN ITALIC

ABCDEFGHJKLMN
OPQRSTUVWXYZ

For a deep raised letter, set-in the outline with a tool whose sweep matches the curves. Enlarge the setting-in cuts and clear the background.

You don't need to lower the background much to create the raised effect. In the photos on p. 189, the background depth is only ¹⁄₁₆ in. You can make the background deeper, but it won't necessarily improve the appearance of the letters or make them easier to read.

Deep raised letters (¼ in. high or more) work well in simple, block shapes, such as the Roman styles shown below and on the facing page, as well as with the curved, Modified German style, used for the shallow relief letter on p. 189.

You can use the same tools to carve a raised letter as you would to carve the letter in intaglio style. Instead of clearing the area inside the letter, set-in the letter and clear the background area around it. I used a 6mm and 12mm chisel to set-in the straight lines of this letter to a depth of about ¼ in. If you're working in a hardwood, you may need to outline the letter first, especially if you're carving letters 3 in. high or more and have to remove ¼ in. to ½ in. of the background. Outlining will relieve some of the stress on the wood and tools caused by setting-in. If you're working in softwood (I used butternut), there is no need to outline the letters first, because there is sufficient give in the fibers to avoid breaking the tool.

I used an 18mm No. 7 gouge to set-in the outside curve, and a 14mm No. 7 to set-in the inside. (Tilt the gouge at a 20° to 25° angle in order to compensate for the bevel and make a vertical cut.) Enlarge the setting-in cuts and clear away the background with a 10mm No. 5 fishtail, as described for the flower on pp. 121-122. Use the fishtail gouge to clear away the wood inside the letter, too. To clear the background areas around the serifs, use a spoon-bent gouge.

BOLD ROMAN

ABCDEFGHIJKLM
NOPQRSTUVWXYZ
abcdefghijklmnopqrst
uvwxyz 123456789

Rounded—A raised letter can be left with vertical sides or it can be rounded. Use a letter style that has rounded shapes and curved serifs, like the Bold Roman shown on the facing page.

The first steps in carving a rounded letter are the same as those for making a deep raised letter. Set-in with a 10mm No. 5 fishtail gouge, a 6mm No. 7 gouge, a 4mm No. 8 gouge and a 12mm chisel. Use the fishtail gouge for grounding-out. Then round off the sharp corners around the edge of the letter with a 6mm chisel, and lightly sand the surface, if necessary.

Beveled—Another way to model a raised letter is to bevel it—this creates the opposite effect of incised lettering.

Draw in the center lines of the shapes of the letter. Make 45° stop cuts with a 12mm chisel where the serifs join the body of the letter, or where a leg and curve meet, as shown in the center photo at right. The cuts should extend from the edge of the letter to the center line. Then, use a chisel to carve a 45° bevel on each side of the center line.

The background of raised letters is as important as the letters themselves. Give special consideration to the final tool marks. They should have a consistent, orderly pattern, so the work looks neat and crisp. You can also stamp the background. Attention to details like this conveys a sense of pride in workmanship, which is an important message in itself.

When a raised-letter carving is stained or glazed, the letters stand out from the background because they are lighter in color. The background is darker because the stain settles into the depressions in the wood and isn't wiped away when the carving is cleaned off.

To make a rounded letter, follow the same steps used to make a raised letter. Then use a 6mm chisel to round off the square edges.

CLASSIC ROMAN

ABCDEFGHIJ
KLMNOPQR
STUVWXYZ

To make a beveled letter, start with the raised letter and draw in the center lines. Then make 45° stop cuts where the serifs or legs of the letter join the body. Use a chisel to bevel the edges of the letter at a 45° angle.

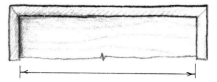

Measure the total amount of space you want the inscription to fill.

Write out the inscription, and count the letters and blank spaces. Then use the formula to find the letter widths. Next, draw three parallel lines. Measure and mark the letters and spaces. Adjust the letter spacing where necessary.

To lay out an arc, use the same method, but mark the letters and spaces on the inside line to keep them from crowding together.

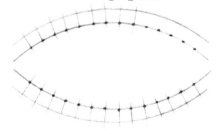

A Sign

The purpose of lettering is to communicate a message. Whether it's sentimental, light-hearted, somber or sacred, the message can be enhanced by the lettering style you choose. The style also plays an important part in whether or not the message is easy to read. A flowing script may be perfect for a plaque in a room where the viewer can stand a few feet away, but the same style would be difficult to read from across the street, even if the letters were quite large.

Size is also an important factor. Letters 1 in. high are legible from about 6 ft. to 10 ft. away; letters 2 in. high from twice that distance. It's a good idea to make a drawing and look at it from the correct distance to make sure the letters are the right size.

Laying out—The real trick to lettering is spacing, because different-shaped letters have different visual space. The distances between letters must vary, or a word will look unbalanced and be difficult to read. In most cases, the greatest distance should occur when letters with vertical lines are next to each other, as in the word *HILL*. Position these letters about one-half letter apart. Round letters can be closer together—their internal space keeps them from looking crowded. Letters with diagonal lines can be placed even closer together. For example, the leg of an *A* can fit close to the base of a *Y*. A round or slanting letter can also fit into the empty space of an adjacent vertical letter.

Correct spacing is very subtle and may require shifting a letter by only a fraction of an inch—but this adjustment is important. We see words and letters all the time and are accustomed to correct spacing, so even slight irregularities are noticeable.

Once you understand the peculiarities of spacing letters, you're ready to position words. Draw a sketch of the inscription. Leave one space between each word, two spaces between sentences for punctuation, and at least a half space at the beginning and end to keep the words from running into the borders. Measure the exact distance the inscription will span, and count the number of letters and full spaces. Divide the distance by the total number of letters and spaces to find the width of each letter. (Most letters occupy a square space, so the width is about the same as the height.)

$$\frac{\text{Total Distance}}{\text{Number of Letters}} = \text{Width of Letters}$$

You can also use this formula to lay out letters of a known height and width. For example, if there are nine, 3-in.-high letters and two half spaces, multiply the number of letters and spaces by the height to find the total length (Number of Letters X Width = Distance). The inscription would require 30 in. This formula will give you a guideline to work from, but it's impossible to measure spacing precisely, so make final adjustments by eye.

To lay out the sign, draw two parallel lines on a piece of paper, as far apart as the letters are high and as long as the inscription. Draw another line halfway between them to mark the midpoint of letters like *A*, *E* and *Y*. Mark the widths along the lines, and sketch in the letters, leaving spaces between words and at the ends. (Or, cut out cardboard letters, position them and trace them onto the pattern.) For inscriptions with more than one line, leave one half to three quarters of the letter height between lines.

To lay out letters in an arc, mark their widths on the inside line, as shown in the drawing on the facing page. If you mark the outside line, the letters will crowd together at the bottom. Don't rush this layout phase. Successful lettering depends on making mistakes on paper, not in the wood.

Before transferring the pattern, clean and smooth the surface of the wood with a plane or with a 20mm No. 3 gouge. The gouge textures the surface slightly and adds visual interest to the background. Transfer the pattern to the wood using carbon paper.

This sign was carved with incised Roman letters. The techniques are similar to those used for chip carving (pp. 94-97). Sketch in guidelines for carving, as you would sketch out *Sechsschnitt* triangles. Mark the centerline of each letter and the intersecting lines that will be formed by the serifs.

Set-in vertical stop cuts along the straight centerlines of each letter using a 30mm carpenter's or carver's chisel and a mallet. Make this cut no deeper than ¼ in. Next, make two angled cuts, one from each side of the letter toward the stop cut, to form the outside edges. The cuts should form a *V*, with the sides at about a 30° angle to the surface of the wood. Don't cut beyond the centerline or you might split the wood on the other side, especially when cutting parallel to the grain.

To incise large, straight letters, use a carpenter's chisel and mallet to make vertical stop cuts at the centerlines.

Lay out your design to make sure the words and letters are evenly spaced. Mark the centerline of each letter, then trace the design onto the wood.

Cut in from each side at a 30° angle to form the V at the center of the letter.

CARVING SERIFS

Mark the intersecting lines that will be formed by the serifs.

Make stop cuts with a fishtail gouge from the serif's center to its edge.

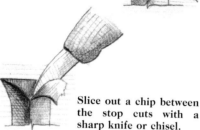

Slice out a chip between the stop cuts with a sharp knife or chisel.

Curved lines are incised in the same way as straight lines, but with a gouge whose sweep matches the curve of the letter. To carve the serif, make stop cuts with a fishtail gouge, and remove the chip with a knife.

To make stop cuts for curved letters, use the same technique, but use a gouge whose sweep matches the curve of the letter. I used a 14mm No. 7 gouge for cutting the small curves around the *J*, *S*, *R* and *U* and a 14mm No. 5 gouge for carving the *C*. For most lettering styles, one or two gouges will fit all the curves. The sweeps of the gouges will vary depending on the size of the letters. Use the same gouge to make the angled cuts that form the edges.

Carve the serifs after the rest of the letter has been carved. That way, you can use the same gouge to make all the cuts at the same time. However, if the straight side of a letter is parallel to the grain, as in the top of the letter *T*, the serifs should be cut first. This is especially important in hardwoods where splits tend to run farther than in softwoods. The serifs serve as stop cuts and prevent splinters from running beyond the end of the letter.

To carve the serifs for these letters, hold a 12mm No. 5 fishtail gouge with the concave side against the wood. Use the corner of the cutting edge to cut into the center of the serif about ¼ in. deep to form the deepest part of the serif. Then swing the handle toward the outer corner of the serif to make a small, curved cut that slopes up to the surface of the wood. Next, take a sharp knife or chisel and slice along the edge of the serif toward the center to remove the triangular chip at about a 35° angle. This technique is similar to those used in chip carving and will leave a crisp edge.

To carve the lowercase letters, use a 15mm No. 13 *V*-tool, as described for the incised letter on p. 187. Hone the point of the inside bevel with a knife-edge, hard Arkansas slipstone. Use the same tool to clean out any splinters inside the capital letters. As a final touch, twirl a 5mm No. 8 gouge between your palms to drill out a small dot for a period, as shown in the photo on p. 184. (This technique can also be used to dot the letter *i* or *j* and make other punctuation marks.)

Hone the inside bevel of a 15mm No. 13 V-tool, and then incise the lowercase letters. Use the same tool to clean out areas with difficult grain.

CELTIC KNOTWORK INITIAL   **Scale: ½ in. = ½ in.**

Initials, monograms and ciphers give you a chance to be creative, and they're fun to carve, too. You can design your own decoration for any style of lettering. This letter is patterned after an example found in the eighth-century, Irish manuscript called Book of Kells. *It is an example of knotwork design, inspired by woven knots or plaited leather and often used by the Celts for designs in wood, metal and stone.*

Architectural Carving 10

Centuries ago, decorating the woodwork of churches and manor houses was the main source of livelihood for the tradesman woodcarver. Because of the expense, this type of work has all but disappeared, and there are few woodcarvers today who can duplicate the intricate ornamentation of the sixteenth and seventeenth centuries.

It's unfortunate that this method of decoration has fallen into disuse. Woodcarving and carpentry can be combined to produce handsome results, and it's a satisfying way for people to add character and interest to their homes. In the past few years, architectural woodcarving has been revived as a means of restoring historical buildings. I feel this is an exciting development, because nothing can recapture the elegance of a bygone era like hand-carved wood interiors.

In architectural carving, just about every woodcarving technique can be used. The molding projects in this chapter use relief and chip-carving techniques. I've also included a linenfold carving, which was a popular Gothic design, that can be used in doors, screens, chests, headboards and cabinets. You can even surround entire rooms with linenfolds, as did medieval carvers, or carve one panel to hang on the wall.

Materials

For the molding projects in this chapter, you'll need a 5mm No. 3 gouge, a 10mm No. 5 fishtail gouge, an 18mm No. 7 gouge, a 4mm No. 8 gouge, a 6mm No. 9 gouge, a 6mm V-tool and a 12mm chisel. For the linenfold carving (p. 206), you will also need a 20mm No. 5 gouge, an 8mm No. 5 back-bent gouge, and 6mm and 14mm No. 7 gouges.

Woodcarving and carpentry can be combined with good results. Linenfold carvings can be used in panels, doors or screens. (Carved by Evan J. Quiros.)

Fireplace mantel and oak newel post. (Carved by Peter Mansbendel, 1927 and 1929. Photos courtesy of The University of Texas, Institute of Texan Cultures at San Antonio.) Front door, carved by Charles Marshall Sayers for his own home. (Photo courtesy of Kenneth Marshall Davis.)

You will also need a few pieces of wooden molding. You can purchase inexpensive molding strips from most lumberyards in a variety of shapes. However, I prefer to make my own molding. I use traditional methods of shaping the contours of molding strips by hand with antique carpenter's planes. Many of these antique planes, like the beading plane, can produce shapes that aren't available commercially. A beading plane has a concave sole and blade and is used to form half-round shapes. Old molding planes can be hard to find, but you can buy a new, metal combination plane with interchangeable blades, and use that instead.

For the linenfold carving, you'll need a rabbet plane, which is designed for cutting rectangular recesses, and used for taking down the edges of panels. You'll also need a plow plane, which is used to cut precise grooves in panel surfaces, or doors and frames for fitting in panels. The plow plane I use has an adjustable depth gauge set into the sole and two threaded, wooden rods that fit through the body. The rods are fastened to a fence that rides against the edge of the panel being planed and determines the distance of the groove from the edge. Plow planes come with blades of varying widths, but I use a ³⁄₁₆-in. blade. To shape the background and the long folds, you'll also need a block plane and a rounding plane. Wooden planes don't require a lot of care. Just rub a little linseed oil into the wood once a month. Wipe a thin coat of 3-in-1 machine oil over the blade after each sharpening to protect it from rust, and these tools will give you decades of use.

You'll also need a mortise gauge, which is an adjustable marking tool with a sharp point, used to score lines. A mortise gauge consists of a block of wood that slides on a wooden shaft and is set with a thumbscrew. To use the gauge, slide the block whatever distance you want to mark away from the point, and tighten the screw. Then place the block against the edge of the board, and lightly drag the point over the wood to mark the distance with a scratched line.

To install molding, you'll need some carpenter's tools. In order for two strips of molding to meet at a corner, they must be mitered to form a 90° angle. Make a miter joint by cutting each strip at a 45° angle, using a 20-in. backsaw, or tenon saw, with 12 teeth per inch. These saws have thin cutting edges and are reinforced with a heavy piece of brass or steel along the back of the blade; a carpenter's saw or Japanese *ryoba* saw can also be used. To make accurate cuts, use a miter box, which is a jig to guide the saw. You can make one from three pieces of wood 24 in. long, 3 in. wide and ¾ in. thick, nailed together to form a trough. Make saw cuts across the miter box to form grooves to guide the saw on both sides: one at 90° and two at 45°.

You'll need finishing nails to attach the molding to walls and ceilings. These are thin nails with small heads that can be set ⅛ in. below the surface of the wood with a nail set and hammer. A 1¾-in. nail, also referred to as a 5d (five-penny) nail, is a good size to use. (The *d* or penny classification dates back to ancient Rome when nails were sold by the hundred for a penny or *denarius*.) After nailing in the molding, set the nail heads and fill the holes with wood dough or a wax crayon that matches the color of the wood.

MOLDING PROFILES

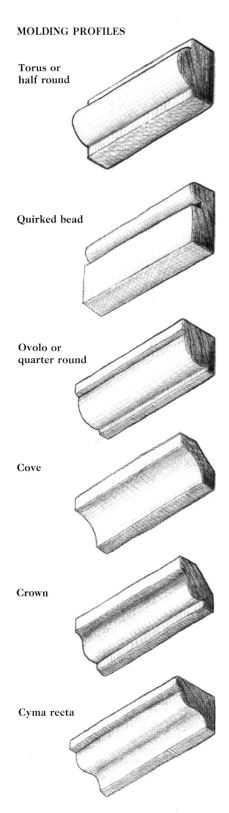

Torus or
half round

Quirked bead

Ovolo or
quarter round

Cove

Crown

Cyma recta

WOODEN PLANE

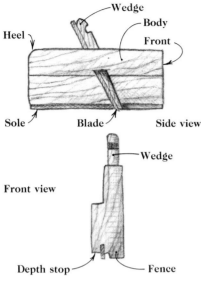

Side view

Front view

Depth stop — Fence

To remove the blade, tap the back of the plane with a mallet. Adjust the blade with a small metal hammer until it makes a thin, even shaving.

Using Planes

Before using a plane, check the edge for sharpness. Remove the blade by holding the plane upside down with the wooden wedge and the top end of the blade supported by your left hand. Then tap the back of the plane with a wooden mallet with several light, sharp blows. (Don't use a metal hammer or you'll bruise the wood and possibly split the plane body.) This tapping motion will loosen the wedge and the blade so they slip out into your left hand. If the plane hasn't been used in a long time, it may take a while to loosen. Test the blade for sharpness against your fingernail, as you would a knife or gouge (p. 29). To sharpen it, rub the flat sides on a fine India or soft Arkansas benchstone in a circular motion. Hone the bevel of molding blades with slipstones—at about a 25° angle for softwoods, 35° for hardwoods. Some plane blades, such as those used for the *S*-shaped profiles of ogee moldings, have irregularly-shaped edges and require a variety of slipstones.

Many antique plane blades were forged with laminated steel— hard, brittle steel bonded to softer steel to make a sharp, strong cutting edge. It takes a long time to sharpen laminated blades because they're so hard, but they stay sharp longer than most modern plane blades.

After sharpening, replace the blade in the plane body. Fit the blade so the edge is about ¼ in. up into the body from the sole. Then replace the wedge and tap it firmly into place with a mallet. Tap the top end of the blade with a small, metal hammer until the cutting edge protrudes slightly below the sole of the plane. Secure a piece of wood to the workbench and make a test-pass with the plane to see if it cuts a shaving. If not, lightly tap the top end of the blade again and make another pass. Repeat this procedure until the plane removes a thin, even shaving. If you tap the blade too far, you'll get a thick shaving, and the surface of the wood will be rough instead of smooth and polished. If so, loosen the wedge, reset the blade and adjust it again. (Don't be discouraged if it takes several tries to get it right—this takes practice.)

To plane a molding, secure the board to the bench using holdfasts or clamps with a piece of scrap between the metal and the wood. When working on long, thin strips, I place clamps about 3 ft. apart and plane the wood in short sections. Stand at the right end of the board (as you face the bench) with your feet about shoulder-width apart, and your body turned so you're looking down the length of the board. In this position, you'll be able to move freely in front of the bench. Place the sole of the plane on the board and work down the length from right to left. Hold the heel of the plane snugly in the palm of your right hand, with your thumb and fingers extending around the sides. Hold the front of the plane in your left hand with your thumb resting on top, and your fingers gripping the sole. The fingers of your left hand act as a fence to guide the plane along the edge of the board. Press down firmly with your left thumb to keep the sole flat against the board, and push steadily until your right arm is extended. Lift the plane off the wood, and repeat the stroke. Don't drag the plane backward on the wood when preparing for the next cut, or you'll dull the edge.

A block plane or jack plane will require about a half-dozen passes to smooth down a board. However, a molding plane has an irregularly-shaped sole, so it takes many more strokes to shape a board. Molding planes have depth stops in the sole, so the plane stops cutting when it reaches the correct depth. Work one section of the board until the plane stops cutting, then release the board from the clamps and reposition it to plane the next 3-ft. section.

Make a few practice cuts to work out the most efficient method of handling the planes, and keep them on the bench in front of you so they can be quickly picked up and exchanged.

Moldings

A molding can be used around the ceiling, doors and windows of a room to soften the corners and edges of the surfaces. You can replace existing moldings and door frames with carved sections at any time. Every winter, when we're more or less snowbound, I replace a molding here or a piece of trim there—all according to a master plan I drew up years ago.

Picture frames are made the same way as moldings, but the mitered pieces are assembled before any carving is done. Gold leaf was later applied to this basswood frame. (Carved by Edmond McKamey. Photo courtesy of artist.)

Planning—The first step in making a molding is to decide on a design. If the building is an 1890 Victorian, you'll want to add carvings with ornate curves and wisps of foliage. An early American structure would look better with folk designs. Historic period homes should have carvings that are consistent with their history and only to replace original carved surfaces. Once you've chosen the design, make sketches of the areas where the carvings will appear to help you visualize the total effect. Or draw the full-size design on paper and secure it with thumbtacks or masking tape to the area where the carving will appear. If you like the design, you can use the drawing as a pattern to trace on the wood.

Looking at sketches in place will also help you determine the scale of the design. A short section of carved molding may look fine in a drawing, but 16 ft. of the same pattern high up on a wall may look entirely different. A heavy, ornate design may be overpowering in a small room, or a molding with repeating designs full of tiny details may get lost in a large room.

To fit molding strips to a wall or ceiling, measure and mark the length you need (measure the long edge for ceiling moldings). Do the carving first, then cut the molding so the designs match at the joint. (Picture frames are made the same way as moldings, but the pieces are assembled first, then carved.) Place the molding in the miter box, line up the mark you made with one of the 45° slots, hold the piece securely and saw the angled cut. Saw the other end of the molding at the opposite 45° angle, then nail that strip into place with finishing nails. Measure and cut the adjacent molding in the same way, and fit the two pieces together.

Carving was commonly used in the sixteenth and seventeenth centuries to decorate the interior woodwork of churches. This is a medieval chancel screen located at Bovey Tracey, Devon. (Carved by Grinling Gibbons. Photo courtesy of The Royal Commission on Historical Monuments, London.)

To carve any style of berry or bead molding, plane a ¼-in., half-round shape with an antique beading plane or a combination plane.

Berry or bead—To make a berry or bead molding, plane a ⁵⁄₁₆-in. half-round shape with a beading plane or combination plane. Next, make a series of stop cuts with a 12mm carver's chisel. Hold the chisel vertically and make ⅛-in.-deep cuts ¼ in. apart. (For hardwoods, use a mallet.) Hold the chisel close to the cutting edge with your left thumb and index finger, as shown in the photo below at left. In this position, your hand rests on the wood and braces the chisel, which allows you to work quickly.

Now invert a 6mm No. 9 gouge to make rounded cuts between the stop cuts. Carve down while swinging the handle up to round one side of the shape. (This technique is similar to rounding the flower's center, described on p. 125.) Repeat this cut from the other direction to form a spherical berry. You can make a continuous row of berries on molding of any length.

Variations on this molding can be carved with the same gouge. Space the berries 1½ in. apart and make ½-in.-long scooping cuts on either side to make the sunken bead shown below. (This technique is similar to shaping the flower petals, pp. 124-125.)

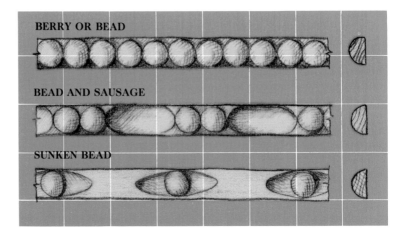

BERRY OR BEAD

BEAD AND SAUSAGE

SUNKEN BEAD

Next, use a 12mm carver's chisel to make stops cuts ⅛ in. deep and ¼ in. apart (above). Make rounded cuts with an inverted 6mm No. 9 gouge to shape the berries (right).

Intertwining ribbon—This is also called strapwork, knotwork or guilloche molding. The earliest example was found in Tutankhamen's tomb, and variations have been found in Africa, Persia, China and Europe. This pattern was used by the Greeks in carved masonry of the seventh century, and is also one of the identifying marks of the Jacobean period of architectural carving and furniture decoration in Britain in the seventeenth century. (The border on the bottom of the St. George carving on p. 144 is another example from this period.) This motif is very versatile; ornate knots can be added and the width of the ribbons can vary to fit narrow and wide moldings. Swiss woodcarvers often used this design to decorate the irregular shapes of chair backs.

When carving a complex, repeating design, like this ribbon molding, use a template to trace the pattern onto the wood, as discussed on p. 61. I used cove molding for this project. Set-in the outside notches with two ⅛-in.-deep stop cuts, made with an

Make a template of the ribbon pattern, and trace the outline onto the wood.

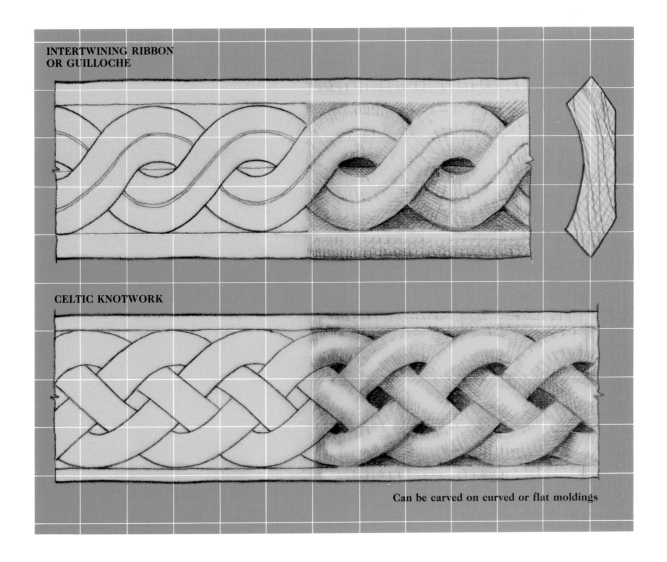

INTERTWINING RIBBON OR GUILLOCHE

CELTIC KNOTWORK

Can be carved on curved or flat moldings

inverted 18mm No. 7 gouge. Next, cut away the waste between the two stop cuts with a 5mm No. 3 gouge. The cuts are made much the same way as for the *Dreischnitt* used in chip carving, except with gouges instead of a knife. Use a 6mm *V*-tool to outline the edges of the ribbons.

To add more detail, sketch a line down the center of the design and incise it with the *V*-tool. The background can be textured with a square or diamond-shaped stamp, or you can incise a double line down the center of the ribbon and use a large, diamond-shaped stamp at regular intervals between the lines.

This molding can be installed so the design continues around corners, but if space is limited, plan in advance so the pattern ends in a logical place. For example, in the Celtic knotwork I used for the door trim shown on p. 211, a decorative knot at each end leads the viewer's eye back into the design.

Next, use an inverted 18mm No. 7 gouge to set-in the notches along the outside of the ribbons by making two stop cuts 1/8 in. deep.

Then make a slicing cut to clear away the chips between the stop cuts with a 5mm No. 3 gouge. For the stop cuts and slicing cuts, the techniques are the same as those you would use for the chip-carved Dreischnitt.

Outline the edges of the ribbons with a 6mm V-tool. To add more decoration, use the V-tool to incise another line in the middle of the ribbons, or texture the background with a diamond-shaped stamp.

Modified egg and dart—All the carving for this molding was done with a 4mm No. 8 gouge and a 10mm No. 5 fishtail.

Draw the pattern onto the wood, and use the 4mm No. 8 gouge to set-in ¼-in.-diameter circles, spaced at 1-in. intervals. Hold the gouge vertically to make the cuts ¼ in. deep, then make a slight twisting motion to clear the small core of wood in the center.

Next, make a series of stop cuts with a 10mm No. 5 fishtail gouge for the triangular shapes on the top of the molding. Angle the gouge so the cuts are deepest at the center of the triangle, as you would when chip-carving a *Sechsschnitt*, then slice out the waste with the fishtail gouge.

At the bottom of the design, use the fishtail gouge to make two stop cuts for each curve, starting the cut below the small circle. Then make two more stop cuts along each bottom edge of the dart, so that the cuts are deepest where they meet the curved stop cuts. Slice out the chips from the small triangles on either side of the dart. Then remove two small chips from the surface of the dart, so that the dart is raised at its center.

This design was carved on a piece of 1½-in. pine that I shaped with a Grecian-ovolo molding plane. The strip could be used as a shelf or bracket on a fireplace mantel, or sliced off the board for a ⅞-in.-thick molding. This design is good for ceiling moldings, which work best with small, repeating designs that continue along the wall and around corners.

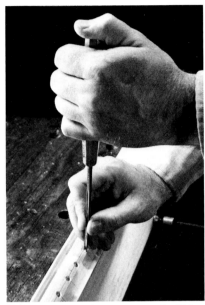

Use a 4mm No. 8 gouge to make ¼-in.-diameter circles at 1-in. intervals. Make a slight twisting motion to remove the small core of wood.

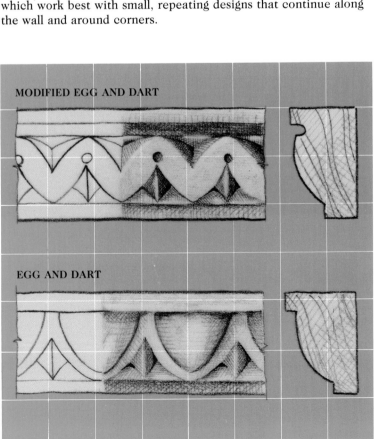

MODIFIED EGG AND DART

EGG AND DART

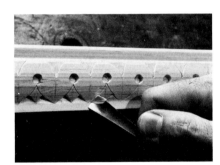

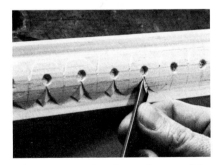

After clearing triangles at the top of the design, make curved stop cuts at the bottom with a 10mm No. 5 fishtail. Clear chips from the small triangles on either side of the dart (top), and two on the surface of the dart (bottom).

TYPICAL LINENFOLD DESIGNS

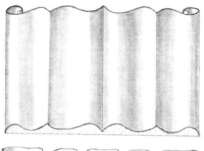

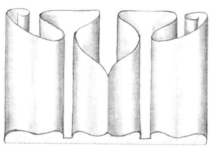

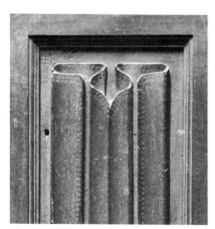

The stamping on this fifteenth-century design creates the effect of embroidery in cloth. (Photo courtesy of The Metropolitan Museum of Art, The Cloisters Collection, 1925.)

A Linenfold Panel

A linenfold is a carved panel that has the appearance of undulating folds of cloth. The design originated with French and Dutch woodcarvers during the early Gothic period, as a means of duplicating in wood the decorative shapes formed by draped altar cloths. Some linenfolds even had intricately carved borders to simulate embroidery. Linenfold carving was also popular among English woodcarvers, and the style became so widely used that it is considered one of the hallmarks of Tudor design. Although early linenfold carvings were realistic interpretations of cloth folds, the design eventually became stylized, and lost much of its subtlety and resemblance to hanging drapery.

Linenfold was usually carved on a rectangular panel, and then fitted into a rabbeted frame. The design was often altered in length, and used as wall paneling in European manors and churches, as well as for panels in doors, chests, beds, screens and other commonplace household furnishings.

Carving a linenfold is a two-step procedure. First, the long folds are shaped with planes, then the ends are carved with gouges. To

Folding screen. (Carved by Peter Mansbendel. Photo courtesy of The University of Texas, Institute of Texan Cultures at San Antonio.)

prepare a panel for linenfold, you might need to laminate several boards to make a wide panel. When gluing the pieces together, it's important that the edges be smooth and the wood grain aligned properly, as discussed on p. 159. Alternate the grain direction in adjacent pieces of wood when you laminate boards edge to edge to keep the panel from buckling. Use pipe or bar clamps to hold the pieces while the glue sets.

Planning the design—An accurate drawing of the linenfold is important because it's difficult to visualize the end result until the final stages of work. Draw a full-scale cross section to show the depths of the long cuts and a clear sketch of the end folds. There are many traditional designs to choose from, and I've included a few examples. Part of the charm of the Gothic linenfolds is the subtle variation between each carving. Carvers would panel entire rooms or hallways with linenfolds, but would keep the design from becoming monotonous by modifying each design slightly. This also kept the woodcarver's task from becoming tedious, and instilled a vitality which set the work apart from later imitations.

To make a wider panel, laminate boards edge to edge. Plane the edges flat, and secure the pieces with pipe or bar clamps until the glue sets.

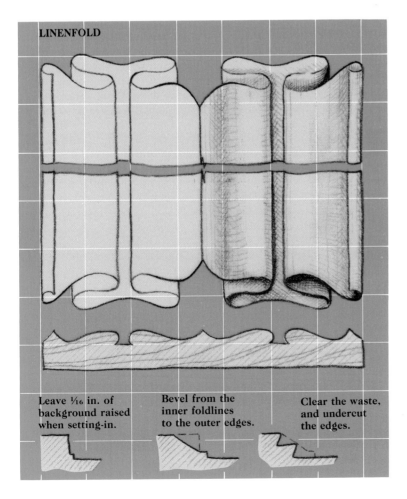

LINENFOLD

Leave ⅟₁₆ in. of background raised when setting-in.

Bevel from the inner foldlines to the outer edges.

Clear the waste, and undercut the edges.

PLANING THE CONTOURS

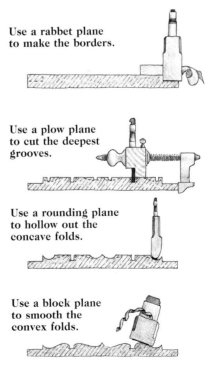

Use a rabbet plane to make the borders.

Use a plow plane to cut the deepest grooves.

Use a rounding plane to hollow out the concave folds.

Use a block plane to smooth the convex folds.

© 1982 FINE WOODWORKING magazine

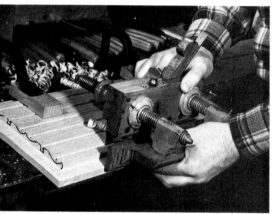

Plane a ¾-in.-wide border on the sides and a ⅞-in.-wide border at the ends of the panel with a rabbet plane. Draw the cross section on the end of the board and use a plow plane to cut the deepest grooves. Then, use a rounding plane to hollow out the contours.

Planing the contours—For this linenfold panel, I used a piece of wood 18 in. long, 9¼ in. wide and ⅞ in. thick. Mark out a ¾-in. border on the sides and a ⅞-in. border at the ends with a mortise gauge. Next, cut down the background edges with a rabbet plane. (Allow 1½ in. extra around the edges if you want to fit the panel into a rabbet in a door frame or furniture carcase.)

Clamp a smooth 1-in. by 2-in. board along the face of the panel as a fence to guide the rabbet plane and to keep the edges of the work straight. The background should not be taken down any more than one-third to one-half the thickness of the panel. I removed about ⅜ in. of the wood. If you remove too much wood, the end folds will become fragile and the entire panel will be weakened. Plane across the end-grain sections first, because splits are likely to occur at the edges of the board. If you plane the ends first, the splits will be cleaned away when you plane the sides.

When the background has been planed, make a cross-section template from the pattern, and trace it on the ends of the wood. Make sure the shapes are symmetrical and line up at both ends of the board, or the cuts will be crooked. Loosen the nuts on the threaded rods on the plow plane, and set the fence and blade for the distance of the cut from the edge of the panel. Tighten the nuts, and set the adjustable depth guide. Set the fence against the edge of the panel, and place your right hand around the heel of the plane, with your fingers curled around the nut. Grip the fence near the front edge with your left hand and push it against the edge of the board, as you move the plane forward with your right hand. Cut a series of grooves that match the deepest parts of the cross section, making repeated passes along the board until the plane stops cutting.

Use these grooves as a guide to keep the next set of cuts the right depth and parallel. Use a ¾-in. rounding plane and carefully hollow out the concave folds. The plane iron should be sharp and the sole waxed with paraffin or ski wax to make planing easier and to keep the cuts true and clean. Next, smooth the convex surfaces of the folds with a small block plane. Use a 12mm chisel or No. 5 gouge to smooth out any ridges left on the surfaces.

Carving the end folds—Make a template for the outer edge of the end folds, and transfer the outline to the ends of the panel. Set-in all the lines with a 6mm No. 7 and 20mm No. 5 gouge and a mallet. Make these vertical cuts ⅛ in. to ¼ in. deep, and then make horizontal cuts from the end to clear out the waste. When setting-in, leave about 1/16 in. of the background depth intact; the outlines will be undercut later to separate them from the background and add depth. If you make the setting-in cuts too deep, they'll show after the folds are undercut.

Round the edges you have set-in with a 14mm No. 7 gouge by carving a curved bevel from the inner fold to the outer fold. Leave a step of at least 1/16 in. remaining above the background at the end of the fold, as shown in the drawing on p. 207. Sketch in the S-shapes of the folds on the beveled surface, then outline the shapes with a 6mm V-tool. Start the cuts of the V-tool at the edges of each fold and work toward the center to prevent splits. Set-in

Next, smooth the convex surfaces of the folds with a small block plane, and smooth any ridges left by the plane with a chisel or No. 5 gouge.

Trace the end folds onto the panel (top). Set-in the lines about ¼ in. deep, and carve a bevel from the inner foldline to the edge of the outer fold with a 14mm No. 7 gouge (left). Then use the V-tool to outline the shapes of the fold, working from the edges to the center (above).

Tool marks add interesting texture to the finished linenfold.

the *S*-shapes with a 6mm No. 7 gouge and a 10mm No. 5 fishtail. Make horizontal cuts in from the end to clear the waste with a 5mm No. 3 gouge. Then use an 8mm No. 5 back-bent gouge to even up the vertical edges of the inner folds, while undercutting them slightly. The action of a back-bent gouge is exactly the reverse of a spoon-bent gouge—practice on scrap before you try it on the carving. You can use a straight gouge for undercutting, but the wood is more likely to split because the tool will apply pressure to the thin edge. Undercut the outer fold and clean up waste and rough spots with the 5mm No. 3 gouge.

As the final step, bevel the edges of the folds with a chisel or gouge with shallow sweep. This bevel reflects light and helps the edges show up from a distance. If the edges were sharp, they would be almost invisible, and the illusion of cloth folds would be spoiled. Lightly touch up any rough spots on the carving with fine sandpaper. Don't smooth over the facets of the tool marks—they add an interesting texture. The beauty of linenfold carving lies in its bold simplicity and crisp detail.

To finish this panel, I used a clear Minwax penetrating resin oil to seal the wood, then I polished it with paste wax. If the carving is going to be used as paneling or fitted into a piece of furniture, it should be finished after it is installed, using whatever material was used on the surrounding woodwork or on the rest of the piece.

Undercut the folds with an 8mm No. 5 back-bent gouge (above), then cut a bevel along the edges with a chisel or gouge so that they reflect light (right).

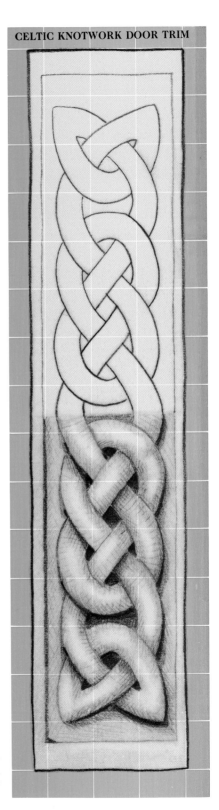

CELTIC KNOTWORK DOOR TRIM

This door trim is a variation of the intertwining-ribbon pattern. There is a knot at each end of the strip to lead the viewer's eye back into the design. This detail had to be planned in advance so that the pattern wouldn't break in an awkward spot and make the design visually frustrating. The length can be varied, so the pattern can be used on moldings as well.

Bibliography

TOOLS AND WORK SPACE
Bronowski, Jacob. *The Ascent of Man*. Boston: Little, Brown & Co., 1973.

WOODS AND FINISHES
Hand, Jackson. *How To Do Your Own Wood Finishing*. New York: Barnes & Noble Books, 1974.

Hoadley, R. Bruce. *Understanding Wood*. Newtown, Conn.: The Taunton Press, 1980.

DESIGN
Bain, George. *Celtic Art: The Methods of Construction*. New York: Dover Publications, 1973.

Franck, Frederick. *The Zen of Seeing*. New York: Random House, 1973.

Hasluck, Paul N., ed. *Manual of Traditional Wood Carving*. New York: Dover Publications, 1977.

Jack, George. *Woodcarving Design and Workmanship*. New York: Taplinger Publishing Co., 1978.

Leighton, John. *Suggestions in Design*. London: Paddington Press, 1977.

Leslie, Clare Walker. *Nature Drawing*. Englewood Cliffs, N.J.: Prentice-Hall, 1980.

Pye, David. *The Nature and Art of Workmanship*. New York: Van Nostrand Reinhold Co., 1971.

WHITTLING
Anderson, H.S. "Andy". *How to Carve Characters in Wood*. Boulder, Colo.: Johnson Books, 1972.

Schroeder, Roger, and McCarthy, Paul. *Woodcarving Illustrated*. Harrisburg, Pa.: Stackpole Books, 1983.

Tangerman, E.J. *Whittling and Woodcarving*. New York: Dover Publications, 1962.

CHIP CARVING
Barton, Wayne. *Chip Carving—Techniques and Patterns*. New York: Sterling Publishing Co., 1984.

Crowell, Ivan H. *Chip Carving: Patterns and Designs*. New York: Dover Publications, 1978.

Hasluck, Paul N., ed. *Manual of Traditional Wood Carving*. New York: Dover Publications, 1977.

Moore, Harris W. *Chip Carving*. New York: Dover Publications, 1976.

RELIEF CARVING
Wheeler, William, and Hayward, Charles H. *Woodcarving*. New York: Sterling Publishing Co., 1979.

WILDLIFE CARVING
Burk, Bruce. *Game Bird Carving*. New York: Winchester Press, 1976.

Clement, Roland C. *The Living World of Audubon*. New York: Grosset & Dunlap, 1974.

Green, H.D. *Carving Realistic Birds*. New York: Dover Publications, 1977.

Pearson, T. Gilbert et al., eds. *Birds of America*. Rev. ed. Garden City, N.Y.: Doubleday & Co., 1936.

Porter, Eliot. *Birds of North America*. New York: E.P. Dutton, n.d.

Robinson, Howard F. et al., eds. *The Gift of Birds*. Washington, D.C.: The National Wildlife Federation, 1979.

Veasey, William, and Hull, Cary S. *Waterfowl Carving: Blue Ribbon Techniques*. Exton, Pa.: Schiffer Publishing, 1982.

LETTERING
Frankenfield, Henry, and Stoner, Charles, eds. *Speedball Textbook*. Philadelphia: Hunt Manufacturing Co., 1972.

Hanna, J.S. *The Marine Carving Handbook*. Camden, Maine: International Marine Publishing Co., 1975.

ARCHITECTURAL CARVING
Bain, George. *Celtic Art: The Methods of Construction*. New York: Dover Publications, 1973.

Boutell, Charles. *Heraldry*. Edited by J.P. Brooke-Little. Rev. ed. New York: Warne, Frederick, & Co., 1970.

Oughton, Frederick. *Grinling Gibbons and the English Woodcarving Tradition*. London: Stobart & Son, 1979.

Rietstat, Johannes B. *Armorial General Precede d'un Dictionnaire des Termes du Blason*. New York: French & European Publications, 1934.

Wheeler, William, and Hayward, Charles H. *Woodcarving*. New York: Sterling Publishing Co., 1979.

Index

Acanthus leaves, 58-69, 145
Adirondack guide and boat, 88-89
Architectural carving, 23, 45, 197-211
Artist's oil colors, 49, 52, 84-85, 143, 149
Ash, 40, 45
Aspen, 41, 45

Balsa, 40
Bandsaws, 14
Baroque curve, 60, 114, 115, 130,
    131-35
Barton, Wayne, chip carving by, 91
Basswood, 40, 44, 45
Beds, carved, 56
Beech, 40, 45
Bench hook, 22, 93
Benchstones, 12, 25, 26-27
Birch, 40, 45
Blanks, for large carvings, 159, 167
Bobcats, 148
Box, oval, 67
Buffing wheel, 32-33
Burning-in. *See* Feathers. Hot Tool.
Butternut, 40, 44, 45
Bütz coat of arms, 137

Carver's screw, 22, 23
C-clamps, 22
Cedar, 41, 45
Celtic:
    alphabet, 188
    knotwork, 195, 211. *See also* Molding:
        ribbon.
Chairs, carved, 68
Cherry, black, 40, 44, 45
Chestnut, 40, 45
Chests, carved, 56, 69
Chickadee, 149-57
Chip carving, 91-113
    finishes for, 45, 91-93
    knives for, 72, 93
    tools for, 23, 93
    wood for, 45, 93
Chisels:
    dogleg, 9
    sharpening, 34
    skew, 5, 6, 7
    woodcarver's, 5, 6, 7
Claws, 179
Clay models, making, 63, 137
Cloth roll, 11
Coat of arms, 136-43
Cogelow, Fred, carving by, 116
Cottonwood, 40, 45
Coyote, 148

Design, 55-69. *See also* Clay models.
    Patterns.
DiGiovanni, Fred M., monogram by, 195
Dogwood, 44
Door, 69, 198
Doors, carved trim for, 211
Drawing, 18, 58
Drawknives, 16
Dreischnitt cut, 94, 95
Duck, 154, 159

Eagle, 186
Elm, American, 40, 45
Eyes, 154, 162, 168, 177

Fan blender, 150
Feathers, 152, 161, 162-63, 172-74

Files, 17
Finishes, 45, 47-53
Finishing:
    and pattern marks, removing, 61
    sandpaper for, 17
    steel wool for, 17
    See also Glazing. Finishes.
Fir, 41, 45
Fleur-de-lis, 65
Flowers, carving, 118-25
    See also Tudor rose.
Fluteroni tool, 6, 9
Foliage:
    detailing, 128-29, 139, 141
    undercutting of, 141
    See also Acanthus leaves.
Fox and geese. *See* Gameboard.
French polish, 45, 49, 50-51
Fur, 168, 169

Gameboard, 113
Gibbons, Grinling, screen by, 201
Glazing, 53, 129, 169, 187
Glues:
    epoxy, quick-setting, 150
    epoxy putty, 150, 176, 177, 180
    for lamination, 159
Gouges:
    back-bent, 8, 210
    care of, 36
    choosing, 9
    firmer, *See* chisels, woodcarver's.
    fishtail, 5, 7, 128, 131, 142
    for roughing-out, 9
    front-bent grounder, 8
    handles for, 9-10
    long-bent, 8
    parts of, 6
    sculptor's, 5
    sharpening, 30-33, 36, 37
    size of, 5, 6
    spoon-bent, 8, 133
    straight, 5, 6, 7
    sweep of, 5, 6
    See also Fluteroni tool. Macaroni tool.
    Veiners. V-tools.
Grain. *See* Wood: grain considerations with.
Grounding-out, 118, 123, 127-28,
    131-33
Guilloche molding. *See* Molding: ribbon.
Gundersen, John, jewelry box by, 92

Handles, 9-10
Heraldry, 137
Hermit, whittling, 78-85
Hickory, 40
Hired Men—Ontario, The, 116
Holdfast, 21, 23
Holding devices, 22-23, 160-61
Hot Tool, 149
Hummingbird, 148

Ironwood, 44

Jewelry box, 92

Knives:
    for chip carving, 93
    chip-carving, remaking, 72
    for whittling, 71-73
    hooked, 4, 149
    sharpening, 28-30
    X-acto, 4

Knotwork. *See* Celtic: knotwork.
    Molding: ribbon.
Kristiansand, Halvor Lie, *kubbestol* by.
Kubbestols, 68

Lacquer, 49, 51-52
Lamination. *See* Wood: laminating.
Landsverk, Halvor, *kubbestol* by, 68
Leaves. *See* Foliage.
Legs, birds', 155, 176, 179-80
Lettering, 184-95
    background of, 187, 191
    beveled, 191
    Celtic, 188
    finishes for, 45
    glazing of, 187
    incised, 186, 187
    intaglio, 188
    layout of, 192-93
    Modified German, 189
    Old English, 186
    outlined, 187
    punctuation in, 194
    raised, 189-90
    recessed, 187-88
    relief, 187, 189-91
    Roman, 189, 190, 191, 193-94
    rounded, 191
    serifs in, 194
    size of, 194
    tools for, 23, 185
    woods for, 45, 185
Lighting:
    in work space, 20
    effects of, 64-66
Linenfold, 15, 196, 199, 206-210
Liquid Deglosser, 102
Loon, 149, 158-65

Macaroni tool, 6, 9
Mahogany, 40, 44, 45
Mallets, 12, 13
Mangle boards, 57, 92, 112, 117
Mansbendel, Peter, carvings by, 69, 198,
    206
Mantels, 186, 198
Maple, 40, 45
Match holder, 98-102
McKamey, Edmond, frame by, 201
Melgaard, Leif, mangle board by, 117
Mesquite, 44
Mirror, rococo, 58
Miter box, 199, 201
Modeling, 118, 119, 124-25, 128
    undercuts in, 141. *See also* Foliage.
    bevel cuts in, 129, 140
    sweep cuts in, 134-35, 141
Models. *See* Clay models.
Molding:
    attaching, 199, 201
    bead and sausage, 202
    bead, 202
    berry, 202
    Celtic knotwork, 203-204, 211
    cove, 199
    crown, 199
    cyma recta, 199
    design of, 201
    egg and dart, 205
    fitting, 201
    half-round, 199
    Jacobean, 203
    knotwork, 203-204

modified egg and dart, 205
nails for, 199
ovolo, 199
planing, 200-201
quarter-round, 199
quirked bead, 199
ribbon, 203-204
strapwork, 203-204
sunken bead, 202
tools for, 197, 199
torus, 199
uses of, 201
Monogram, 195
Mortise gauge, 199
Mounting, 156-57, 167, 179-81
Myrtlewood, 44

Newel post, 198

Oak, 40, 44, 45
Odden, Phillip, acanthus leaves by, 145
Oil finishes, 45, 49, 50, 53, 142, 143
Old English alphabet, 186-87
Old Mountain Phelps. *See* Hermit,
    whittling.
Osage orange, 40, 45
Osprey, 146-47, 149, 154, 170-81
Otter, 149, 166-69
Outlining, 9, 118-20, 127, 131
Owl, 182-83

Paint:
    acrylic, 149
    alkyd, 149
    applying, 45, 49, 52, 152
    artist's oil colors, 149
    enamel, 52
Paintbrushes, 150
Panels, 56, 92, 145, 206-10. *See also* Doors.
Patterns, 55, 60, 61-62, 203
Picture frames, 117, 201
Pierced carving, 138
Pine, 41, 44, 45
Planes, 14-15, 200-201, 208
    beading, 199, 202
    block, 15
    care of, 199, 208
    combination, 202
    jack, 15
    molding, 15, 201, 205
    plow, 199
    rabbet, 199
    sharpening of, 200
Platter, 116
Pliers. *See* Puzzle, whittling.
Poplar, 40, 45
Punches. *See* Stamps.
Puzzle, whittling, 86-87

Rasps, 17
Redwood, 41, 44, 45
Relief carving:
    finishing, 45, 125, 129
    modeling of, 118, 119, 124-25
    pierced, 138
    tools for, 23, 118
    techniques for, 118-25
    types of, 115, 123
    woods for, 45
    See also Baroque curve. Flowers.
    Tudor rose.
Rifflers, 17
Roman alphabet, 189, 190

Rosettes, 103-113
    double-hexagonal, 107
    heptagonal, 109
    hexagonal, 105
    octagonal, 108
    pentagonal, 110-11
    quatrefoil, 106
    spiral, 104, 113
Roth, James, knife by, 149
Roughing-out, tools for, 9
Round Hand Script alphabet, 187
Rudser, Thelma, platter by, 116
Ruffed grouse, 148

Sandpaper, 17, 102
Sassafras, 44
Saws:
    band-, 14
    hand, types of, 14
    for miters, 199
Sayers, Charles Marshall, door by, 198
Screens, 201, 206
Scrolls, folds in, 142
Sechsschnitt **cut,** 94, 96
Setting-in, 118, 119, 121-22, 131
Sharpening:
    of chisels, 34
    of gouges, 30-33, 36, 37
    importance of, 25
    of knives, 28-30
    of planes, 200
    stones for, 12, 25-27
    of V-tools, 34-35
Shellac, mixing, 50-51
Siengaard, Ole, box by, 67
Slipstones, 27, 36
Spokeshaves, 16
St. George and the dragon, pattern for, 144
Stains, 45, 48, 49, 143
Stamps, 18
Steel wool, 17
Strapwork molding. *See* Molding: ribbon.
Strops, 12, 27, 29
Sweep cut, 97
Sweeping cut, 134-35

Tails, adding, 171-72, 173
Talons, 179-80
Tarldseth, Rolf, carvings by, 58, 69
Teak, 40, 45
Tools:
    cabinet for, 19
    care of, 3, 10, 11, 20, 36
    by carving types, 23
    handles for, 9
    See also Sharpening.
Trunk, carved, 69
Tudor rose, 126-29
Tupelo, 44

Undercutting, 141

***V*-tools,** 6, 7
    crosshatching with, 125
    letters with, 194
    outlining with, 118, 119, 120, 124, 127,
        129, 131
    sharpening of, 34-35
    winged, 6, 9
Varnes, Jacob, picture frame by, 117
Varnish, 45, 49, 51
Veiners, 6, 7
Vises, 21, 22

Walnut, black, 40, 44, 45
Wandfeuerzeug. *See* Match holder.
Wax, paste, 45, 49, 53
Whittling, 23, 45, 70-89
Wildlife carving, 23, 45, 146-83
Wings, joining to body, 173-75
    See also Feathers.
Wood:
    choosing, 44-45
    grain considerations with, 40, 43, 60, 74,
        75, 120
    hard, 40, 41, 44, 46
    kiln-dried vs. air-dried, 46
    knots in, 42
    laminating, 159
    pith of, 41-42
    sapwood in, 42
    seasoning of, 45-47
    soft, 41, 44, 46
Work space, 18-20
Workbenches, 20-21

X-acto. *See* Knives: X-acto.

Zip Sander, 102

Editor: Laura Cehanowicz Tringali
Design Director: Roger Barnes
Assistant Editors: Deborah Cannarella, Scott Landis
Assistant Art Director and Illustrator: C. Heather Brine
Art Assistant: Karen Pease
Staff Artists: Lisa Long, Kathryn Olsen
Indexer: Harriet Hodges
Manager of Production Services: Gary Mancini
Production Manager: Mary Galpin
System Operator: Nancy-Lou Knapp
Production Assistant: Claudia Blake Applegate
Darkroom: Annette Hilty, Deborah Mason
Typeface: Caslon Book 9½ point